P9-DMC-324

What's
Holding
You
Back?

What's Holding You Back?

CRITICAL CHOICES
FOR WOMEN'S SUCCESS

Linda S. Austin, M.D.

BASIC BOOKS

Published by Basic Books,
A Member of the Perseus Books Group

Published by Basic Books,
A Member of the Perseus Books Group.

FIRST EDITION

Designed by Elliott Beard

Library of Congress Cataloging-in-Publication Data has been applied for.

ISBN 0-465-03262-1

00 01 02 03 04 / 10 9 8 7 6 5 4 3 2

To my parents, Robert and Elpidia Gozalez Smith,
and my children, Matt and Stephanie Austin

Contents

You see, I want a lot.
Perhaps I want everything:
the darkness that comes with every infinite fall
and the shivering blaze of every step up.

So many live on and want nothing,
and are raised to the rank of prince
by the slippery ease of their light judgments.

But what you love to see are faces
that do work and feel thirst.

You love most of all those who need you
as they need a crowbar or a hoe.

You have not grown old, and it is not too late
to dive into your increasing depths
where life calmly gives out its own secret.

RAINER MARIA RILKE

Breaking the
Psychological Glass Ceiling

No one will ever create a bolder vision of your life than you are able to envision for yourself.

IT WAS THE FIRST SESSION of a psychotherapy course I taught to the third-year psychiatry residents. "In what way," I asked brightly, "would each of you like to be great?"

I posed my question in part to warm the room, to encourage the residents to let me know them as individuals. But the question itself intrigued me, for I had begun to wonder how much of women's career trajectories was determined by whether they could dream of greatness.

The men in the group had a variety of responses, reflecting a mixture of personal and professional goals; almost all, however, said they wanted to be great psychiatrists. Six of the seven women in the group replied: "I want to be a great mother." Only one said, "I want to be a great doctor and a great mother."

I was truly taken aback by the women's responses. Their inability to dream of professional greatness astounded me because of who they were. Their average age was about thirty. Each had graduated with sterling grades from four-year colleges, then completed four years of medical school, and were now in the third of their four years of residency. They were women who had sacrificed enormously for their education and careers, and each stood on the brink of finally being able to enjoy the fruits of her immense personal investment. Each of them would be a practicing physician in two years. With determination and discipline, each had the potential to become a *great* physician. Yet, in their twenty-third year of formal education, *something* restricted their ability to experience and acknowledge their full ambition.

Surely these women had been initially motivated by deep ambition. Had they become so worn down in the course of their long educational journey that their drive was now flagging? Were the pressures, needs— and pleasures—of family living catching up with them, making them feel it was necessary to limit their aspirations? And if so, why wasn't this true for their male counterparts? Had their young lives as achievers become too taxing, too conflicted, too *inconvenient* for them to hold on to their visions of accomplishment? Before my eyes, I saw the course of female ambition personified.

THE PSYCHOLOGICAL GLASS CEILING

Much has been written about the infamous "glass ceiling," the external barrier in the corporate and professional worlds that limits women's career advancement. This book is about the *psychological* glass ceiling that we women unconsciously erect within our minds. Despite its invisibility, it influences every decision we make in our careers and is far more life-defining than any external barrier could be.

At the beginning of my own professional training at twenty-one, I believed that the obstacles impeding women's drive to the top were, in fact, all "out there." It was 1973 and I had just entered Duke Medical School. It was a historic time for women doctors: the number of women entering med school in the United States had tripled to 30 percent of admissions in just two years. It was the heyday of the women's liberation movement, and at Duke there was so much to liberate. A pathology professor showed *Playboy* slides in class. Another had just published a textbook using pin-up pictures to demonstrate gross anatomy. The ob-gyns called all their patients "girls."

I was part of a happy, noisy cadre of young women who stomped through the halls of academia, decrying the misdeeds of insensitive males. (It was also the era of miniskirts, so we did our stomping in skirts so short that they barely covered our rears. In fact, when we were given scrub dresses that did not display enough leg we ripped off the bottom inches of hem—the Dr. Daisy Mae look.) We were in our element, certain that if external forces would only equalize for the two genders, we women would take our places in the ranks of great achievers. If only all women had equal access to higher education, as we did . . . if only women could compete equally for the best jobs . . . if only child care were widely available . . . if only the world could be free of gender bias, *then* we would all stand alongside our brothers as leaders.

But despite several decades of enhanced opportunities, women have not gained positions of power or been recognized for significant accomplishments in parity with our male peers. While we have made great gains in equalizing our numbers in entry-level positions, our representation dwindles disturbingly at the top levels of the achievement pyramid. We currently receive 53 percent of all bachelor's degrees and 52 percent of master's degrees. Yet at the next level, only 40 percent of doctoral degrees are awarded to women, meaning that a male will have a 50 percent greater likelihood of obtaining this advanced training. Overall, women hold roughly 10 percent of top-level jobs. We are less than 6 percent of corporate executives, 13 percent of upper-echelon federal employees, 10 percent of judges, and 10 percent of full professors in academic medical centers. In other words, a man is about nine times more likely to reach the highest levels of achievement than a woman is.

The traditional feminist explanation for these dismal numbers, of course, is gender discrimination. This discrimination now comes less often in blatant, tangible ways, but rather occurs in the form of myriad tiny, imperceptible differences in opportunity. The nature and degree of these differences vary greatly from setting to setting: an introduction not made, a case not shared. Nonetheless, the comments of the women residents in the class I taught seemed to constrict their dreams of the future beyond what external issues alone demanded. After all, they had developed in a subculture that had been very supportive of their ambition. They had excelled in science courses in college. They had gone to medical schools in which 45 percent of their classmates were women. They had entered a profession, psychiatry, in which women were well represented, and they had trained in a residency class with more women than men. At the medical school where I teach, 60 percent of entry faculty positions are held by women, positions into which my students, too, would soon be welcomed. Further, psychiatry is a field remarkably well suited for working mothers.

Clearly, they had all displayed a real capacity for achievement. For years their lives had been organized around their ambition, and they had made many sacrifices. Yet as they neared the moment when they would make critical decisions about their career directions, something *internal* rose up to prevent them from shouting their exultation in their achievements from the mountaintops. They seemed to be saying: *I will fully and completely develop my intellect—but then I'll put it on the back burner. I'll have a career—but I won't be a career woman. I'll be good, but not great.*

I have spent the last twenty-five years as a psychiatrist in academic medical centers, treating patients and teaching students and residents. I've developed educational programs for lay people, which led to a call-in public radio program and other large-scale, interactive programs at grade schools and colleges. This work has allowed me to study, up close and personal, the psychological issues that limit women. I've treated—and taught—scores of women from all fields whose internal barriers prevented them from achieving at their fullest potential.

I'm convinced that a woman cannot begin to clear institutional hurdles if she is tripped up by her own psychological stumbling blocks. If she is unable to think of herself as a great achiever, she will begin to scale down her expectations of herself, making choices that compromise the development of her intellect, power, and authority. She will pay insufficient attention to opportunities that could help her advance. She will never reach the point where a door bangs in her face, because she will have slipped out a side exit first.

Yet I've also been able to observe women who were not internally constricted, women whose psychology has permitted an expression of ambition that has allowed them to soar. These are women who have shaken themselves free of traditional female limitations and anxieties. Something *internal* has guided these women to make daily choices that propel them toward their goals—and that internal something can be learned by others.

I predict that women as a group, examining our frustration about our ongoing underachievement, will soon reach a point similar to that of my patients who enter psychotherapy filled with hurt and anger about their experiences in the world. In therapy there comes a turning point when attention shifts from what goes on "out there" to what goes on in one's *inner* world that plays a role in shaping life events. This shift does not negate the reality that "out there" can be a tough, unfair place indeed. But the shift is essential for attaining emotional health and strength, for it signifies a determination to achieve mastery over one's destiny, regardless of external issues.

For all the years we spend in formal education, we receive virtually no instruction about ourselves and our inner life. This book is written to help women learn about themselves in the context of their dreams of accomplishment and achievement. By sharing research and observations of the issues that lead women to succeed as well as fail, I hope to give readers the tools to take their own personal psychology in hand, to purposefully shape their thoughts and behaviors to optimize their ability to reach their goals.

THE SEARCH FOR ANSWERS

That jarring moment, as I listened to my women residents describe their limited career aspirations, was a defining one for me, crystallizing a decision to learn as much as I could about the psychology of female ambition and to share my findings in a book. Since that day, I have studied these issues from every imaginable direction. I began to pay more attention to the ways my women patients struggled, at work and at home, with their conflicted feelings about ambition. I watched closely the mixed-sex groups of first- and second-year medical students I taught, observing how the young males and females barely out of college learned, studied, and led each other in group activities. I listened to how my women residents in psychotherapy supervision approached their patients. I observed my academic peers as they struggled for promotion and tenure, and I analyzed the behavior of a some great women leaders whom I knew personally. I was fortunate during this period to participate in a year-long fellowship at MCP Hahnemann University, the Hildegard von Ameringen Executive Leadership in Academic Medicine for Women, which allowed me to meet for several week-long retreats with thirty-five upper-level women academicians who were also passionately interested in these same issues. Most of these women had met the challenge of achieving academic success while raising their families, and I learned much from our intense and revealing discussions.

Since the field of medicine represents only a small fraction of ambitious women, however, I moved outside to other professions as well. I interviewed scores of women in a variety of fields. As an invited speaker for women legislators, therapists, lawyers, and businesswomen, I had the opportunity to try out my ideas before hundreds of women and hear their experiences and ideas as well. I conducted focus groups in different parts of the United States and Canada, particularly targeting highly successful women to learn how they had succeeded.

And finally, I read everything I could find about women as leaders, visionaries, and achievers—particularly scientific articles from areas removed from standard psychology fare. I looked at the scientific literature to answer the most interesting questions: *How much of feminine behavior is nature? How much is cultural? Are certain behaviors universal? Are they affected by hormones that ebb and flow throughout the life cycle, or by genes exerting stable influences over many years?* To answer these questions, I not only looked at psychobiological and neurohormonal studies, I studied the fascinating literature on female primate behavior, for the millions of years of primate brain development is a far more powerful determinant of our behavior than the mere two hundred thousand years of human evolution. My goal was to answer the question: *If there are innate, biologically determined behavioral and psychological differences between males and females, how can we women make optimal use of our distinctly feminine psychology in the service of achieving our goals?*

BRAVERY

As I studied women of ambition and achievement, I identified eight psychological issues that most determined their ability to achieve. These were: a powerful motivation driven by a sense of meaning; the capacity for risk-taking; the ability to focus intelligence; the ability to find and define great problems to work on; a willingness to compete in hierarchies as well as individually; the ability to tolerate and learn from failure; significant skill with difficult people; and the development of autonomy and power. This book is organized around these topics, and each chapter defines the psychological choices women face with each of them.

One force, however, united all eight issues, and powerfully influenced how women shaped their careers. That force was the *feminine drive to affiliate with others*, a drive numerous scholars have described as the most gender-specific aspect of women's psychology. Throughout human history, this female drive has been narrowly focused to promote the welfare of the family and, to a lesser degree, one's immediate community. Women of achievement, however, while profoundly motivated by affiliative needs, channel this energy in nontraditional, often very bold directions. From the need to connect, support, and protect others, these women draw the motivation to achieve, the desire to take risks, and the vision to find unique problems. Freeing the affiliative drive from traditional constraints and channeling it into the service of achievement requires real bravery, however, for it compels a woman to confront her deepest wishes about how her life should be defined.

While courage is surely an important trait for the achieving man, women must be even more psychologically brave than their male counterparts to succeed. After all, it is so clearly within the scope of expected male behavior to take independent, autonomous action. The bolder a man of achievement is, the more he is actually conforming to his gender stereotype: his social position becomes safer than ever, and he thoroughly gratifies the expectations of his parents, family, and society. For a woman, boldness puts her distinctly at odds with the role that society expects of her. She leaves the safety of conformity to group expectations for a solitary adventure that is hers alone. Bravery leads her to a final step of the process that psychologists call "separation-individuation," the forging of a unique, authentic, self-determined sense of identity.

SEPARATION-INDIVIDUATION

It was, in fact, a female psychoanalyst, Margaret Mahler, who first described the process of identity formation that is central to the development of emotional health. Mahler noted that while physical birth is a discrete, observable event, psychological birth unfolds slowly over many years. The infant, born in a helpless state of symbiotic attachment to her caretaker, only gradually develops a sense of being a separate person. During the first two years of life, her emerging physical independence lays the groundwork for her emotional independence, as she gradually distinguishes "Me" from "Not-me." The development of the capacity for non-anxious autonomy is referred to as "separation." Throughout childhood and adolescence, she gradually develops traits, opinions, and tastes that are different from her parents and eventually from her peers; this is the process of "individuation," the establishment of a unique personality.

For a woman to become ambitious and achieve requires a step beyond the normal process of separation-individuation that males and females experience. The achieving woman must, in fact, separate and individuate from socially determined gender norms, which to this day decree that a woman is good, not great. At every step along her path she is challenged to draw upon her courage to assert her individuality. As each of the choices described in this book illustrates, achievement requires the ability to determine a unique sense of meaning, often radically different from what society suggests. The way a woman develops her intelligence and defines the problems that intrigue her are highly personal and even idiosyncratic. She must develop her own version of what it is to be female. The phenomenon of women defining individual interpretations of feminine identity is historically unique, for neither women of previous generations nor males of any era have been challenged to individuate to such a high degree.

At the heart of it—or perhaps even at the start of it—ambition itself is a brave choice for a woman, immediately distinguishing her from others of her gender. This is, perhaps, what underlay the reticence of my women residents to articulate their dreams: merely thinking of themselves as ambitious challenged their gender identity and their social acceptability. To think the thought, much less say the words *"I want to be great"* is an act of ultimate courage.

GOING AROUND FOR VOTES

"Ambition" is a provocative word, defined as "an eager or strong desire to achieve something, such as fame or fortune; will to succeed." Embracing ambition, with all its headaches and heartaches, is one of the most important choices a woman can make, for it defines the course of much of her life. At hidden levels, women have always been ambitious: humans have survived because mothers had strong determination that they, and their families, should thrive. Historically, though, women have had to minimize our ambition with disclaimers, cloaking their desires in terms of what is good for others, especially their families.

The modern term is derived from the ancient Latin word *ambitio*, which originally meant "going around for votes"—and at that certainly our gender, even in this day, is unsurpassed! Before we allow ourselves to pursue our dreams, we typically ask our "voters"—our husbands, lovers, children, parents—if they approve of our ambition. More significantly, though, many women do not begin to allow themselves to dream big dreams because they imagine that the "voters" would be too put out.

Women working hard, inside and outside the home, is far from a modern invention. In undeveloped, agrarian societies women have always had responsibility not only for maintaining the home and family but for working in the fields as well. A survey of 186 indigenous cultures revealed that in only 3 percent did mothers stay at home to take exclusive care of their own children; in 40 percent of societies children were cared for more than half the time by someone other than their mother. The Swedish International Development Agency describes a typical day for a poor, rural African couple:

> The woman's day begins with kindling the fire, breast-feeding the baby, making breakfast, eating, and washing and dressing the children. She then walks about one kilometer to fetch water, which she carries home; she then feeds and waters the livestock and washes her cooking utensils. Next she fetches more water, washes clothing, breast-feeds the baby, and brings food to a field a kilometer away where her husband is working. After returning home, she walks another kilometer to another field, which she weeds; on the way home, she breast-feeds the baby and gathers firewood. At home she pounds maize into flour, fetches more water, kindles the fire, prepares the evening meal, serves and eats it, breast-feeds the baby, washes up, puts the house in order, and is the last one in bed.
>
> The man's day begins when breakfast is ready. After eating, he walks one kilometer to the field where he works until his wife arrives with his food. After eating, he resumes working in the field and later returns home, rests, eats dinner, and walks to the village to visit with other men before going to bed.

Throughout Europe during the centuries of the premodern era, working-class girls typically left their homes in early adolescence to work as servants for a decade or more to earn their dowry. Upon marrying, these women continued their hard work in their own homes, and many also worked as domestic servants or in factories or on farms to support their families. A prime consideration during these times was for daughters to stabilize the family's social position by marrying well, so it was the job of the mother to train her daughter to become a desirable candidate for marriage. Obviously our foremothers were intensely ambitious for themselves and for their children.

We have not lost the wish to work in meaningful ways, ways that really make a difference to ourselves and others. But with the advent of the technological era, the ways that both men and women work have changed, and therefore what feels meaningful has also changed. Women's desire to contribute, to experience themselves as centrally important to a group mission, has remained constant, however. Some women maintain their outside interests throughout the period of having young children. Many others find that until they are needed less by their children, they are less drawn to produce and create outside the home. But the fundamental wish to engage in a meaningful exchange with others through our labor is the legacy of our female heritage.

If the drive to work and to be ambitious has always been part of our emotional life, there clearly are also powerful forces opposing our wish to work effectively. Society in general, and men in particular, have never really minded us toiling; their opposition came when we started to work in ways that made us powerful as individuals or as a group. In the prefeminist era the opposition came in concrete, definable forms. We were blocked from access to education and entry into professional guilds. We were refused consideration for promotion to higher ranks. We were paid at lower rates. Child care was difficult to obtain, and we could not divest ourselves of full responsibility for household management. Appropriately, the early decades of the feminist movement focused attention on these tangible barriers, and the result has a been a significant, though not complete, removal of some of those obstacles, particularly in the area of acceptance into educational programs and entry-level positions.

HIDDEN PETTICOATS

What we have not paid enough attention to, however, is how cultural hostility toward womanly ambition shaped our psychology for thousands of years and continues to define our emotional lives. The cause of this age-old anger has always been that our ambition is so terribly inconvenient to others. It is inconvenient to our husbands, who feel deprived of a home environment that makes few demands on their time and energy. It is inconvenient to our children, who must learn to be independent and to contribute to the family maintenance. It is inconvenient to a society that has traditionally assigned us the job of stabilizing life for everyone else.

This cultural hostility creates subliminal anxieties within us that take as many forms as the snakes on Medusa's head. Consciously they are expressed in relationship terms. *What if my husband feels threatened by me? What if my children feel abandoned? What if my friends feel jealous?* These issues drive us, as women, to make choices that limit the scope of what we can achieve. It is not success per se that we fear. Rather, we worry that the behaviors that lead to success may not meet with the approval of others.

These anxieties may be a howling wind or they may be gusts of unexpected breeze, arising when you least expect them. Even as a gentle breeze, however, they have the capacity to throw you just enough off track that you never reach your intended destination. Perhaps you work, but hold yourself back from reaching your fullest potential. You achieve, but not so outstandingly that your personal relationships are threatened. You feel some ambition, but not so strongly that others might actually notice. Like the women in my psychotherapy seminar, you have your career, but you fall short of what you could achieve and contribute. You wear your ambition like a petticoat, a supporting undergarment of which only a peek might occasionally be possible. You keep it hidden, and above all, you keep it pretty.

I'm not speaking here about *conscious* decisions to delay career development in order to spend time with young families. I'm speaking of women who have made the conscious decision to work fully, but *unconsciously* hold back. Further, I'm not speaking of one single, organized unconscious decision to hold back. Rather, there are patterns of behaviors that undermine a woman's progress, patterns that spring from discomfort with ambition and from identification with traditional female behavior. These patterns lead you to cooperate but not initiate; produce but not invent; participate but not lead; reflect but not create. In other words, compromise behaviors are often less about the ways you *do* work as about the ways you *do not* work.

I present the eight patterns of behavior as choices you make on a daily basis, choices that determine whether you will reach your destination or are blown off course. You will notice that the choices are not between good and bad behaviors; rather, they are between good and transcendent behaviors. Good choices are those that allow you to work in conformity with what is expected of you and with what you expect of yourself. Good choices inconvenience yourself and others only moderately, and you reach respectable levels of achievement. Transcendent choices are those that allow you to leverage your intelligence and energy to produce and create at a level beyond "good enough" to outstanding.

WHY BOTHER?

If you have always described yourself as unambitious, you're probably wondering: *Why bother?* You may feel you're doing well if you can run your morning car pool and still make it to work on time. Perhaps you're the first member of your family to graduate from college. Isn't it good enough that you went to grad school, whether or not you fully make use of your degree? Or if you and your husband are both contributing incomes, does it really matter if you're paid highly or not?

I say it does matter, for several reasons. First, since you probably work anyway, whether it's inside or outside the home, you might as well work in the cleverest way possible, putting your energy into projects you'll be proud of. You might as well earn a higher salary rather than have that money diverted to your male associates. You might as well develop more control and power to determine your work life, because you're going to be working those hours anyway.

Women often avoid prestigious jobs for fear of the stress and long hours they might entail. In fact, no one works harder than women at the low end of the pay scale, for without the financial means to pay for help in the home they put in a back-breaking double shift, day in and day out. As you rise in your organizational hierarchy, you will find you have more freedom and flexibility to arrange your work schedule as you need to and more financial power to buy relief from domestic chores. Your life will become more like men's traditionally have been, with more responsibility at work but greater independence and power in your life overall.

A second reason to bother, and the one that motivated me to write this book, is that the world really needs what you, and the rest of womankind, have to offer. By underachieving, you and we miss out on the glory of what you might contribute. Consider this passage from Dean Keith Simonton's book *Greatness: Who Makes History and Why*. In this five-hundred-page volume, published in 1994, a full seven pages are about women. There you will read:

> In the diverse histories of cultural attainments, the names are overwhelmingly male. In Western civilization, for example, women make up only about 3% of the most illustrious figures of history. And many of these females, some might argue, entered the records in part by luck, birthright or marriage. . . . In the annals of science, fewer than 1% of all notables

are female. . . . In classical music, the proportion of female luminaries may shrink to near zero. . . . Among the giants of literature, about 1 out of 10 are female.

One could argue that Simonton wasn't counting right. There were certainly many great contributions by women that were neglected or stolen. But even if his figures were multiplied by five, our major contributions still have been disturbingly few. How much richer the world would be if we had had twice as many scientists, composers, artists, and humanitarians! If women had been political and military leaders, would we have repeatedly sent our sons to die by the millions on battlefields? If women had been religious leaders, might we have developed more rational approaches to population control?

Another issue, yet more abstract, is the reduced quality of life that gifted women have experienced because they couldn't fully develop and express themselves. Imagine the individual women who could have been Shakespeares, Beethovens, or Lincolns. Those women couldn't have been aware of their genius, for they had no opportunity to develop and demonstrate it; how impoverished their lives were compared to what they might have experienced. I'm convinced that potential female geniuses are in our midst now, though many of them will never have a glimpse of all they could have been had they known how to develop themselves. If you have some awareness that you might be using your talent and energy more productively, this book is written for you. But if you do not have that awareness, this book is also meant for you, for I want to help you understand how to use your own mind more effectively and authentically. The simplest goal of the book is fairly humble. It is merely to get you to think more broadly, and from a different perspective, about the countless choices you make during your daily life that will shape your career life. And the outcome of your new approach will not be humble at all.

The process of achievement will make you a different person than you were before: more capable, confident, and resourceful. Resculpting your own psychology to promote achievement is itself an ambitious goal, one that is certainly not accomplished with a single stroke of determination. It occurs imperceptibly, as each small experience or success creates the confidence that the next risk or effort can be just a bit larger. But the process of psychological growth must begin with a decision to love your ambition, convenient or not.

MOTIVATION

Derailed by Anxiety or Inspired by Meaning?

THE BEDROCK of all ambition is motivation—an intense and sustainable drive toward a specific goal. Any effort you make to increase your ability to achieve must begin with an examination of your motivation, with an eye toward how you can increase and maintain your drive. Traditionally, women's motivation to contribute has been most powerfully expressed within the home. Achieving *outside* the home requires harnessing that same motivational energy and directing it toward goals that are less safe and familiar. This shift of motivation is challenging, often opposed not only by social and familial forces but also by internal anxieties and self-doubt. How have those women who have achieved managed to find the determination to succeed?

To explore this, consider the motivation of three great women of history: Hildegard of Bingen, Harriet Tubman, and Florence Nightingale.

I have always remembered a fact I learned in medical school: The seventeenth-century British anatomist William Harvey is called the father of modern cardiology because he asserted that blood circulates through the body, rather than ebbing and flowing in the blood vessels. I was therefore stunned to read just recently that a woman, Hildegard of Bingen, beat Harvey by *five hundred years* in a scientific treatise that suggested not only the circulation of blood, but also a link between diabetes and sugar, and transmission of signals from the brain to the body along the nerves.

Although Hildegard was well versed in the medical theories of her era, her scientific insights were actually a sidebar in her career as a religious leader. Hildegard, born in 1098 in Germany, began experiencing religious visions at age three. At thirty-eight she became abbess of a Benedictine cloister. Five years later she reported to her confessor that her health was suffering because she had refused a command from God to write down her revelations. She subsequently began to record them in a body of work titled *Scivias vias domini* (Know the Way of the Lord) and was formally declared by the church to be the recipient of divine revelations.

Once she had been confirmed as a bona fide mystic, there was no stopping Hildegard. She founded a new convent and "persuaded" the abbot to vacate the monastery and turn it over to the nuns for their new order by telling him she'd had a vision that God's judgment would destroy him if he did not comply. She was successful in opposing the male hierarchy of the church on numerous occasions by exploiting her status as a mystic this way. Hildegard worked as a public preacher and teacher, writing two more books describing her visions. She composed a symphony consisting of a cycle of seventy-seven songs to be performed on the feast days of the saints; these works are still being performed and recorded today, and are widely available commercially. She remained active throughout her long life; at age eighty, for instance, she was involved in a dispute with the local church officials that led to their placing the severest form of sanction, an interdict, against her abbey. Hildegard succeeded in having the sanction overturned by once again invoking divine revelation.

What motivated Hildegard to accomplish deeds we're still reading about some nine hundred years after her death? She must have been fiercely intelligent, and yet there have been countless women of great brilliance who lived and died unnoticed. She was well educated for a woman of her day, but the vast majority of highly educated women do not become historical figures. She was born into a family of religious distinction but could have just as easily become another nun, living quietly in the shadow of a male-dominated church.

What distinguished Hildegard was not only that she had a unique and bold vision but that she felt irresistibly compelled to *express* her vision and was able to maintain the stamina to do so throughout her long life. A product of her time and her religion, she experienced her compulsion as coming from God in the form of visions and revelations. Her achievements sprang from a conviction that she had an obligation to live a life of significance, to use every ounce of her being to express the views and values that defined her. She was driven by a sense that her life should have meaning and purpose. At the most fundamental level, Hildegard became who she was because she was able to say in the most vigorous way: "Hey, listen to me. I have some great ideas—so great that they actually came directly from God. And if you don't pay attention to my great ideas, God is not going to be very nice about it."

The biographies of great women and men show that all outstanding achievers share one trait with Hildegard: They have all been convinced of the importance of their ideas, and they pursue those ideas with great tenacity. In most cases, in fact, their lives began in rather ordinary circumstances, and the ideas they devoted themselves to were not always brilliant, original, or unique to them. But because they were sure their ideas were worthwhile, they steadfastly persisted in getting others to recognize them. During their lives of achievement, they surely felt deep anxiety at many points and from many sources, but the conviction that their personal journeys had great meaning allowed them to overcome this anxiety.

Harriet Tubman was born in 1820 on a slave-breeding plantation in Maryland. She began to work the fields by age seven but was brutalized many times; on one occasion her skull was crushed, which resulted in periodic epileptic seizures that plagued her all her life. She married a freedman at age twenty-four, and experienced powerful yearnings to be free herself. Aware of this, her father began to teach her how to survive in the woods.

At age twenty-nine, after learning she was about to be sold, she escaped the plantation with her two brothers. Though they turned back, she continued her escape alone. Subsequently she made nineteen round trips to help slaves escape and relocate in Canada, resulting in a forty-thousand dollar bounty on her life. After the Civil War began, she served as a spy, scout, and nurse for the Union army. On numerous occasions she wore a disguise and led groups of black men behind Confederate lines; one such campaign resulted in the rescue of eight hundred slaves. After the war, Harriet campaigned for women's rights and worked on behalf of orphans, the elderly, and freed slaves. At age eighty-eight she established the Harriet Tubman Home for Indigent and Aged Negroes.

The year of Harriet's birth also produced another great woman, Florence Nightingale. Throughout her childhood she yearned to have an occupation other than the typical social obligations common to girls of the British upper class. At age sixteen she wrote, "God spoke and called me to His service." Due to opposition from her family, however, it was not until another fourteen years had passed that she was able enroll in nursing training. Three years later she was appointed superintendent of nursing at the English military hospitals in Turkey, where the Crimean War was being fought; she was the first woman ever to have been employed to nurse wounded soldiers. Due to her ceaseless efforts both to reform military nursing and to personally provide bedside care, she became a national heroine on her return to England. She founded the Nightingale Training School for Nurses in London in 1860. In 1907, she was the first woman to receive the prestigious Order of Merit.

Hildegard, Harriet Tubman, and Florence Nightingale all shared a core set of values that they might have described in this way: "I have been created with particular talents and strengths, and I feel compelled to develop my strengths in order to live my life most fully. I wish to make a contribution that will enhance my life and the lives of others. I am more than willing to endure discomfort for the sake of achieving my goals."

I would doubt that these women could have predicted at the beginning of their journey how far they would actually go; as young women, they could not possibly have foreseen what they would eventually achieve. I suspect that beyond the wish to live lives of passion and meaning, they simply decided to go as far as they could go, one day at a time, decision by decision.

THE SCOPE OF YOUR WORLD

"Wait a minute," you're thinking. "Hildegard, Harriet Tubman, and Florence Nightingale made history. Very, very few such people exist, male or female. I don't have a sense of world-changing mission. I'm not that talented, that special, that brilliant. Am I really to be motivated by the same sense of meaning that inspired *them*?"

My answer is yes, you may indeed find and define great meaning *within the scope of your world*, a world you create for yourself, defined by the people whose lives you touch: your family, friends, and the people who are affected by your work. If you're a teacher, your world includes the children in your classroom. If you're a nurse, it includes the patients in your care. If you're a journalist, it includes your readers. It is within the world you have created that you live out your destiny. If you are a teacher, you can be a great teacher. If you are a nurse, you can be a great nurse.

As you look back on your own life, you will probably see that the size of your sphere of influence is inversely proportional to the impact you have been able to have on a single life. In my own life, I spent five years in a private psychiatric practice engaged in psychotherapy with twenty or so patients in any given week—a rather small world. Years later, when I began my radio show, my voice reached thousands. Yet the impact I could have on any one listener was very small relative to what I offered my psychotherapy patients. If you have chosen for yourself a small world, the influence you can have on each person may be enormous—and those individuals will eventually pass your gifts on to others.

Clearly, society needs both those who have a small impact on many people and those who have great impact on very few people. For many women, much energy in the early midlife years is spent on mothering, a small world/high impact activity, while later midlife offers opportunities to expand their sphere of influence. How you define your world reflects your values and aptitudes, and you may anticipate that your scope will expand or contract from time to time.

MEANING AND MOTIVATION

Just as our foremothers needed physical stamina, you require a source of psychological energy to fuel your ambition, energy that is derived from a conviction that your work has meaning. This energy will be obvious in all aspects of your life, not only in your work but also in your friendships, your parenting, and your romances; paradoxically, women who approach their work with passion find that that passion spills over into all the important areas of their life. High energy becomes the norm. The achieving woman naturally and consistently engages with life, moment by moment, encounter by encounter. She abhors passivity, choosing instead to dive into experience, pursue learning, and seize opportunity. Faced with the question "Does my life count?" the motivated woman answers: "Of course it counts. Of course I am here for a reason. Of course I want to leave my mark."

Researcher Sally Reis conducted an in-depth study of twelve women, ages fifty-five to eighty-nine, who had achieved eminence in a variety of fields after the age of fifty. Among their remarkable traits, the quality of emotional vigor was particularly notable. Reis found that all of these women had exhibited great determination throughout most of their lives. They demonstrated the ability to strive for success and to work hard despite setbacks.

These women cited a variety of motivations as driving them. Some described a need for a sense of purpose in life, others a desire to produce, to leave a mark upon the world, or to experience the sheer joy of creativity; the overarching motivation of all of the women was to improve the human condition. Reis commented on the vigor these women displayed:

> [A]ll of the women emanated a type of energy and an enjoyment of life. Some were enthusiastic while others were quiet; some laughed frequently and moved constantly, others were very calm and almost reserved. However, each exuded an energy and intensity about her life and work, and a spirit of satisfaction about the direction her life had taken.

My own interviews with great women achievers revealed that *motivation is derived from a personal system of meaning.* I was impressed that when I asked these women how they attained a sense of meaning, they were rarely surprised by the question, and in many cases had already grappled with it. For instance, Anne Darby Parker, a renowned photographer, explained to me how her passion for her work came out of her sense of meaning in this way: "My goal is that in every creative process, I bring an everyday dignity to the person I am photographing—a dignity that allows the soul of the person to be experienced. I feel that way about everything I do. If I'm setting the table, my act should reflect the celebration of our family coming together. My work is successful when the beauty or dignity of the person or environment is pulled out. My passion in life is to be a creative person—whether what I am creating is my art or my children. I think that creativity is central to the meaning of life."

The psychologist Jacquelynn Eccles, who has studied women's achievement motivations for twenty years, has determined that personal values and confidence of success are the two biggest influences on women's achievement-related choices at all levels, from what courses they select in high school to what occupation they choose to enter and how energetically they develop their career. Gender-role socialization may lead men and women to develop very different core values, to give various long-range goals different weights, to define success differently, and finally, to show different degrees of focus vs. scatter in the breadth of goals selected.

And what are these gender-specific values? Gifted women typically endorse social and aesthetic values, while gifted men endorse theoretical, economic, and political values. Further, women tend to value having a job that allows them to help others and do something worthwhile for society, whereas men tend to value becoming famous, making lots of money, seeking out challenges, and doing work involving math and computers. Significant gender differences in a sense of meaning begin to appear in adolescence. In studies of American high school seniors between 1977 and 1991, girls were more likely than boys to express concern and responsibility for the well-being of others, less likely than boys to accept materialism and competition, and more likely than boys to indicate that finding purpose and meaning in life is extremely important. These differences were observed across social classes throughout the period from the mid-1970s to the early 1990s and have shown little sign of decreasing.

Women's Need for Relationships

The impact of values should be considered not just in terms of male vs. female differences but in the hierarchy of values that women develop for themselves; herein lies part of the answer to why women have traditionally not achieved on a par with men. Eccles's findings demonstrate it is not so much that women as a group do not value achievement, but rather that relative to men, they value it less than they do family and relationships. When a choice has to be made, it is often the achievement-related alternative that is sacrificed. This pattern can be traced throughout the life cycle of females; beginning in childhood, for instance, girls rate making occupational sacrifices for one's family higher than boys rate it. A body of research has documented that women are much more likely than men to limit their careers for the sake of family. The Terman Genetic

Study of Genius, which followed exceptional boys and girls from 1922 to 1972, traced the patterns of familial sacrifice made by gifted women and found that many of these women later regretted the career opportunities they had missed.

Nancy J. Chodorow, an eminent psychoanalyst who has written extensively on the development of gender identity, concluded that psychological differences in gender development are based on the different social environments for boys and girls that result from the fact that the first and strongest relationship is usually with the mother. Girls maintain this relationship throughout their early years and base their feminine identity on this unbroken connection. Boys, on the other hand, must break their identification with their mother in order to identify with their father. As they pull away from her, they lose their deep sense of attachment to their first and primary love. As a consequence, a boy's sense of maleness is connected to a sense of detaching from his closest relationship, Chodorow wrote.

Building on this concept, the psychiatrist Jean Baker Miller explored how the masculine emphasis on independence has led to a devaluation of the feminine emphasis on relationship. Miller called for a "new psychology of women," noting that "eventually, for many women the threat of disruption of an affiliation is perceived not just as a loss of a relationship but as something closer to a total loss of self." While acknowledging a considerable body of literature that suggests this equation of self with relationship leads to a variety of psychological ailments in women, Miller noted that women's priority on relationship contains "the possibilities for an entirely different (and more advanced) approach to living and functioning . . . [in which] affiliation is valued as highly as, or more highly than, self-enhancement."

Pursuing this line of thought in another direction, Harvard psychology professor Carol Gilligan explored how the need for relationships influences the development of a sense of ethics and morality in women. Gilligan observed that for women, moral issues are experienced as reflecting the need for inclusion that all humans experience. Males, by contrast, experience morality as reflecting "certain truth" without particular reference to attachments. Faced with dilemmas such as whether to invest time and energy into one's own development or in the welfare of their family, women are more likely than men to choose the latter.

To return now to the central question of this book: At a psychological level, why have women as a group, throughout history and to the present day, failed to reach their potential as achievers? I suggest the following:

We women routinely invest our emotional energy so heavily in the quest for love relationships that our capacity to invest in achievement-oriented personal development is significantly limited. It is not that we fear success per se, but that we have failed to develop a value system that includes high achievement to begin with. Our capacity to surmount obstacles is weakened by our halfhearted commitment to the pursuit.

The psychoanalyst Ethel Spector Person has suggested that this issue comes into play even during childhood, shaping the development of basic skills and abilities:

> [Girls] are preoccupied with social relations in childhood and adolescence, during those crucial years when many boys are laying down passionate interests and acquiring techniques of mastery. A preoccupation with relating crowds out other pursuits. The acquisition of social skills too often takes priority over the acquisition of other skills. Active aims are bent toward being chosen by the male. Vague ambitions persist but without clear-cut goals. This constellation of goals and interests predisposes to a fear of failure.

Person delineated a number of dynamics that may inhibit a woman's ambition:

- Role conflicts related to the shift in social definition of the ideal feminine role.

- Ambition without clear-cut goals, occurring when vague ambition combines with passivity to block the delineation and pursuit of specific interests.

- Fear of failure, which is commonly associated with a low self-esteem that makes the risk of shame and embarrassment unbearable.

- Fear of deviance, or anxiety that high achievement will result in a loss of feminine self-perception.

- Fear of success, whereby a woman fears she will lose the love of others if she succeeds.

An individual woman confronts external obstacles to success with a particular psychology that diminishes her capacity to challenge them. Faced with work-related problems that contain a unique twist for women, she lets her anxiety-charged wish to protect her love relationships above all else influence the way she solves them. For example:

Kimberly graduated from a prestigious medical school at the top of her class and desired a career in academic medicine. Married to a business executive, by age forty she had relocated four times as he climbed the corporate ladder, for she and her husband had decided that his would be the primary career. By the time of the fourth move, she had come to see herself as a benchwarmer in the world of academics; confronted also with the reality of a system in which only 11 percent of full professors were women, she had fundamentally abandoned her goal of attaining the highest rank at a university. Five years later her husband left her for a younger woman, and at that point Kimberly finally began to invest herself more fully in her career.

Nancy, the daughter of an attorney, had herself considered becoming a lawyer. A straight-A student in college, she had plenty of intelligence and drive. She was, however, engaged to a young man who also wanted to become a lawyer, and they could not financially sustain both of them in school simultaneously. Troubled, she consulted with her father. "Sweetie," said he, "law is really a tough business for a woman. Look at my firm: Only three out of twenty partners are women, and they've really had to sacrifice their family life." Lacking support from her fiancé and her father, anticipating an uphill fight to become a respected attorney, and driven, above all else, to establish herself as loving and supportive to her future husband, Nancy chose to become a paralegal instead.

These examples of challenges to a woman's capacity to choose a path of achievement may seem unusually dramatic, but many women do experience similarly stark choices. Further, such big decisions are set within a context of the daily, tiny choices women make that are so different from those men face. Will I spend my lunch hour reading a report or picking up a gift for the birthday party my child has to attend? Will I leave work at five to be home with my children, or will I stay until 6:30 like the men in my office? If I take time off to be classroom mother, will I be seen as a lightweight by others in the office?

Whether the decision is large or small, the psychological process underlying these choices is often the same. To the degree that a woman believes it is women's lot to be sacrificial, she perceives these choices in a narrow either-or frame of reference, as entailing a painful threat to either her love relationships or to her commitment to her work. Such beliefs will unconsciously lead her to constrict the way she conceptualizes her options. No matter what she chooses, she will feel unhappy.

The result of such either-or thinking is an inability to formulate creative solutions to problems, so-called third choices that happily answer both aspects of a woman's life. She might, for example, choose to delight her child's friend by slipping a ten-dollar bill into a birthday card and thus be able to meet her work deadlines. She might choose to ask her boss's permission to do some of her work at home after the children are tucked in at night so she can get home earlier in the day. She might not be able to be a classroom mother, but could take her daughter on an annual weekend trip of her own choosing. She might ask her husband to buy the birthday present, come home at five, or be a classroom father.

How we arrive at these large and small decisions affects our work life and our love life as well. Clearly, the goal should be neither to reflexively make the self-sacrificing choice every time nor to always avoid that choice. Rather, the goal is to live a life that reflects a balanced sense of meaning, allowing for a free range of choices and creative problem-solving that begins with the assumption that it is possible both to love and to work without feeling like a martyr in the process. Developing such a value system involves both clarifying and developing a sense of meaning that honors both love and self.

The central purpose in *clarifying* a value system is to disentangle whether relationships are a rich, mutually satisfying experience of love and intimacy, or whether you're using them to answer anxiety-based issues. A hypertrophied valuation of relationships might come from expecting a relationship to help bolster self-esteem, to ward off depression, or to serve as a buffer from fears of independence.

Developing a value system involves accepting, or even welcoming, that throughout the life cycle, whether or not you have children, the way you experience a sense of meaning will evolve. Women accustomed to defining their sense of meaning as supporting and helping others may be surprised to find a shift to other values in midlife. One of the most delightful parts of being a woman is that we are allowed a broad range of choices in defining a sense of meaning, and as externals in our lives change, we may permit ourselves to alter how we define meaning.

Women's Value Systems

If the nurturing relationship is central to the emotional life of women, it should not be surprising that achieving women often derive their sense of meaning from work that reflects their connection to the human world. Many of the women I interviewed said the values that guide them in their work life are the same values that inspire them in their home life and their play time. Unlike men, who at times display one set of traits at work and a very different set at home, these women seemed to be guided by a unified set of values in all spheres of their lives. The value systems they endorse tended to fall into several categories:

The opportunity to experience and express love. Women who truly love their work almost always experience affection and commitment toward their students, patients, parishioners, and clients. This affection is quite similar in quality, though not in quantity, to what they feel toward their families. Numerous women I spoke to mentioned this emotion:

An attorney practicing domestic law and mediation: "If I'm working with a couple going through a divorce, they are usually in a state of enormous turmoil and psychological despair. Shepherding them through that awful period and guiding them to make the best possible choices is enormously rewarding."

A professor: "I always have a few students each year whom I really care about. They're the ones I know will come back to see me. Sometimes they're the ones who have really struggled the most, or who I know come from tough backgrounds. It's an incredible thrill to watch them grow and eventually succeed."

A doctor: "Last year I got to try out a new experimental medication on a patient who had been ill for years. She was at a point of desperation and we didn't have much hope that anything would help. I couldn't believe it. She got her life back."

From time to time, a psychotherapy patient will ask, "Do you care about me?" I will respond that of course I care and that I try to show my caring by offering the best help I can. Occasionally the patient will respond, "But how can you care? After all, you were assigned to be my doctor. You wouldn't see me if I didn't pay you money."

Many relationships are "assigned" rather than chosen; even parents and children are assigned to each other. Further, there are many relationships in which a transfer of service and money takes place; teaching is such an example. But within these assigned relationships, and notwithstanding the flow of services and money, of course powerful feelings of affection and loyalty can develop that give enormous richness to life. In work life, love is most healthily expressed in a highly disciplined, structured way. The professional demonstrates her love by not transgressing private boundaries or burdening the recipient with her own issues and problems; respect for these boundaries is what allows the relationship to endure.

The opportunities to experience and express love are by no means limited to the helping professions. Most work settings provide the opportunity to initiate and sustain many types of rewarding relationships with colleagues, bosses, employees, and clients. Being part of a group of people working toward the same end fosters a wonderful sense of affiliation, and over the course of a lifetime these relationships can become meaningful and fulfilling.

Contribution to a cause: As Harriet Tubman surely knew, a powerful source of meaning is the conviction that one's efforts contribute to something far larger than oneself. Just as family represents a cause larger than the individual, so does work, whether it is humanitarian, environmental, cultural, or even commercial. Associating with the cause yields a spiritual sense that one's life has meaning as part of a larger whole.

Well-managed companies, though driven by a profit motive, can instill the concept of dedication to a cause in their employees; after all, it is private enterprise that is responsible for much of the progress of civilization. Great salespeople genuinely believe that the customer will get satisfaction from a well-designed product that delivers what is promised, whether that product is computer software, a manufacturing system, or a new pharmacologic agent. Companies also offer their workers the chance to improve the lot of their fellow employees; a spirit of teamwork is established with the understanding that each person contributes to the ability of the corporation to make life better for all workers.

It is for this reason that the ethical basis of organizational life is so important. If the leadership of an organization is perceived as dishonest or self-serving, employees lose their sense of dedication to the group cause, regardless of how noble the cause might be. Likewise, even in the most obviously profit-driven organizations high ethical standards and demonstrations of concern and loyalty to employees instill a sense of dedication.

Personal development and self-expression: For many people, the drive to expand intelligence becomes a lifelong pursuit extending throughout work and home life. The thought behind it might be summarized in this way: I am responsible for the development of my brain, body, and soul. It is my duty to guide that development as well as I can to fully express the potential I have been given.

Out of this sense of responsibility to develop the self, a desire to *express* oneself follows naturally. In my conversations with women of achievement, this drive repeatedly surfaced. In fact, it was often expressed not just as a *wish* to express oneself, but as a *need*.

Jill, a violist, commented, "They always say that you should not become a professional musician unless you really have to play. The life is very hard; the pay is low, the competition is intense, and the travel is very tiring. But I really felt that I had no choice but to play."

Paula, an artist, echoed this sense. "I always knew I wanted to be an artist, but it was a passion I couldn't fully express while my boys were young. Now that I can devote my life to my art, I feel younger, immensely happier, and that I am living the life I was meant to live."

Stephanie was a minister who developed a reputation in her community as a gifted orator in the pulpit. Under her leadership, her church's membership swelled. As she entered her forties, however, her goals shifted. She gave up pastoral work to devote more time to writing. "My work has changed because my sense of meaning in life has changed. Originally it was derived from inspiring and encouraging and consoling other people. However, that sense of meaning did not sustain me because it left out a crucial ingredient—which was *me*. So now I seek meaning from coming to know and appreciate the ever-deepening realms of my interior world, and out of that, creating and articulating my vision through my art. It gives me a sense of meaning and even joy in the moment of doing it, and it isn't dependent on whether the other person responds to it. Earlier in my life I believed that the experience of spirituality had to be expressed by service to other people. It wasn't until midlife that I began to realize that there could be other ways, legitimate ways, to develop and express my spirituality."

At a roundtable discussion with a group of women physicians, I commented that I couldn't imagine being anything but a psychiatrist. All the women at the table, representing a variety of specialties, echoed the same feeling. The surgeon *had* to be a surgeon, the pediatrician *had* to take care of kids, the researcher *had* to spend her life in the lab. The passion to express one's unique talents, skills, and knowledge is an enormous source of meaning for women of achievement.

Stimulation: Many women speak of an element of fascination in their work, seeing it as a great source of intellectual stimulation. Typically such women are intellectually alive in their relationships as well, sharing intense interests with their families and friends in conversation and leisure activities. The psychiatrist Irvin Yalom, writing about various types of meaning, has called this form of meaning *hedonism*, referring to the pure pleasure derived from exploring an intriguing subject.

Awe is a particular form of fascination that can be the source of enormous productivity. It was awe that led Rachel Carson to become absorbed in her study of the environment, for instance, which ultimately led to her landmark book, *Silent Spring* (1962), in which she called for the protection of the earth against pollution by industrial toxins. It is awe for the beauty of music that leads performers to work at their instruments day after day. Awe draws the participant to become one with the object of her appreciation.

The opportunity to master a childhood issue: The field of psychotherapy has traditionally held that how a person constructs her own family life as an adult reflects childhood issues that need to be worked through. The need to rework and master old issues is similarly revealed in work choices; the same emotional themes color both spheres.

An example of using work to complete the "unfinished business" of childhood is illustrated by Aletta, a highly respected judge, whose passion for fairness first manifested itself when she was a little girl. Aletta was raised by her aunt's family after her own mother died. Although they were kind and loving people, Aletta always felt like an outsider, and she remained keenly aware of the unfairness of the loss of her mother. In her adopted family she often played the role of the peacemaker with her quarrelsome relatives; she felt she could "earn" her place by bringing tranquillity into the home. Unconsciously, she was pulled to the profession of law in order to master her need to establish a belief in a fair world; in the courtroom, she could be a force for a just solution to conflict. To have limited herself in her career would have only reinforced her old feelings of being on the second tier of an unfair world. For her, clearly, work expressed a spiritual solution to her childhood tragedy. She commented, "There are really two parts of the work I do that are important to me. First, I love the process of legal thinking itself. There is a crystal logic to it, a step-by-step understanding of each of the legal issues in a particular case, that has an internal beauty of its own. But the second part of it is that the concept of fairness is so important to me. When I was a lawyer my greatest strength was that I could always see both sides of a case, and that helped to clarify what was fair both to my client and the other person. I would always try to help both parties in a dispute understand the other party's concerns as well as their own, and so usually both sides would come away feeling they had reached a fair settlement. As a judge, I have even more opportunity to influence that fairness."

Work can be a wonderful way to right an old wrong. Often the meaning of work can be found in giving to others the support, counseling, education, or healing that one missed as a child. Frequently, doctors choose specialties because of a desire to help others suffering from illnesses that their parent or a sibling died of. Organizing one's life to respond to a threat one felt powerless about as a child can be a source of enormous inspiration.

And what about money? In focus groups I've held across the country, one source of meaning in work often mentioned is the capacity to earn money. Money, after all, is necessary to feed, clothe, and house yourself and your children. It is also a way to freedom, independence, and power. Money lets you experience the extraordinary range of cultures, foods, music, art, and recreation the world has to offer. Money brings you security from worry as you age.

When a woman says to me, "I work because I want to make as much money as possible," I translate that to mean she wishes to use her energy to buy as much freedom, security, stimulation, and delight in her life as she can. Obviously the quest for money can go too far, obscuring more important values; love of money *can* be the root of much evil. But poverty can also be the root of evil. Clearly, it is not money itself that is either inherently good or evil, but the humans who make use of it.

For Jerilyn, the owner of a women's boutique, the wish to make money is a significant, if not primary, part of her motivation to succeed. After her husband suddenly died, it was clear that she had to earn a substantial living to support herself and her children. As a teenager, she'd loved to sew and took extensive tailoring classes that gave her an appreciation for high-quality cut and construction of garments. She savored everything about fine clothes: the feel of exquisite fabrics, the drape of a beautiful fit. She took out a loan and started a high-fashion boutique. Ten years later she has a thriving, lucrative business. "The driving force behind my success came in response to the overwhelming devastation, and even stark terror, that I felt after my husband died," she said. "It was not only that I had lost my best friend; in addition, I was now the only parent my children had for guidance, support, and discipline. And on top of that, I had to figure out how to support us all financially, and I really wanted them to have as many opportunities as they would have had Charles lived.

"After he died, I went to bed for three days—I just could hardly move. As I lay in bed, I tried to understand why Charles had died, what possible meaning there could be in it. I don't really believe that God had him die for a purpose. Yet if any possible meaning could be extracted, it was only in the challenge, even demand, it created for me to rise to the occasion with as much grace, energy, and determination as I could muster to create a good life for my children and me. And that challenge has driven me all these years."

Yet even though money is perceived as an important motivation for working, salary alone is rarely a good predictor of job satisfaction. For both men and women, career satisfaction has been shown to be determined far more by subjective job rewards, such as social support, stimulation, and opportunity for growth. This explains why women are found to be equally satisfied with work as men, despite earning less money—the so-called Female Paradox.

Love, contribution, self-development, stimulation, emotional mastery, power, freedom: all these values could be gathered under the heading "engagement with life." Fundamentally, the wish to achieve is the wish to be as deeply engaged as possible: engaged with your own mind and creativity, engaged with people, engaged with solving the problems of the world. Each of the choices that follow this first fundamental choice of meaning not only enhances your capacity to succeed but inexorably draws you into a deeper romance with life.

What If You Find No Meaning in Your Work?

For many people, of course, work has no intrinsic meaning beyond generating income. A retired woman I interviewed, for example, described having spent twenty-five years at a job she hated *every day*. "I did it strictly for the money," she said "and because it provided great benefits. I'm so thrilled to be retired, because my husband and I have a great life, thanks to my retirement package." Of course a great retirement is wonderful—but is twenty-five years of hating the way you spend five days a week worth it? And what if she had died without ever having enjoyed her retirement?

If you find no meaning in your work, consider the possibility that the work you do directly conflicts with values you hold dear. Or perhaps the people you work with do not command your respect or even liking. If you feel genuine antipathy toward your colleagues, your workplace will begin to feel like a bad marriage—a toxic environment you stay in only because change is scary. Or perhaps you've simply been working at the same job for so long that it doesn't provide the stimulation and opportunity for growth it once did.

If you find no meaning in your work, find work that does have meaning.

This advice may seem obvious until you consider how utterly common it is for women—and men—to remain stuck in a job long after it has stopped providing any sense of fulfillment. Finding different work might mean taking on new activities in your current job; it could mean doing the same work for another organization; it could mean a complete change of occupation. If, in the course of thirty years of work life, you continue to mature and develop, it logically follows that the work you enjoy will change as well. Further, in a fast-changing society, the variety of work possibilities continues to grow—why not be part of that change, if it might bring you new opportunities?

RESILIENCE

If a sense of meaning is the bedrock of motivation, a second psychological trait is necessary in maintaining motivation: resilience. This is the ability to stay motivated despite the myriad setbacks that inevitably occur over a lifetime of ambition.

The concept of emotional resilience first appeared in the psychological literature almost fifty years ago in the work of Jack Block, who has continued his research on this topic ever since. While defining resilience as the capacity to restore psychological equilibrium after stressful events, Block notes that more than just acquiescing to reality is involved. In his view, resilience implies resistance to undue anxiety as well as the capacity for positive engagement in the world and openness to experience.

In a recent study, Block noted that many of the characteristics of resilience are also qualities of intelligence—for example, a high degree of what psychologists refer to as "executive functions." But by performing a statistical analysis that allowed him to tease out so-called pure emotional resilience from pure intelligence, Block found that the resilient young woman has qualities distinctly different—in fact, almost opposite—from the resilient young man. Specifically, emotionally resilient young women possess the capacity *not* to yield to social pressures to overcontrol their impulses. In his words, she "values her independence, is self-indulgent, colorful, interpersonally skilled, relatively less over-controlled, and not submissive." By contrast, young males who are resilient are characterized by ethical and responsible behavior, conservatism, predictability, internal consistency, and an acceptance of society's limits. Block suggests that women need a measure of spontaneity in order to resist societal pressure to be passive, indecisive, and cowed by the opinions of others. For boys, however, the capacity for socialization helps to modulate testosterone-driven aggression and competitiveness.

The fact that these particular female traits of resilience are not correlated with IQ explains in part why there is often not a direct correlation between IQ and achievement. Gifted but overly conforming females often feel trapped between wanting to be "nice" and wanting to achieve. In a study of multiethnic girls between third and sixth grade, the psychologist Lee Anne Bell heard five gender-role themes emerge repeatedly. The girls worried about whether their winning achievement contests might hurt someone else's feelings; whether they would be seen as bragging if they were openly pleased with their success; whether they were beautiful enough; and whether they were too aggressive in getting their teacher's attention. These girls also tended to overreact to failure.

The overwhelming wish to "be nice" is not quickly outgrown, unfortunately. Marianne, a medical student in a small, interactive class I taught, was brilliant, but so quiet that her grade was suffering. I urged her on several occasions to speak up more in class, but to no avail. Then, after the group members had shared comments about each other at midterm, she said: "When Dr. Austin asked me to participate more for the sake of my grade, that was one thing. But when my classmates asked me to participate more so that they could have a better learning experience, I really started taking my problem more seriously." In other words, she could be motivated by the fear of disappointing others, but resisted change for the sake of promoting herself!

The problem of "making nice" continues to the highest levels. Commenting on his views of what women need to do to advance in organizations, a male senior executive commented, "The women who get ahead here are those who are not afraid to speak their minds. Some, in fact, can be a bit abrasive at times. Women seem to worry so much about whether what they say will be offensive. Men never worry about that—they just say it."

For women, then, resilience requires a bold capacity to remain relatively unconcerned about the judgments and opinions of others. This quality allows the achieving woman to focus on her goals despite lack of support from others. She is able to endure defeat and to bounce back from uncomfortable, even painful moments in order to achieve her goals. Precisely *how* she endures these tough times is highly variable; some women are stoic and dignified, while others are outspoken and opinionated. It matters far less *how* she rebounds than *that* she rebounds. It is not necessary to get an A for style or grace.

GOAL-DIRECTEDNESS

The third core element of motivation is goal-directedness, the capacity to focus your energy on a particular, highly defined target. Goal-directedness allows you to conserve your energy for what is most important to you, giving you the ability to distinguish the meaningful from the mundane, the vital from the trivial. The achieving woman maintains her vigor and resilience by not wasting her energy on minor conflicts and meaningless pursuits, refining her sense of priorities as she goes.

Goal-directedness inspires the ambitious woman to avoid the bane of the modern working woman's existence, fragmentation. Our society assumes that women will instantly respond to whatever demands arrive from an infinite number of directions and that men should be spared these interruptions. The tacit assumption that fragmentation is the norm for women leads to the intense stress that so many women experience, a stress that depletes vigor and weakens resilience.

Abundant research documents that males are far more focused in their goal-directedness than females are. Males are significantly narrower than females in their interests—a topic we will return to in the discussion of intelligence. Girls are likely to express interest in a variety of subjects, boys only in traditionally male-related areas. A study of graduate students in mathematics found that the men were most concerned about their professional status and their mentors' views of them, while the women were most concerned about the impact their studies had on family life. This reflects a recurrent theme in studies of the achievement motivation of men and women. Men perceive that their achievements will benefit their families by providing a more secure standard of living, while women perceive that their achievement will detract from their contribution to family life.

By no means is this to say that men's relative unidimensionality is necessarily superior to women's multidimensionality, but it is important to recognize the effect of this difference on women's productivity. It is highly challenging for a woman to compete with her male peers on an equal footing during the years when she chooses to direct her energies in multiple directions. To avoid a sense of victimization about her different career trajectory, the multidimensional woman must appreciate and accept the impact that her diversity of goals has on her capacity to achieve at work. It is not that she cannot achieve her goals but that her achievement will be delayed; this consequence may be well worth it, if the woman can remain patient and can tolerate the frustration of seeing her male peers advance faster than she.

Further, it is often women who reinforce men's unidimensionality: we allow our time to be directed to activities that diffuse our energies while protecting men's work and leisure time. Married women with jobs tend to assign themselves all household tasks, freeing their spouses of an equal sense of obligation. Whether the job is making the beds, sorting laundry, or washing windows, it is usually the wife who does it.

Is it possible for a woman to pursue two major goals—raising a family and pursuing a meaningful career—simultaneously? *Absolutely*; many women do this. However, it is not possible to do both well while allowing energies to be scattered in meaningless ways. If your time at work is limited, you do not have the luxury of pursuing activities that are not central to your work goals. You have limited time for social chatter with workmates. You especially do not have time for any activities that could be appropriately delegated elsewhere, particularly to support staff.

Anne Darby Parker, the photographer, spoke of the parallel issues at home: "Too many women run themselves ragged on such inconsequential matters. I do all my shopping at the nearby Bi-Lo, and my friends will always ask me why I don't go to the deluxe grocery store that's a mile further up the road. I don't have time for that. I just can't be bothered with driving all over town. If my family life starts getting too crazy I'll look at where we can cut back—so what if my kids go to two birthday parties instead of four? I'd much rather have a happy family life."

Achieving women do have time for a happy family life—but we do not have time to waste in meaningless frenzy. A fulfilling home life is not to be confused with deluxe groceries or a dizzying social schedule.

Translating Motivation into Action: The Strategic Plan

To benefit maximally from your sense of motivation, try writing out a Strategic Plan. The process of actually writing down your strategy helps organize a jumble of wishes, impulses, and fantasies into a course of action. The purpose of the plan is primarily to get you started; you are likely, in fact, to change the details and even some of the goals as you go along. Without a plan, however, you may never initiate the first concrete steps of turning your achievement wishes into reality.

Begin your Strategic Plan with a *vision statement*. Your vision should be painted in very broad brushstrokes and should express your ultimate dreams, couched in terms of your sense of meaning in life. Don't be afraid to be grand; in fact, your vision should be magnificent in scope. Some examples of vision:

"To join in the fight against breast cancer, so other women won't experience what I did when my sister died."

"To know myself as a spiritual being and to express that in a way that inspires others."

"To become involved in the political process to be able to work on issues that matter to me."

"To help African Americans achieve power and control of their lives."

A vision statement doesn't express *how* you are going to accomplish your ends, just *what* you want to accomplish and why it is important to you. Although it is purposefully vague, a vision statement serves as a psychological lighthouse, drawing you toward your goals and reorienting you when you veer off course.

The next part of your Strategic Plan, the *mission statement*, should address the *how* of your goals. If your vision is to fight breast cancer, do you want to do that by becoming a researcher studying tumors, an ob-gyn or nurse midwife, or an employee of an organization that promotes women's health issues? If you wish to express your spirituality, would you like to do that as a minister, a counselor, a writer, or an artist? If you wish to become politically active, will your mission be to run for office, or will it be to work for a political party or government agency? If you wish to help African Americans, will you do that as a teacher, community leader, or writer?

The third section should be the *activities section*, divided into a long-range plan and short-term goals. Think of your long-range plan as developing over five years or so, enough time for you to have accomplished something quite concrete and tangible. The concept of a five-year plan is particularly important if you are at a phase of your life in which career is relatively dormant, often the case with mothers of young children. This dormancy can be an important period for taking a respite from the pressures and value system of the workplace, allowing you time to reconsider your goals. It may be, for instance, that you wish your ultimate career path to take a very different direction from what you had imagined in your early adult years. You might use your five years to get a master's degree half-time, to learn a second language or another skill, gain work experience by volunteering in a field related to your interest, or to cultivate acquaintances who might be leads to important contacts.

Your short-term goals should be extremely concrete and explicit, focusing on what you need to do today, this week, or this month to move forward. A long-term plan can be reached only by the accretion of short-term goals successfully met. If your goal is to write a book, your short-term goal may be to write three pages a day, a chapter by the end of the month. If your goal is to get a degree, you may start just by writing away for catalogs.

The fourth section of your Strategic Plan should consider *constraints* and *resources*. Make a list of the various obstacles in your path; examples might be lack of child care, money, spousal support, or proximity to educational opportunities. Now struggle with each one, analyzing to what degree you can limit the impact of the constraint, or to what degree the constraint may slow down your development. As you analyze each constraint, assess the resources you may need to deal with each one. Remember that "luck" is not a resource. If you are unable to modify the constraint, you may be forced to ask yourself whether your goals are unrealistic. In fact, you may even have to wonder whether you have chosen an unattainable goal as an excuse for inaction.

Besides enabling you to clarify your core priorities, your Strategic Plan will enable you to establish rules for what you will *not* do. Years ago, as a junior faculty member and single mother of two young children, I drew up a Strategic Plan with the help of a friend. At that time I realized that my chief interest was public education in mental health. My friend suggested that I limit myself to using only electronic media in the strategies I would pursue. That meant, for example, that I would turn down requests to give talks to small local groups—an enjoyable, meaningful, but exhausting activity that would have robbed me of time in the evening with my children or productive work time during the day. Years later, when I was given charge of public education activities for the medical school where I teach, my staff and I decided that our priority would be activities that would have a statewide reach; local and national projects would be lower on the list. The clarity of deciding up front not only what I *would* do but also what I *wouldn't* do was an essential part of maintaining goal-directedness.

Consider drawing up a Strategic Plan for your home life as well. What is your vision? If it is, presumably, a happy, serene home life, what are the choices and behaviors that thwart that? What is your mission? If your mission is to provide support and nurturance to your family, which activities are central to this mission, and which siphon off your energy? Next, what are your resources? Compare your current activities to your Strategic Plan; to what degree do you invest time in activities that have little meaning to you and do nothing to promote your mission?

Throughout this chapter I have used terms like "meaning" and "values" as if all of us really understand and can articulate what it is we really care about. In fact, however, a gap often exists between what we *believe* we really care about and what our behavior indicates are our true values. If, for instance, you routinely feel you do not spend enough time in conversation with your child, and yet have time each day to watch television, paint your nails, or talk with a friend on the phone, it may be that what you truly value is quite different from what you believe you value. If you feel you do not have the money for a housekeeper who could free up your time to allow you a saner family life, and yet you spend an extra $10,000 buying a new car rather than a used car, what really are your core values? If you have money to spend on great clothes but none to take your family on a vacation, what does this say about what you care most about?

A Time for Honesty

The process of developing a Strategic Plan may reveal a truth to you that you have not articulated previously: Your motivation to achieve may, in fact, be limited right now. Limited motivation may arise for unfortunate reasons, such as poor self-esteem, depression, passivity, or apathy. But there are also excellent reasons for low motivation at certain points in your life. You may, for instance, be at a time in your life when other pursuits, such as a love relationship, the birth of children, or a spiritual journey, take precedence over your drive to achieve. There may be external situations beyond your control that limit the reality of what you can achieve—for instance, a responsibility to care for a sick parent, or recovery from an illness of your own.

If this is the case, it is far better to limit your goals than to take on overly ambitious projects and fail. You might, for instance, choose a modest goal and work intensively at it on a part-time basis. You might choose to merely "hold your place" at work, until a more opportune moment comes. The challenge, of course, is not to become derailed for life, but to prepare yourself for the time when a shift in your sense of meaning allows investment in a goal worthy of your talents.

But what if the exercise of articulating your Strategic Plan clarifies a reality that you have not fully grasped before: that your goals really *are* important to you, perhaps more important than other ways you are spending your time and energy? If you see in your plan the elements of a journey that truly is exciting, it is time to get started on your path.

CHOICE

INVESTING YOUR ENERGY

Nest-Building or Risk-Taking?

SURELY IT IS possible to reach goals simply by virtue of steady, grinding, daily perseverance. But taking an occasional intelligent risk allows you to leverage your energy for greater achievement, enabling you to leapfrog over the tedium of a slow accretion of tiny gains.

Leeda Marting is a wonderful example of a woman with a great willingness to take risks for the sake of long-term, ambitious goals. Marting, well known in New York City as a successful foundation administrator and fund-raiser, decided to open a garden shop in Charleston. I first met her while she was buying an old wreck of a building just off the beaten tourist path to renovate for her business. Determined that her business would be called Charleston Gardens, a name coveted by another woman with a similar idea, Marting was in the middle of a costly legal dispute.

Leeda was delightful, but I found her plan mystifying. Why, I wondered, would anyone leave a glamorous lifestyle in New York for Charleston, especially someone with no personal ties to the area? Why did Marting think Charleston needed one more garden shop, when we had excellent nurseries just outside the downtown area? Why was she willing to risk so much money renovating an old building just to sell some pots and a few lawn chairs? And why was she so intent on the name Charleston Gardens that she was willing to engage in a legal wrangle?

In the several years since that time, I have watched in amazement as Leeda Marting's business has grown. The renovation was nothing short of spectacular; the two-hundred-year-old building was gutted, but the charming facade and all original brickwork remain. The interior is an open, airy space with wonderful architectural details that opens to a walled garden behind the shop, complete with trees, ponds, and fountains. Marting's inventory is impressive, consisting of upscale imported garden items—furniture, pottery, garden sculpture, and clever accessories. She has also developed a national catalog featuring her products against the backdrop of historic Charleston architecture and is currently preparing capital for the next wave of expansion to secure a central position in the national upscale-garden business.

Simultaneously, Charleston itself has exploded as a tourist mecca, moving into the top ten national vacation destinations. In the decade since Hurricane Hugo in 1989, the city has successfully embarked on an ambitious plan to develop its parks and a range of tourist amenities; the downtown residential area with its magnificent private and public gardens is frequently featured in garden and travel magazines. Thus the name Charleston Gardens reflects both a business and a tribute to a very special city. Every one of the hundreds of magazine articles featuring the gardens of Charleston indirectly promotes Leeda's business as well!

Marting's success appears to be the result of a lucky gamble. A gamble it certainly was, but much more than luck was involved. As soon as she had her first inklings of developing her own business, she undertook extensive market research and determined that gardening is the number one hobby of the huge baby boom generation. Further research revealed that Charleston was about to take off as a tourist site and that it was beginning to develop a national reputation for its gardens. She researched the site of her building, correctly predicting that it was ideally suited for expanding tourist traffic and that it would soon be perfectly geographically positioned for foot traffic. In other words, she actively and aggressively got her ducks in a perfect row before she made her move.

The trait that distinguishes Leeda Marting from many other intelligent, hardworking women is a certain *boldness* that infuses her vision, her thinking, and her spontaneous behavior. It is, of course, precisely this trait that has been most discouraged in women throughout history. Our collective psychology has been based on a denial of our boldness. Claiming this trait is a critical element in developing a psychology of ambition.

WOMEN, MEN, AND RISK

Women have traditionally taken a curious approach to risk. If you were asked to take a risk that required you to invest all your finances, personal security, and emotional stability in a proposition that carried a 50 percent likelihood of failure, you would probably balk. Yet this is precisely what marriage entails, given the current high rate of divorce. Historically, female risk-taking has always been through another person, namely, a husband. We took one giant risk in yoking our lives to theirs; they took risks in interacting with the world.

Throughout history, human cultures have decreed that women be "protected" from risk. It was men who sailed the seas and discovered new lands. It was men who first climbed mountains, explored the ocean floor, and orbited the planet. It was men who went to war and ran for office. Even in our era, it remains enough for individual women to be the first *woman* this-or-that; we are almost never the first *human* to explore new frontiers.

All our lives, we are bombarded by overt and covert images and messages that perpetuate the notion that risk is for men, not for women. On Saturday afternoons throughout America, our televisions blast us with

images of men colliding into each other on the football field, men whack-
ing each other with hockey sticks, men crashing their cars on a racetrack.
The message is clear. It is men who take risks. In our daily lives, custom
mandates that when a woman is in the company of a man, it is he who
should perform such dangerous feats as driving the car down the road or
walking on the curb side of the sidewalk.

These are images of physical risk-taking behavior. But research documents gender differences in the approach to risk in virtually *all* areas
studied. But before I describe these studies, an explanatory note about
how to interpret this type of gender-based research is in order.

A Caveat and a Note of Encouragement

Throughout this book I cite studies to support observations of gender
differences in a variety of psychological functions. Although I report only
on studies in which either the number of subjects was very large or where a
significant number of studies found similar results, you should be aware
that gender differences reported, though statistically significant, are generally small—sometimes not more than a few percentage points on a scale.
Further, there is enormous overlap between males' scores and females'
scores, so that these studies do nothing to predict differences between a
specific woman and a specific man.

Despite these caveats, these gender-based trends are important to
understand, for one simple reason: *however small each difference is, the
number of achievement-related traits where such differences are observed is
large.* Imagine, for instance, that relative to your male colleagues you are 5
percent less likely to take risks, 5 percent less likely to be goal-directed, and
5 percent less likely to value achievement. Add these deficits together, and
the impact is significant. But the good news is that you don't need to rein-
vent your personality in order to become more successful. Rather, think in
terms of becoming, say, 10 percent more risk-taking, goal-directed, and
achievement-valuing—you'll surpass your male friends!

Foolish Risks and Smart Ones

The observation that in virtually all types of risk studied, males take chances far more readily than females do has profound consequences, both positive and negative, for both genders, because taking risks increases the likelihood of very good or very bad things occurring. Relative to women, for instance, males have attained far greater accomplishments that have won them fame and fortune; but that same risk-taking impulse has also won them the dubious distinction of being far more likely than women to end up in prison, in wheelchairs following accidents, in drug rehab, or in an early grave.

First, the up side to the female aversion to risk. Relative to men, women are far less inclined to take physical risks that might expose us to bodily harm, an aversion that serves us well in many aspects of daily life. Relative to males, we are less likely to engage in behaviors that endanger our health, such as ignoring seat belts, carrying weapons, using tobacco, alcohol, and drugs, and indulging in unsafe sexual practices. Boys are much more likely to take risks that may lead to physical injury than girls are. Women are more concerned about risk from environmental toxins and nuclear accidents than men are. One study of male and female soldiers in a computer-simulated exercise on minefields documented that males are more inclined to take risks even in cyberspace.

These are dramatic instances of physical risk in which discretion may indeed be the better part of valor. But sex differences in risk-taking also carry over in subtle, insidious ways that may not serve us so well. Research by the psychologist Elizabeth C. Arch suggests that the female aversion to risk holds true in social contexts and presents a powerful impediment to achievement. The linguist Deborah Tannen has pointed out that in verbal situations men take risks by dominating conversations and asserting their opinions, while women retreat from controversy with phrases that reflect tentativeness and defuse conflict. In situations where they are being evaluated, women are more likely than men to worry, feel lower self-esteem, and become less willing to participate than men.

Studies of gambling behaviors are especially interesting because they more directly reflect risk appraisal and are less complicated by cultural issues than the other behaviors. In several lab studies, males repeatedly waged larger amounts of money than females did and described a greater "illusion of control" than females did. In real-life situations such as the race-track, men gamble and bet more often than women do and for larger stakes.

Observations of entrepreneurship in women, one of the most poten-tially rewarding forms of risk-taking, suggest that women are beginning to change the way they approach risk. Before 1970, less than 5 percent of businesses were owned by women. Since the mid-1990s, however, women have surpassed men in starting new business by a ratio of 2:1, an encouraging sign. However, of the 8 million businesses that are owned by women, 3.5 million are run out of the home, suggesting that when we do start businesses we avoid the risk of significant capital outlay, and these numbers may be inflated by many businesses using women as fronts.

Risk-taking is a complex behavior, the end product of a series of calcula-tions that have important psychological determinants. Before you take a chance, your unconscious mental computer sorts through a series of issues. *Do I enjoy the prospect of something novel occurring, or do I find change anx-iety-provoking? Do I have faith that I can optimize the chance of a good out-come, or do I doubt I have the capabilities to ensure success?* Even more gen-erally, *Do I perceive that I have the ability to shape events, or do I see forces outside my control determining the course of my life?* How you answer these questions will determine whether you are willing to roll the dice. In fact, men and women often appraise these issues quite differently.

Sensation-Seeking

Psychologists and psychiatrists studying risk-taking behaviors have looked at a trait believed to be an antecedent to the urge to take a chance: sensation-seeking. People who take risks, as it turns out, tend to like new and different situations; they are more easily bored with routine, and they search out stimulation. Researcher Marvin Zuckerman and his colleagues have studied basic psychological differences between the genders in sensation-seeking and the genetic factors that may cause them. On Zuckerman's "Sensation-Seeking Scale," which measures *thrill- and adventure-seeking*; *experience-seeking* (including the pursuit of new experiences through the mind and the senses, such as through the arts, traveling, meeting unusual people, and certain types of drugs); *disinhibition* (including impulsive activities such as sex and gambling); and *susceptibility to boredom* in routine activities, males score higher than females in all four categories, though the difference is most dramatic in the area of disinhibition. Zuckerman suggests a variety of biological factors associated with sensation-seeking, including the male sex hormone testosterone.

But whether this difference is nature or nurture is still unresolved. Women, after all, have been culturally conditioned through the ages to tolerate the boredom of domestic chores and to limit their range of exploration if it conflicts with family responsibilities.

Confidence

A second element of taking chances is self-confidence, for how you appraise your own competence affects your perception of your odds of success. Study after study have found significant sex-based differences in confidence: men overvalue themselves, often beyond their true ability, while women either assess themselves realistically or undervalue themselves. These studies confirm what many women have always believed: men just *think* they're *soooo* smart! A body of research has documented this disparity in diverse groups, finding, for example, that men believe they are more knowledgeable than women about current affairs; male teachers are more secure than females about their teaching skills; male athletes are more self-confident than their female equivalents; and male financial analysts are more sure of their abilities than female analysts are of theirs. In one study, late-adolescent females rated themselves as less confident than their male classmates, despite the fact that they were better qualified academically than the boys. Another particularly disturbing study rated the self-concepts of

301 boys and girls who had won prestigious Westinghouse awards for research in science, math, or social science during their senior year of high school. Even in this group of proven high achievers, girls rated themselves lower than boys on all self-concept scales.

Janie, a resident in a group I teach, illustrates a thought process that many women share. Though one of the most competent students in the group, Janie usually prefaces her remarks by saying, "I don't really understand x very well, but maybe the group could help me." She then proceeds to demonstrate impressive knowledge about the subject, but highlights the few areas that remain unclear to her. Unlike the men in the room, she places greater emphasis on what she *doesn't* know than what she *does* know. This appears to be neither a ploy nor a social nicety, but rather the fundamental way she evaluates her own knowledge and competence.

It is altogether too easy to be overwhelmed by displays of male confidence, mistaking their assertiveness and certainty for superior competence. Like Janie, many women would benefit from allowing themselves a mental "correction factor"—a reminder that they can validly add on a few self-evaluation points to compensate for the tendency to underestimate themselves.

A few studies suggest that even beyond the realm of personal competence, women as a group may be less optimistic in general than men. Michael Malinchoc and his colleagues used the MMPI in a study of 1,315 boys and girl ages 13–17 and found that girls were significantly more pessimistic than boys. This paralleled their earlier, similarly large study of adults, which also found that males are more optimistic than females. Though intriguing, these findings raise as many questions as they answer. Just why are we a bit more pessimistic? Is it because we have grown up in a culture where we have traditionally been seen as the "weaker" sex? Is it perhaps because we are more realistic than men, especially as historically things have not always gone so well for us? Research has yet to answer such questions, and they remain open to debate.

Locus of Control

Another construct that may help us understand gender differences in risk is the locus of control. People who have an *internal* locus of control tend to believe that they are in charge of events; those with an *external* locus of control perceive consequences as due to outside forces. A number of studies have shown females to have an external locus of control more often than males. For example, one study divided up control issues into four categories: luck-chance, fatalism, powerful others, and personal control, finding that in all four categories females were more external than males. This difference appears to be transcultural, for a study of more then 4,500 managers and employees in fourteen countries also found women's locus to be more external than men's. Further, those in powerful positions had a more internal locus than lower-level employees, regardless of gender. It should not be surprising that women are more likely than men to have an external locus of control, for the lives of women *have* been largely controlled by men until quite recently. Remember, it has only been since 1920 that American women have even had the right to vote. For millennia our collective identity rested on the accurate acknowledgment that our lives were indeed controlled by external forces, and the ideals we developed for ourselves stressed the importance of traits such as patience, tolerance, and humility; small wonder that we have some work to do before we can begin to feel more thoroughly in charge of our lives.

Tolerating Anxiety

We pay a hefty psychological price for our avoidance of risk, and men gain an invaluable psychological advantage by their immersion in it. *They learn to tolerate anxiety.* Beginning when they're small boys, their preoccupation with fantasy figures like Batman and Superman leads them to tuck fear into the deep recesses of their unconscious. Forays into high school football or hockey force them to swallow pain and keep pushing themselves. For many young men, military training teaches them to conquer, or at least hide, their fear and weakness. As they learn to deny or repress their fear of physical challenges, they also develop mechanisms for tolerating emotional danger.

As a mother, I have been struck by the differences in exposure to risk that my son and my daughter experienced in their developmental years, which conform to research studies of boys' and girls' behavior. Starting in preschool, Matt and his buddies seemed to try to outdo each other on the playground, vying to see who could jump from the highest perch or who dared to drag himself around in the mud beneath the merry-go-round. In junior high school when Matt began playing football, he once confessed to me how scary it was to be tackled by the bigger boys; yet he and the others lined up play after play, game after game, struggling to master their fear. Girls, of course, also have their own anxieties to conquer, but these are primarily social in nature. For young boys, the process of taking physical risks is a day-in, day-out experience.

The experience that young boys provide themselves in *purposefully* exposing themselves to fearful situations parallels the way cognitive-behavioral psychologists train patients to tolerate anxiety. Psychologists have long observed that in a naturalistic setting an individual has only two choices in response to anxiety: either to flee from the situation or to "push through" the experience and tolerate their psychological discomfort. Whichever choice is made has important consequences for establishing patterned responses. Choosing to flee demonstrates that anxiety can be *temporarily* lessened by avoiding the scary situation. Ironically, though, the more often one chooses to flee from fear, the more anxiety-prone one becomes, for smaller and smaller doses of "danger" are required to trigger anxiety. When this process becomes exaggerated, it may even result in a phobia or other anxiety disorder.

The process of "pushing through" the scary experience—the choice that boys tend to make—teaches a different lesson: that anxiety actually is a self-limiting experience. If you repetitively expose yourself to a particular scary event, eventually you will become desensitized to the fear. The process of purposeful exposure to anxiety actually increases the dose of "danger" required to elicit anxiety, and it becomes easier to tolerate risk.

Fueled by testosterone, boys drive themselves into physically scary experiences. Reinforced by cultural pressures to deny and hide fear, they tolerate their anxiety and in the process increase their psychological immunity to anxiety. Small wonder that by the time adulthood is reached they develop the propensity to embrace risk. Relative to women, the experience simply doesn't feel so uncomfortable. For a female to increase her risk-taking capacity requires a conscious effort to tolerate increasing doses of anxiety.

This process of self-desensitization is all the more challenging because anxiety may present itself in many forms. Sometimes you may indeed feel it as a heart-racing, sweaty-palmed impulse to bolt from an intimidating situation. At other times you may experience anxiety as a night of lost sleep or a few weeks of rumination about the possible consequences of a decision you are making. As uncomfortable as those experiences are, at least they are clearly recognizable as anxiety and offer you the opportunity for self-desensitization.

What is most challenging, however, is that anxiety often presents itself in disguised, unconscious forms. If you are an author or journalist, anxiety might cause a writer's block that keeps you staring at a blank computer screen. If you are an athlete, you might experience anxiety as a sense of lethargy that prevents peak performance. If you are a salesperson, you might feel an inexplicable urge to procrastinate about making the final call that could secure a new account. These insidious forms of anxiety manifest themselves as a holding back, often *just* at the moment when success is within easy reach.

There simply is no magic trick for pushing through such times. They represent the moments when ultimate courage is required, for the enemy that is seeking to defy you is not outside but within. Recognizing that your anxiety is about to sabotage your efforts is your first challenge; finding the determination to persevere nonetheless is the second; and the sheer grit of pushing through your psychological paralysis is the third. It helps to remember that each time you go through this painful process you become stronger, more able to accept the discomfort of risk-taking that is essential for real achievement.

NEST-BUILDING

The traditional way that women have dealt with the anxiety of risk-taking is to retreat to the nest. I use "nest-building" as a metaphor for the activities—thinking, feeling, talking, and acting—whereby one devises and dwells in a protective structure of familiarity. Since women's primary role in civilization has been to build the family's nest anyway, using it as a hideout from the scariness of risk-taking comes naturally.

Optimally, both men and women should experience an easy, natural oscillation between risk-taking and nest-building behaviors. Within the nest that is your physical home, you find love and nurturance from the relationships that give meaning to your life. Within the nest that is your network of friends, you find support and understanding. Within the nest that is your guiding beliefs and principles, you find moral strength for living your life. Ideally, the stability these nests provide allows you to venture out into the world of risk.

But for most of human history, it has been men who have been expected to do the venturing, returning to the nest only for quick gulps of nurturance. Small wonder that they have often felt detached from the home-as-nest, particularly when the clamor of family life renders the nest less than serene. With the growth of feminism and the softening of gender expectations, some men are taking an increased interest in sharing with their wives the responsibilities and pleasures of maintaining the nest. But in the overwhelming number of households it is still women who bear this responsibility.

The question for any individual woman, never easily answered, is when is nest-building a healthy, meaningful investment of creative energy, and when is it used to avoid the scariness of taking a risk? Throughout your life, on a daily, even hourly basis, you are faced with choices between known and unknown, safety and risk. These choices begin with the tiniest thoughts that flit across your mental screen. At this most microscopic level, you have the most freedom to take risks lavishly and wildly because thoughts, by themselves, have no consequences. But even thoughts may be perceived as dangerous. It is at this level that we tend to be most restrictive, confining ourselves to safe trains of thoughts. Translating a risky thought into bold behavior in your daily interactions is a second level of risk. Here you will rein in your wildness a bit, because your behavior does indeed have consequences. At the third level, the setting of life goals, you want to apply your most analytic thoughtfulness, for your choice of goals will shape the course of your life.

RISK-TAKING IN THE REALM OF THOUGHT

The greatest achievers are invariably those who have presented revolutionary ideas that have radically changed the way other people think. And within the minds of those achievers themselves, a change of thought patterns had to occur, a change that is often resisted for long periods of time.

An example of this resistance is, oddly enough, the story of Simone de Beauvoir, whose radical feminist book *The Second Sex* established her as one the most significant thinkers of the twentieth century. Until the publication of this book in 1949, Beauvoir was perhaps best known as the companion of Jean-Paul Sartre, though she had written several well-received novels. In the mid-1930s, Beauvoir's close friend, the feminist writer and political activist Colette Audry, was beginning research on a book about women, out of her deep frustration with women's lot. But Beauvoir felt no frustration at all, largely because she was content with her relationship with Sartre. By the mid-1940s, however, Beauvoir began writing of her relationship with Sartre and came to "the very profound and astonishing realization" that she was different from Sartre "because he was a man and I was only a woman." Later she explained her thinking:

I had not yet settled on the idea of woman as the other—that was to come later. I had not yet decided that the lot of woman was inferior to the allotment of men in this life. But somehow, I was beginning to formulate the thesis that women had not been given equality in our society, and I must tell you that this was an extremely troubling discovery for me. This is really how I began to be serious about writing about women—when I fully realized the disparity in our lives as compared to men. But [in 1947] none of this was clear to me.

Even for a radical thinker, taking risks with new thoughts can be disturbing: "I must tell you that this was an extremely troubling discovery for me." For Beauvoir to challenge the complacency she had felt about her role as a woman, her position in society, and her relationship with Sartre must indeed have been a troubling process. By definition, great ideas are disturbing, because they force a reassessment of the entire body of assumptions they are connected to.

The tendency to become entrapped within our own thinking is easily observable. The next time you catch yourself in reverie—while driving your car or lying awake at night—stop for a moment and review everything you were thinking about. You will probably notice that your train of thought was familiar to you; you may well have experienced the identical thoughts, in a predictable order, about the same topic hundreds or thousands of times with little variation. You can probably identify particular sequences that you have thought about several times a day for years.

You might find yourself ruminating about a terrible injustice that has befallen you. *How could he have been so unfair? Couldn't he see I was really trying?* Or perhaps you have become stuck thinking about a situation about which you feel guilty. *If only I had gotten Mother to the hospital a little earlier.* The more painful or traumatic a situation is, the longer it may take you to "metabolize" your response.

Even when you receive a stimulus that might encourage you to change a given thought program, it is very difficult to do so. Many times in your life you have undoubtedly made a suggestion to a friend or relative you thought might dislodge them from unproductive thoughts or behavior. You notice they light up and seem to agree, only to revert to the same thought pattern again by the next time you talk. This is why the process of psychotherapy can be so lengthy and repetitive, for thought patterns are deeply entrenched.

The stubbornness of your thought patterns is inherent in the way your brain is wired. Nerve cells make connections with each other that are either strengthened by repeated use or gradually weakened by disuse; these changes are actually observable with electron microscopy. These patterns allow you to react instantly to stimuli. They form the neurological basis of personality, the predictable way you respond to your world. The more a particular pattern is repeated, the harder it is to dislodge. That is why, for example, it is easy to change your first impression of a new acquaintance, but not so easy to change your feelings about your mother, no matter how hard you try.

Small wonder, then, that it is so challenging to leave your comfortable nest of thoughts and feelings: staying there is exactly what your brain is wired to do. Fortunately, however, Mother Nature has supplied us with a countervailing force: the tendency to seek novelty in order to relieve boredom. Individuals vary greatly in novelty-seeking behavior, and there is good evidence that this trait is genetically influenced. Even infants show significant differences in their approach to or withdrawal from novel situations, and geneticists have clues about how this trait is handed down.

Thus Zuckerman's research on sensation-seeking has real relevance for women. It is only by exposing yourself to novel situations and ideas that you will be stimulated to create the new ideas you need to become a thought leader. If you are naturally a sensation-seeker—if you become bored with the mundane and you like to move beyond the comfortable and predictable—your challenge is much easier and you will probably spontaneously stimulate your thinking throughout your life. If you recoil from the shock of the new, you may need the discipline of placing yourself purposefully in settings that will stimulate your growth—signing up for a course, joining a discussion group, or volunteering for a task that will force you to learn new approaches.

If you find yourself reluctant to take a risk, you may need to walk yourself through the process step by step. Begin with the "Great Idea" that you care about actualizing. Now consider: What is that idea worth to you? How much might you be willing to risk, possibly lose, to see if you could actualize your idea—in other words, what are you willing to put on the table? If the answer is "Nothing," it may be that either your idea is not terribly important to you, or you have come to so overvalue the time, money, or energy you might need to invest that you're unwilling to risk any portion of it. If so, challenge yourself on that unwillingness. Time and energy, after all, cannot be saved up for future use; the period of time you might invest in a project will be used up regardless. Confront your finances, and determine whether you really have no money to spare or whether you've become overly attached to your nest egg.

Radio talk show host Bobbi Conner described to me the risk-taking she demonstrated when she decided to launch her award-winning program, *The Parent's Journal*:

> At the time, I was newly divorced and I had two small children I had to support. But I did have a small amount of money set aside that would support us for nine months, so I decided to use those nine months to get the show going. I knew at the end of that time I could always get a job at a college library.
>
> So I put together a press kit about the program and began knocking on doors looking for a sponsor. I would send out my press kit to any and all corporations I could think of and I'd try to get into their marketing or public relations departments. Of course no one was interested in a show that had never even been broadcast, but I was too naive to know that. Finally, after probably 200 corporations said no, Gerber suddenly said okay, simply because they had had a recent PR problem. It was right at the end of that nine-month period.

Conner went on to launch a program now heard on 145 public radio stations nationally. Even now, though, her career is not risk-free, for sponsors are notorious for withdrawing their funding on short notice. Because she decided to tolerate that risk, she has a career she loves.

EMOTIONAL RISK-TAKING

To reshape your psyche so it supports greater achievement, you may need to take risks at an emotional level as well. Emotional risk-taking occurs with the thought, "What if some of the emotional 'facts' I believe in aren't really true?"

The emotional "facts" worthy of scrutiny cover a wide range: the sanctity of nest-building, the sanctity of marriage (even a bad one), the wisdom of staying in an unsatisfying job until a better one comes along.

The majority of us will someday endure the loss of a relationship that we had once hoped would be lifelong. When this happens, through death or divorce, we will face one of the most significant risk-taking thoughts possible: *What if I, and I alone, am responsible for my happiness, my success, and my overall well-being?* Yet accepting this notion, even if you are in a successful relationship, is often a key to fostering a personal psychology of ambition.

Actress and award-winning playwright Marjie Rynearson is living proof of the importance of emotional risk-taking. Early in adulthood she had committed herself to raising her children with her husband, Bob, with whom she had a wonderful marriage. His job, as a department chairman at an academic medical center, had drawn the family to a small town in Texas. Her dream was to become an actress, and she started a repertory theater in town. Her dream, however, was larger than her small town could support. What she really wanted was to act in significant productions in major theaters and to write her own plays.

She told me how she finally decided to change her life. "For years, I realized that someday I would need to find work that I would enjoy as much as I had enjoyed raising our sons. Finally, one day, after our youngest had gone to college, I found myself sitting in front of the television, watching a soap opera. A soap opera! That was when I knew I had to get out. Then the question became not would I go, but would Bob come with me."

But Bob did not want to go with her. He had himself begun to realize that he no longer wanted to be a doctor: he wanted to be an artist. He was taking sculpting classes, importing multi-ton blocks of luminescent marble from Italy. He wanted to work outdoors year-round on his sculpting and therefore wanted to stay in Texas rather than move to Chicago with Marjie. They chose an unusual solution. He remained in the family home, she moved to Chicago and began an acting career, and they stayed married.

Ten years have passed since their decision. Marjie is happier than she has ever been, and Bob continues to thrive in his life as a sculptor. She had a lead role in a movie and won a significant award for a play she had written. They spend one weekend a month together, but talk on the phone twice a day. They are able to take wonderful trips together. Their marriage, now in its fortieth year, remains strong. She recently mused about her career to me. "The other day I had to get a new passport, and I compared the picture to the old one. Despite the fact that I was ten years older in the new one, I actually looked younger—because I'm so happy now."

Their story is unusual: I suspect very few couples would be able, or would wish, to maintain a long-distance relationship on an indefinite basis. But their story is worth telling because their remarkable ability to think flexibly and creatively about how to achieve their dreams can be emulated.

SPEAKING UP

Research suggests that females consistently respond less positively than males do to situations of competitive challenge, especially if they contain the possibility of criticism. This research echoes Deborah Tannen's observations of female silence in group situations, which clearly limits our ability to rise to positions of leadership, to gain respect, and to influence important events.

The overwhelming majority of risk-taking activity involves using your voice. Talking is the way humans forge alliances, resolve conflicts, strategize new initiatives, and establish leadership. By using our voices, we sometimes avoid the deadly combat other animal species engage in. This is why our female unwillingness to risk speaking up is so detrimental to our progress.

Far too frequently I observe the female medical students and residents whom I teach retreat to the seeming safety of silence in group settings. Silence, after all, has traditionally been a sanctioned behavior for women. In fact, the response of silence is not at all safe because it can be so easily misinterpreted. *Is she bored and uninvested? Poorly prepared? Does she have no opinion? Is she passive, withdrawn, or even depressed?* In a group setting, *some* response, *any* response is better than no response at all, because it at least establishes that you are an interested, active participant.

Your goal should not necessarily be to monopolize more air time in meetings, but to be ready to assert your opinion at critical moments, tolerating the anxiety that your views may be unpopular. Because the pace of discussion is often extremely quick, your readiness to take risks with your voice must be reflexive. Many years ago when I started my public radio show, I expressed concern to my executive producer that I might say something wrong—give misinformation, give bad advice, or exhibit poor taste. My producer pointed out that if I worried too much about saying the wrong thing I also would not say the right things; I would lose spontaneity and become flat.

Eleanor, a participant in a focus group of ambitious, successful women that I organized in order to learn more about how women interact at upper levels of organizations, told a story that expressed the female tendency to lose our voice just when we need it most. She and her associate Michael were both top executives at a multinational corporation that was planning to hold a major meeting in their city of executives of all branches. One morning they were called into the office of their supervisor, James. "We have a unique opportunity," he said. "We have been given an entire morning of the conference to present our division's projects as a model of our company's productivity. I'd like to ask the two of you to work together on the presentations. For the breakfast session we'll need a keynote speaker, who should be someone from our branch. Then there will be a number of break-out sessions as well."

Eleanor began to think. If she could give the keynote, it would be a fabulous opportunity to enhance her visibility. Maybe she could suggest highlighting her group's product, which would make her the natural candidate to speak. Or perhaps she could subtly suggest the speaker should be a woman, since the company was trying to broaden its image. Or maybe . . .

"Great!" said Michael. "If I may be so bold, I would love to give the keynote myself, because I have some issues to present that are important for the future of the company. Eleanor, maybe you could pull together a preliminary list of participants."

"Good," said James. "Get back to me when you have established the agenda."

Eleanor, beaten to the punch, howled at herself internally for having been slow to speak up. Yet even at that moment, she again had a choice. Instead of taking the traditionally feminine peacemaking approach and agreeing to Michael's proposal, she could have said something like, "I also have some ideas for the keynote. And I think we should share in putting together the agenda, since it will be considerable work for whoever takes on that task. I'd suggest that both Michael and I sketch out our thoughts for the keynote, and let you decide, James, which direction you'd like to go."

By speaking up, Eleanor would have taken a definite risk in several ways. She would have knowingly created an awkward situation by exposing her sub rosa competition with Michael. Likewise, she would have exposed rather than covered over his tendency to view her as the corporate hausfrau who would automatically shoulder unglamorous tasks. She would have risked her colleague's resentment (although he clearly had not been concerned about whether she might resent him). Finally, she would have made her boss take her more seriously as a significant contender for promotion—a risk of a different order.

For many women, the impulse to promote harmony is so powerful that it stifles their psychological freedom to allow emotional discomfort to occur. Their challenge is to allow themselves to step out of the traditional peacemaker role *when necessary*. I am not suggesting that Eleanor should blindly lunge at every opportunity that comes her way, but that she should be able to *choose* to do so when the rewards are important to her. Niceness should be a choice, not a compulsion.

RISK-TAKING IN EVERYDAY LIFE

Of course, risk-taking extends beyond talking, to the choices you make about whether to expand or constrict your sphere of influence. Think of your world as only those people, places, or situations that touch you directly. Whether that world is small or large dictates what you will experience and ultimately achieve.

At a focus group of high-achieving women in New York City, several of us were standing around chatting before the session began. Then Judy Barker, another participant, arrived, and suddenly the energy in the room seemed to quadruple in intensity. First, Judy warmly greeted the two or three people she knew, then she said to one of these women, "I'd love to talk some more, but I already know you. I need to get to meet some of the people here I've never met before." When the evening was over, Judy had spoken at length with each of the women in the room. The next day, she was one of two participants who made it a point to call me personally and tell me how much she had enjoyed the evening and that she hoped we would become friends.

As I subsequently learned, Judy Barker is in fact a most remarkable woman. As an African American, she has surmounted not only gender but also racial barriers as she has pursued her successful career; she is currently president of the Avon Foundation and a global vice president of Avon, Inc. Judy did not graduate from college, but achieved her prominence on the basis of her innate intelligence, informal education, and real genius at human interaction.

During the group session, when I asked each participant to describe aspects of herself that they felt accounted for their success Judy spontaneously described herself as a risk-taker. Indeed, what I observed the moment she entered the room, choosing not to linger with those she already knew but to seek out strangers, was a striking example of interpersonal risk-taking.

In fact the theme of risk-taking was raised again and again in this focus group. One woman described leaving her Midwestern town for New York City because she longed for "brighter lights and louder music." Arriving without a job or a place to live, she built a successful career for herself as an executive in a not-for-profit agency. Another woman had recently left a position as head of European marketing for IBM and had launched a new career as a professional lecturer to communications industries.

As impressive as these risk-taking adventures were, I was more intrigued to observe the risk-taking dynamics within the group. These successful women were not afraid to make startling announcements about their lives and opinions. If several women began speaking of their faith in God, the next would announce that she had no such faith and that it was only by relying on herself that she had gotten anywhere. If several spoke of the importance of support from their spouse, the next would announce that she preferred having affairs with married men. There was none of the typical let's-make-nice-and-all-agree pleasantries that usually characterize the conversation of women who don't know each other well.

Clearly, the high-powered women in this group had the capacity to take major, life-altering risks—and they had developed this capacity by taking risks in their daily behavior on a minute-by-minute basis. They actively tried to meet new people. They were not afraid to use their voices. Further, they were not afraid to reveal themselves, even when they knew others might not agree with their personal values or even lifestyle. As a result, they enjoyed very successful, fascinating lives.

A frequently voiced observation in the focus group was some variation of "If I could have foreseen when I was twenty where I would be now, I never would have believed it." This comment suggests that much of what happens in life doesn't result from setting a major life goal. Rather, if you are able to push yourself to take risks, you will inevitably expose yourself to new opportunities, and these will lead you in unpredictable directions. But this process starts with taking very small chances, one person, conversation, or event at a time.

EXPERIENTIAL RISK-TAKING

Experiential risk-taking refers to specific choices—such as getting an educational degree, marrying, having children, taking a new job—that require a degree of ongoing commitment. Experiences that are less immediately life-altering, such as going in a new direction at work, taking a course in a new area, or becoming serious about an artistic interest, also qualify as risk-taking. By choosing a particular new experience, you open the door to another set of options. You change the balance of particular responsibilities and liberties in your daily life. Often there is an exchange of free time for committed time, or unstructured activities for discipline.

A simple question tells you whether you have an experiential risk in your future: *Are you satisfied to live fundamentally just as you are now, forever?* If the answer is yes, then you will have no need to take a major risk. You will try to hang on to what you've established for yourself. You will respond to change by trying to minimize its impact on your life. If the answer is no, then risk is in your future. The more significant the change you seek, the bigger the risk you will have to take.

During their thirties and early forties, many women concentrate on nest-building in every sense of the concept and spouse and children constitute the closest circle of personal relationships. Maintaining a house demands a commitment of time, money, and energy. Yet even during this period of intense nest-building, the possibility for taking risks exists. In fact, an active portfolio of risks, even during the most concentrated nesting phase, can be an antidote against an explosive midlife crisis. Couples who become too immersed in the predictable routines of nesting can be unaware of the stagnation they feel. When they suddenly perceive it, they often blame their ennui on the marriage, and the quickest solution is a casual (but potentially destructive) affair.

Perhaps more than at any other phase of life, gender differences in nesting vs. risking are sharp in this early midlife period. Even women who are not married may find that preoccupation during this period with finding a mate absorbs enormous energy and attention. Some men, also, may find their energy directed toward the nest, but almost never as powerfully as women do. In fact, for many men, the early midlife period is their most extreme period of risk-taking, for it is at this time that the successful man's career takes off. In all areas of achievement these are most commonly the years of greatest productivity.

Women, therefore, have two types of psychological challenges. First, at the point in their lives when the pendulum has swung closest to the side of nest-building, can they maintain at least some energy and interest in risk-taking? Or will they so single-mindedly set their sights on being perfect wives and mothers that they forget their early dreams of being great achievers? Will they begin to rule out important opportunities and make career choices that will forever limit what they might have achieved?

Second, once the reality issues that require intense investment in nesting begin to subside, will a woman allow her psychological pendulum to once again swing back in the direction of risk? It is possible to achieve a trajectory of productivity beginning later in life that parallels trajectories beginning in early adulthood. The challenge for a woman who postpones her entry into the world of risk is to eventually make a psychological shift back to the risk-taking spirit of the earlier years.

The Defensive Use of Reality

The thought process you use to retreat from the anxiety of taking risks is what my mentor Dr. Larry Inderbitzin calls "the defensive use of reality." In psychoanalysis, the concept means that the patient dwells on mundane events to keep herself from perceiving psychological truths. More broadly, it involves distorting or overemphasizing day-to-day issues in order to avoid the anxiety that might accompany a change in your life.

Imagine that you were offered an opportunity that was exciting yet frightening. Perhaps it would make you more independent, and you unconsciously prefer to see yourself as weak and helpless. Perhaps it would change the dynamics of your marriage, revealing problems you are scared to face. Perhaps it would inflame your competitiveness, which you have neurotically tried to squelch your whole life. If any of these were the real reason you found your opportunity frightening, you probably could not consciously admit it to yourself, much less to others. Rather, your mind would seize upon so-called reality issues to block you from taking action. "Well, this is a bad year to take a course because we're renovating the house, and I should be around. . . . Well, I really shouldn't think about getting a job because John needs me to help with his accounting. . . . Well, I've already committed to be PTA president and I really shouldn't take on too much." But these are not the real reasons for your retreat from the opportunity.

Tracy, a woman in her forties, came with her husband to see me for therapy because of her frustration in the marriage. Her husband had inherited the family farm, and she felt lonely and isolated out in the country. She focused all her attention on her two children, but as teenagers they now needed her less and less. She had become increasingly angry with her husband because he refused to consider leaving the farm, even though he had a reasonably good offer to join his brother in business in a nearby city.

I asked her whether she had considered taking a job in town herself. Predictably, she cited a slew of "reality" reasons to explain why this was "impossible." Her experience was in nursing, but she had a bad back and couldn't return to that occupation. The kids needed her to be at home to supervise their homework. Besides, who would run the house if she weren't there? Finally, she didn't want to make it too easy for her husband to just "do his thing" and ignore her wishes and needs. *He* should be the provider, but *they* should decide these matters as a team, she insisted.

As is so often the case with women in therapy, Tracy was so immersed in her familial identity that she had no psychological room to consider her own wishes as a separate person. Her approach to problem-solving relied exclusively on manipulating others—"Pack your bags, we're going on a guilt trip" seemed to be her guiding principle in managing her family; she was master of the well-timed weep-fest. We discussed at length the idea that to the degree she could accept her husband and children as autonomous, separate beings, she could be one as well.

I repeatedly challenged Tracy to take a risk: to hold herself, alone, responsible for her life and her happiness. Whatever the reality issues, the simple, undeniable fact was that the life she was leading was making her miserable. Eventually she developed a five-year plan, which included going to graduate school to get a degree in business so that she could support herself if she eventually decided to separate from her husband when the children were grown. As soon as she made the decision, her husband said he would be willing to move the family to whatever city had the best program for her—an unexpected happy resolution of what had seemed an impossible situation.

"Reality" is frequently used as an excuse for not exploring a wide range of options to reach goals. As a therapist, after I've listened to the typical litany of reasons, excuses, and rationalizations for why a particular change cannot possibly be made I ask a pointed question: "Okay, if your life depended on getting around these 'reality' reasons and solving this problem, what would you do?" Haltingly, the patient comes up with an answer. "Great!" I say. "Now tell me five even better ways of solving the problem." When it becomes clear that reality can actually be dealt with, we get down to the business of why the patient's wish seems so scary.

MUST YOU BECOME A RISK-TAKER TO SUCCEED?

One participant in a focus group took issue with the notion that only risk-takers succeed. "What about all the scientists, for example, who go to the lab, doing the same experiments day in and day out, but finally collect enough data to reach an important conclusion? What about the engineer or the computer analyst who becomes successful just by dint of sheer daily discipline?"

Her point is a good one, for certainly there are high achievers who do not seem to be significant risk-takers, and there may even be some fields—engineering, for example—where risk-taking would be foolhardy. Even scientists and engineers, however, occasionally have to make major decisions that entail risk. Will the scientist choose to do experiments that confirm the findings of other researchers, or will she choose a question that breaks new ground in her field and may lead to important new insights? Will the programmer or engineer choose projects that tax her ability, forcing her to learn and grow, or will she stay comfortably with familiar and safe projects?

Risk allows you to leverage your abilities and energy beyond what simple daily hard work might do. By confining yourself only to what has been proven by others to work, you are performing activities that many other people are doubtless also able to do. By definition, because risk draws you into the realm of the unproven, you have the opportunity to capitalize on creating skills, products, or competence in a unique niche.

Precisely how you accomplish a goal is not nearly so important as just beginning somewhere, *anywhere*. Because risk-taking can be uncomfortable, consider these tips to make it easier:

• Identify the particular type of risk-taking that is essential for your success. Different types of work demand the capacity for different types of risk-taking. Corporate life, for example, requires the ability to take managerial and financial risk. Excellence in the arts requires creative risk, but little interpersonal risk. You need not become a global risk-taker in order to achieve, but you should take seriously the particular demands of your chosen field. The process of becoming a risk-taker will feel less formidable if you can concentrate on a few specific areas of risk.

- Identify your own strengths and weaknesses as a risk-taker. Are you so extroverted that interpersonal risks come easily, but you flinch at the thought of taking a risk with your money? Are you inventive and creative, able to imagine and produce, but are intimidated by the thought of having to market yourself and your ideas? Clearly, your path will be easier if your work requirements and your personality are well matched.

- Analyze yourself to determine which antecedents of risk-taking are strengths and which are weaknesses. Watch yourself for evidence of your weak areas and try to remind yourself that the time has come to think differently. If you are low in self-confidence, challenge your negative thoughts simply and easily, letting go of them with a sense of humor when they come into your mind; above all, do not engage in criticism of your own negativity! If you find yourself ascribing control of situations to external forces, ask yourself this question: *If my life depended on it, how would I make this situation go my way?* If you find yourself pulling back from novelty, use a little personal discipline to encourage yourself to open up a bit, much as you would gently but firmly encourage a child to try a new experience.

- Meet others in your field who have succeeded in ways you would like to. Ask them about the risks they took and what the consequences were. Experienced people not only love to give advice, but relish the retelling of old defeats. If you're like most people, you'll find these stories oddly comforting, for they will reassure you that you, too, can take a risk and that life as you know it will continue if your gamble fails.

- Find a knowledgeable coach or mentor who will stick with you and guide your development. This person may be a boss or older friend who has a sincere interest in your advancement. If such a person is not available, consider hiring someone as a consultant. If you choose well, this person can help you avoid unwise risk and encourage you to persevere.

- Analyze the risky situations presented to you and weed out those that are high-risk/low-payoff. If you have always been risk-averse and are trying to change, begin in areas where you have either a high likelihood of success or minimal negative consequences if you fail. Use your intelligence to learn to distinguish good risk from bad; your goal is to become a thoughtful, discriminatory risk-taker. Educate yourself thoroughly about the merits and flaws in any project you are about to undertake. The goal, after all, is not risk for its own sake, but only as a means to accomplishment.

- If the nature of your risk-taking goal is behavioral, remember to practice steadily. Be sure to bring a level of authenticity to your efforts. If, for instance, your goal is to become more assertive in meetings, begin by listening more carefully to what others are saying and do background research so that you can make useful contributions. If your goal is to be more open to meeting new people, take the time and energy to understand something important about each new person and to share something meaningful with her about your own life.

- Write down your goals for risk-taking on a piece of paper and put it out of sight in the bottom of your sock drawer. Someday, long after you've forgotten you wrote your goals out, you will find your piece of paper again and will be amazed at how successful you have been.

THE PERSONAL PIE CHART

The way you divide your energy between nest-building and risk-taking is bound to change from time to time. Clearly there is a yin and yang to these two behaviors, a balance to be struck that may shift over the course of your life. To think about the balance of nest-building and risk-taking in

your own life, you might think of the famous pie chart that investors like
to display. I first learned of this concept from a financial adviser who was
asking me questions about my investment "style." "Are you the type of
person who likes to take really big risks, the kind that could net you really
big profits?" I warmed to the words "really big profits" and nodded happily. "Or are you the type who wants really secure investments, so that
you never have to worry that there will be something there for you?"
That sounded pretty good, so I nodded yes to that one, too. She looked
confused. "What I want," I said, "is to be absolutely certain of really big
profits."

Clearly, there are plenty of people like me out there, the investors who
want big returns while maintaining total security. Investment counselors,
therefore, have created the pie chart, so that one chunk of money goes
into riskier investments that may really pay out, while another chunk goes
into safe-but-low-yield investments. In the financial world, the relative
portions of the pie change depending on your age and personal circumstances.

Throughout your life, think of your nesting-vs.-risking decisions as
your personal pie chart that will determine what you are able to achieve.
As with finances, a portion of your emotional investment should be in
safe, dependable nesting activities. Another portion should go into activities of moderate risk that add spice and interest in your life without com-
promising your basic security. But keep at least a sliver of your pie available for a really big, audacious risk, the kind of risk that just may lead to a
great achievement.

FOCUSING YOUR INTELLIGENCE

Scattered Light or Piercing Laser?

ACHIEVEMENT TAKES many forms, requiring a variety of skills according to the type of goals you set for yourself. The psychologist and former reporter Daniel Goleman has propounded the notion of "emotional intelligence." In ascending order of importance, Goleman's "first domain" of excellence is pure IQ—that is, one's global intelligence as measured by the intelligence quotient tests. The "second domain" is expertise, which he defines as "common sense plus the specialized knowledge and skill we pick up in the course of doing any job." The "third domain" is emotional intelligence, consisting of skills in the realm of feelings and interactions.

While I don't dispute the importance of emotional intelligence, clearly the relative influence of such competence on achieving your goals depends heavily on context. In business and organizational life, emotional intelligence indeed is often the overriding factor determining success; in fact, Goleman takes most of his examples from the corporate world. But, if your goal is to leave a legacy in other realms, the issues go beyond pure IQ, expertise, and even emotional intelligence. For instance, if your goal is to leave your mark as a true thought leader, changing the way those in your field conceptualize issues, or as an artist, writer, musician, or poet, something beyond Goleman's three domains must be considered, a "something" that is the subject of this chapter. You must analyze how you take your raw intellectual potential in hand and purposefully, willfully stimulate, nurture, and direct it so that your mind becomes capable of generating unique ideas that go beyond what others in your field have been able to generate.

Gender and Intellect

Whether significant *innate* differences exist between male and female intelligence has been a hotly debated topic for centuries. Seasoned researchers who have reviewed the *same* studies have been far from unanimous as to whether such disparities exist to a significant degree. The issue itself is politically and ideologically charged. Throughout the nineteenth century, it was generally assumed that the smaller physical size of the female brain meant women were intellectually inferior. When it was pointed out that if intelligence were directly related to brain size, humans would be dumber than many animals, a revised theory offered: intellect was related to brain surface convolutions, and women had fewer of them. Again, it was pointed out that this theory would place humans in an intellectually inferior position to sheep. The debate over biological brain differences continues, focusing on such issues as the size of various brain structures, brain lateralization, the effects of hormones on the brain, and, most recently, rates of metabolism in various brain substructures.

Colloquially, we refer to intelligence as a single, monolithic entity. We describe someone as a "brain" without specifying just what her specific intellectual strengths are. This approach is reinforced by the ease of reducing a person's intelligence to an IQ score, or even an SAT score, as if a number could capture the uniqueness of each human's intellect. Seeing this approach as too reductive, the psychologist Howard Gardner has proposed seven distinct types of intelligence: linguistic, logical-mathematical, spatial, musical, body-kinesthetic, interpersonal, and intrapersonal. And within each of these categories are numerous subcategories. For instance, linguistic abilities might be measured as vocabulary, speed of reading, memorization of words, creative writing. In even such a short list it is easy to imagine a person with varying degrees of ability in each area. Therefore, in any research study that purports to show gender differences in intelligence, questions arise about how a particular subintelligence is defined and precisely what aspect of intelligence is being measured.

A point of intense controversy is the question of *how much* difference is a real difference. Because the variability of test scores *within* sexes is so much larger than the mean difference *between* sexes, the consensus of most prominent researchers in the field is that the gender differences are close to meaningless. The eminent researchers Hyde and McKinley, for instance, have concluded:

> There are essentially no consistent gender differences in measures of verbal ability, with the sole exception that women tend to perform better than men do on tests of speech production. Men tend to perform better than women do on some measures of spatial ability, but the magnitude of the gender difference varies markedly with the demands of each specific test. There are essentially no consistent gender differences in measures of mathematical ability, with the sole exception that beginning in high school men tend to perform better than women do on tests of mathematical problem solving. Differences between men and women on measures of science achievement are small, and their magnitude varies as a function of the specific area of science being tested.

However, one noted researcher, Diane Halpern, argues vigorously that the gender differences *are* indeed significant and that how statistics are analyzed and reported has enormous impact on how differences are interpreted. For example, imagine a test in a given subject on which males scored just 4 percent higher than females. If the scores of the two genders were plotted on two bell-shaped curves, the males' curve would be shifted just a bit to the right of the females'. This slight shift could account for males having 60 percent of test-takers above the combined average score, while females would only have 40 percent above average. There are numerous scholarships and programs for which the cutoff occurs at a given score, resulting in large differences in males and females being accepted.

How could such controversy about gender differences in intelligence persist when seemingly objective tests are being performed? One issue relates to the age of subjects being tested: Girls show early superiority in verbal and mathematics skills, which tends to fade around the time of puberty. Often large numbers of studies are statistically analyzed together in one large study, called a meta-analysis. If the meta-analysis includes many studies of young children, the results may be very different from those involving older age groups.

Another important issue is gender differences in the "tails"—that is, the extreme ends of the bell-shaped curve, which represent the lowest and the highest scorers. This issue is obviously important for those interested in very high achieving students. Males are more variable than females in many tests of various intellectual skills. In other words, the males' bell-shaped curve is shaped differently than females', with more scores distributed at each end of the curve. This finding appears to hold true not only for math and science, but also for traditional female intellectual strongholds, such as verbal and language skills. The impact of this effect is significant, for it equalizes the numbers of males and females who are high scorers in verbal areas and magnifies the male advantage among high math scorers.

Finally, there is controversy over what test scores really mean, anyway, and concerns about gender bias possibly influencing the writing of test questions. Most intelligence tests have been designed so that males' and females' scores are similar, though gender differences in subtests persist. This means individual questions that elicit disparate answers from male and female test-takers are systematically eliminated from tests, making it yet harder to look at differences.

Finally, the predictive value of standardized tests is quite limited. For example, though women on average produce lower SAT scores than men, they earn better grades than men in college. What, then, is really being tested? Yet thousands of young women lose out on scholarships because of test performance; for example, only one-third of National Merit Scholarship finalists are women. When New York State started using both SAT scores and grades instead of SAT scores alone in evaluating candidates for Regents' Scholarships, women won a majority of scholarships for the first time in that state's history.

Although innate gender differences in global intelligence may be small, women as a group do tend to take a quite different approach to developing their own minds than men do. Our typical approach has some serious limitations that must be understood if we are to overcome particular problems that have plagued our gender. But the female approach does have enormous potential for a very useful *type* of intelligence, if we learn how to harvest its rewards. To understand the distinctly female ways that we typically develop our minds, compare these two stories of gifted and successful people, one female, the other male.

Female Greatness: A Case Study

Heather Paul is the highly successful executive director of the National Safe Kids Campaign in Washington, D.C. Under her leadership and driven by her boundless enthusiasm, the organization has expanded its annual budget from $2 million to $10 million. She has accomplished this by forging innovative, creative liaisons with industries such as Johnson & Johnson and General Motors. She routinely appears on national television and testifies at congressional hearings as a premier expert on childhood safety.

Undoubtedly Paul developed highly specialized knowledge in the area of childhood safety along with the leadership skills required for her job. Here is the path that led to this combination:

She graduated from college in 1968 with a degree in English. For the next few years she worked as an English teacher and a social worker. After spending one year obtaining her master's degree in English, she accompanied her husband on his military assignment to the Philippines, where she directed an adult education program to service personnel but also became fascinated with foreign cultures and social science. On returning to the United States at age thirty, Paul began working on her Ph.D. in American Studies, writing her dissertation on the history of the first department of sociology at an American university. During this period her daughter was born. For the next year and a half she was a health policy associate with the U.S. Department of Health and Human Services. Next she moved to Cleveland because of her husband's career, but she continued to work in health care policy. Upon returning to Washington at age forty, she took a job in futures research with the Institute for Alternative Futures, in which she was a consultant to private industries in their strategic planning. From there she became vice president of the National Health Council for two years and subsequently assumed the directorship of Safe Kids. As director, she has been instrumental in political processes leading to adoption of tough child safety laws as well as guiding a network of nearly 300 grassroots coalitions through the United States to promote child safety.

Male Greatness: A Case Study

Rusty (L.T.) Williams, a fellow student of mine at Duke Medical School, had twin interests—science and music—which began at a very early age. By age ten he became absorbed in ordering science kits and performing experiments. At thirteen he developed his first significant experiment: measuring the effect of thyroid hormone on rat metabolism. As a senior in high school he entered two projects in the state science fair under two different names, and tied himself for first prize. As an M.D.-Ph.D. student at Duke, he published twenty papers on heart cell receptors. He completed his training program at the prestigious Massachusetts General Hospital, taught at Harvard, and then became a full professor of medicine at the University of California, San Francisco. He eventually became a Howard Hughes Medical Institute investigator and is currently one of the world's leading authorities on growth factors and their cellular targets, clarifying cell mechanisms that lead to the development of heart disease. Most recently, he left the safety of academia to join private industry, becoming the chief scientific officer of Chiron Technologies, the world's second-largest biotech firm. Doubtless, his research there will continue to make important contributions to saving countless lives as well.

Had I not revealed the gender of these two individuals, it would nonetheless have been easy to guess who was the female and who was the male. Rusty Williams's story would have been recognizably masculine because of his interest in science, his early absorption into the world of experimentation, his narrow, well-defined interests, and his meteoric rise as a scientist. Heather Paul's story would have been recognizably female because of the breadth of interests, her social, interactional orientation, the rather roundabout path she took to success, and her slower ascent to the upper ranks of her field. Yet both have made brilliant, life-saving contributions.

It is doubtful that any career counselor would ever advise a young person to follow the circuitous path Paul took, although she ultimately has integrated the talents she developed in her many jobs into leadership skills at Safe Kids. Six years of teaching fostered superb communication skills, and her time as a social caseworker gave her insight into how people really live. Since Safe Kids is a national organization, the knowledge and appreciation of diverse cultures she acquired in the Philippines have been helpful, and her experience as a mother has guided her in designing practical programs aimed at young families. The maturity and sophistication she gained in her consulting work with industry and government provided a seasoning that would come in handy when negotiating with leaders of top industries.

Yet for every Heather Paul who is able over time to synthesize her diverse interests and talents and become highly successful, there are many more women of great potential who never reap the harvest of their intelligence. Unlike the logical, step-by-step career development of Rusty Williams, career paths such as Heather's are extremely vulnerable to disruption and derailment. Many women fail to find opportunities that knit together the full diversity of their experiences. Others begin to not take their careers seriously or are not taken seriously by others in positions of power who might offer real support. Some women find themselves racking up a long list of small accomplishments, but fail to develop a body of significant achievements in a single area that would give them real credibility. Often such women remain diamonds in the rough, contributing their intelligence and energy to supporting the visions of others.

Paul's story illustrates the two gender differences in intellectual style that influence the trajectory of women's careers: *the type of subject matter* that generally interest women, which numerous studies as well as common wisdom suggest is very different from what interests men, and women's tendency to develop *a broad array of interests*, a breadth that can be either our greatest strength or our greatest weakness.

Intellectual Preferences: People vs. Things

What you like to learn about and *how* you like to go about the business of learning shape the way your mind works and how you approach your work life. Typically, women tend to be more interested in learning about the human world, and even those women who are oriented toward math and science share this fascination. Women develop an intelligence I think of as *holistic human intelligence.*

Women acquire this intelligence with every social interaction. In earliest childhood, a little girl is far more likely than her brother to be fascinated by a new baby. As she plays with, hovers over, and coos to her new sibling, she begins an intuitive learning process about child development. In her play with friends she creates a fantasy world with dolls; her brothers, meanwhile, are collecting model cars or building with Leggo's. As she grows older, she and her friends talk endlessly about themselves and each other. Her social life is orchestrated around learning about people. While her brother's sleepovers are rowdy and prank-oriented, hers are an immersion in the inner world of other girls. As she grows into adulthood, she maintains this curiosity. What is often scornfully dismissed as "gossip" is a way of learning about people. Even the personal interviews with famous people in the magazines she reads cater to her deep interest in what is *really* going on inside others. Her drive to understand the lives of others is as intense as any scientist's research motivation could ever be. While many of these behaviors are disparaged by men, they represent an ancient, adaptive means of understanding the human world. We learn who the players in our world are, how their alliances have formed, and what their true desires might be. We learn whom to trust and whom to avoid. Such information has been and will always be crucial to survival in our complex social world.

Researchers David Lubinski and Camilla Benbow have found that gender differences in intellectual preferences give rise to striking differences in the cognitive development of gifted boys and girls. The "people" fascination of young girls eventually matures into humanistic interests such as the arts, languages, and psychology. This contrasts with the "things" fascination of young boys, which drives an eventual interest in the manipulation of the world of objects: engineering, math, and science. It is the immersion in these respective worlds—"people vs. things"—that eventually shapes the nature of the intelligence of the individual.

Breadth of Interests

Women's intense interest in people naturally gives rise to a second characteristic of our intelligence: our tendency to be interested in a broad array of subjects. Lubinski and Benbow have found that even mathematically talented females are more socially and aesthetically oriented than boys are and have interests divided among math and science, social, and artistic areas. Their study of high school boys and girls who score in the top 1 percent of math ability found that girls were enrolled in math/science and English/foreign language courses in equal ratios, while boys were six times more likely to enroll in math and science than in literary or language areas. Following these students through their higher education, they found that only 1 percent of the females pursued doctorates in math, engineering, or the physical sciences, while 8 percent of boys did. Other studies have noted that within the sciences, women were turned off by inorganic science, vastly preferring biology and medicine. These findings were echoed by a Duke University study of 947 academically gifted adolescents, which noted girls chose summer enrichment courses that were different from what their regular school offered and would make them more well-rounded; boys chose courses they were confident they would do well in and that would further their academic and career goals.

These studies revealed a pattern: During their formative years, girls tended to develop a broad range of diverse interests, while boys began at a fairly early age to focus their interests, often to math, science, and technical fields. And even women choosing majors in traditionally male fields such as biological sciences, fisheries, forestry, engineering, mathematics, and business administration expressed significantly greater interest in the arts and service than males did.

Developing Lasered Intelligence

The traditional female inclination has been to develop an intelligence that is analogous to a lightbulb. A lightbulb produces a type of light called *incoherent light* because it has many colors, from infrared to ultraviolet. The light of a bulb scatters in many different directions, creating a soft glow.

We would do well, however, to aim to become more like lasers. Laser light is of one frequency, so it is called *coherent light*. Rather than diffusing off in all directions, the light rays point in the same direction, running parallel to each other to a tiny target. Because of this extraordinary focus, a laser light can perform microsurgery, melt a hole in a diamond, create a holograph, or even reach the moon.

The combination of our passion for human issues and our passion for a broad variety of interests makes it challenging to translate our incoherent light into lasered energy. But, this combination also suggests that women can make extraordinary contributions to the world *because* of our diverse abilities. Women doctors, for instance, combine their skills in medicine and science with their people genius to develop themselves as healers. Many women lawyers specialize in domestic law, where their interest in human relationships is an enormous advantage. Women politicians often develop special expertise in issues relating to children.

As you begin to focus your multiple skills and interests toward one small target, you find yourself able to do things others cannot. Women with academic interests, for example, may be excellent teachers or administrators, their people skills allowing them to convey their subject expertise in a uniquely vivid way.

Our people orientation and breadth of interests are the two major aspects of our intelligence that define the direction of our achievement. These traits, however, are expressed under the constraints of limited time.

THE TIME ELEMENT

Perhaps the day will come when men and women participate completely equally in the raising of children; men will then no longer refer to their child care activities as "baby-sitting" any more than mothers do now. Maybe someday housework will be divided up fifty-fifty, no questions asked; currently, however, the average American wife devotes twice as many hours to household labor as her mate does, regardless of other obligations. It is conceivable that one day science will extend women's years of fertility, and the concept of a "biological clock" will become obsolete. But I doubt that any of these events will occur in our lifetime, and until they happen, women's sense of time will remain drastically different from men's.

Of all external issues that affect a woman's productivity, those related to time are the most important. As a young woman begins to think of career directions, questions of when to pursue education and advanced training hinge on whether she expects to take time off for child care. She may ignore many career possibilities because of her perceptions, justified or not, that they might not allow her time for a family.

The way women and men experience time may be very different on a day-to-day basis as well. High-achieving women with families often describe a sense of urgency about managing time in their daily lives. They organize their schedules carefully; they limit nonessential activities; and they often feel they're cutting corners, at home, at work, or both.

The Ten-Year Rule

Researchers studying the development of genius have observed that a minimum of ten years is almost always required to achieve real mastery of a subject or skill. Herbert Simon, the great economist and social scientist, studied human intelligence as a basis for creating artificial intelligence. Simon observed the thought processes of chess masters as a model for learning, because chess is a relatively simple intellectual skill to analyze. Chess masters demonstrate an uncanny ability to memorize patterns of pieces on a board; some masters, in fact, are able to keep track of a dozen or more games simultaneously while playing *blindfolded*.

This is a type of genius one might assume to be innate. Not so, however, and Simon's research reveals how this ability is developed. He divided chess players into three groups: masters, experienced players, and novices. He then showed each of the three groups chessboards with pieces arranged as they would be during an actual game. Not surprisingly, he found that the masters remembered better than the experienced players and the novices remembered least well. However, when he showed them boards that had the pieces arranged completely randomly he found that all three groups remembered about equally well!

Simon proposed that the masters' ability to recall actual games depends on "chunking" data; that is, the masters remembered clusters of chess pieces grouped together in commonly occurring patterns that they had seen many times before. Chunking is the same type of thought process that makes it easy to recall a phone number whose digits can be converted to a word, or to remember a name that is drawn from a familiar language rather than an unknown language. Simon calculated that it takes about ten years for the average devoted chess player to remember the fifty thousand chunks that are required to become a master. In other words, genius-level chess playing is a matter of putting in the time it takes to learn the chunks.

Other researchers found that in virtually all fields of endeavor, the capacity to group individual items of information into chunks is the basis for learning, and in almost all areas studied it takes about ten years to learn enough chunks to become an expert. For example, it is rare for composers to produce a truly great work until they have been composing for about ten years. Mozart began composing great works at age fourteen—but remember, he started composing at age four! Artists in other genres also note that it seems to take a solid decade of significant effort to begin to create works of excellence. In medicine, one does not begin to practice until one has spent four years in college, four years in medical school, and four or more years in a residency.

Lubowski and Benbow's math-gifted males begin narrowing and focusing their interests in high school. In summer enrichment programs they seek out technology-oriented programs. They choose science and engineering majors in college and have relatively less interest than females in becoming "well-rounded." They then go to graduate or professional school for some years. By the time they are finished with their education in their mid-twenties, they may already be close to the ten-year minimum.

A gifted young woman will typically pursue a different course. She may have a sense that she wishes to work in a social service area. In high school she chooses enrichment programs oriented toward her humanistic interests. In college she decides to major in psychology, anthropology, sociology, or political science. Perhaps she is not sure what direction to go in next, so she works for several years for a foundation. Only after several years—or even after starting her family—might she begin graduate school in a social science. When she finally gets that degree, she goes to work for an agency, institution, or foundation, and it is here that she discovers the niche in which she would like to specialize.

The years of experience in diverse, humanistic fields are all extremely useful for her in her work; in fact, she couldn't possibly be as effective as she becomes without that broad background. But because she comes to her area of specialization relatively late, her timetable will be different than her friend's in engineering. Yet studies have shown that careers that begin at a later age can have the same trajectory of excellence as those started in young adulthood—the peak of achievement is just reached later in life. Further, in various disciplines the peak of achievement typically occurs at different ages. Artists tend to peak in their forties and show a rather steep decline thereafter. Those engaged in scholarship, such as historians and philosophers, tend not to peak until age sixty, and they remain active throughout their lives. Those in science peak at about forty but their decline is midway between artists and scholars.

As a group, men frequently have an early lead on us; during the years while we are still sifting through a broad area of interests, or nurturing our young families, or even just beginning to understand how much achievement means to us, men are already spending long hours at their work, year after year. By the time we have reached our thirties, when the dust may be just settling after the upheaval of starting a family, our male counterparts have achieved their ten years of mastery.

Most men do not sustain their high level of productivity throughout their careers, but rather begin to show a decline at midlife. This is just the time when many women are freed enough from family responsibilities to devote more energy to work. The challenge is for women at this stage *not* to have already typecast themselves as second-tier achievers, nor to become discouraged or feel left behind. The challenge is to re-find the excitement of achievement they experienced in young adulthood.

Given the reality of most women's lives, if women are to succeed fully we must extend our expectation of the age when that achievement will occur and actively nurture the development of our intellect to allow that to happen. Current norms in American society decree that by forty a person will have determined the trajectory of her productivity. Such expectations once made sense. After all, it was only two generations ago that average life expectancy was fifty. It was only one generation ago that few women were employed. We are obviously in the midst of a revolution of lifestyles and life cycles, which can and should liberate us from age-based expectations of achievement. Women with family responsibilities may not reach their peak of achievement until their fifties or sixties. Further, as men begin to share more fully in child care responsibilities, their age of peak productivity may also occur later in life.

The life of Zira DeFries illustrates that the process of intellectual growth may continue throughout the life cycle. DeFries graduated from medical school and practiced as a generalist before specializing in neurology. She subsequently retrained as a psychiatrist and practiced psychoanalysis until age seventy-nine. DeFries subsequently relocated in Florida and began yet another career as a writer. She joined a writing club and set aside hours each day to develop her skill.

Yet if women are to drastically extend the age range during which we are highly productive, like Zira, we must become more serious about our personal development throughout the life cycle.

Lifelong Learning

Virtually all human societies display a peculiar attitude to the development and nurturing of intellect. We make an enormous financial and emotional investment in the education of our children, spending large amounts of money on their schools, debating the curriculum they are offered, disciplining them if they fail to study, grieving if they are not accepted at the best colleges. Yet we fail to place the same value on *our* ongoing education. We cluck about the amount of time our young people waste in front of the television, but rarely count the hours we spend mindlessly ourselves. We take it for granted that our children's brains require education in order to develop, but fail to understand that our own brains can lose skills, knowledge, and reasoning power without ongoing stimulation. We assume that just by being out and about in the world, we will be stimulating our minds. While that is partially true, if you don't thoughtfully seek out the type of stimulation you require you may shortchange the fullest development of your intellect. You may instead be stuck with a vague, multidimensional intelligence that cannot be harnessed in the service of tangible achievement.

Musical training is one of the purest models of how the brain develops with disciplined, regular, intense exercise. Throughout their lives, musicians teach their brain extraordinarily complex patterns by endless repetition. Professional musicians practice hours every day for decades of their lives. The result is the ability to play their instruments with astonishing virtuosity; in addition, many musicians seem to defy the laws of the aging brain, maintaining their mental acuity throughout their lives.

I was fortunate to observe this process firsthand during my adolescence, when I took piano lessons from an amazing woman, Clara Brass. Mrs. Brass was a demanding teacher who would never allow me to leave a piece until I could play it perfectly; she was, in fact, the first teacher I had who insisted on high standards for achievement. At times she would play for me on the enormous Steinway concert grand that dominated her small home. I would marvel at the lightning speed of her fingers and the ripple of arm muscles beneath her paper-thin skin, as she dazzled me with Liszt, Beethoven, or Chopin. She often played from memory, piece after piece, and her face seemed transformed by the passion she felt for her music. Mrs. Brass was in her eighties. Yet she was by no means unique in maintaining her musical intelligence; the musical roster has numerous examples of world-class musicians who continued to perform into their eighties and nineties: Horowitz and Rubinstein in the classical genre, Cab Calloway and Alberta Hunter in jazz and blues. If you consider the daily life of a musician, the longevity of their intelligence is not surprising. As they read music, their visual cortex is activated to rapidly interpret the notes on the printed page. Messages are sent through the motor cortex to direct their fingers with extraordinary rapidity, coordinating the right and left hemispheres in extremely complex rhythmic patterns. Meanwhile, their auditory brain centers are listening to the sounds they are producing in order to guide their pacing, tone, and volume. Other centers of the brain are responding to and interpreting the emotional content of the piece. Performers regard the exercise of their brain as a matter of personal discipline, essential for maintaining their expertise. Day in, day out, hour by hour, they stimulate and develop their mind.

If such purposeful, guided, disciplined mental exercise is important for musicians, it is no less important for anyone, male or female, who wishes to achieve fully. Our brain is incapable of maintaining intelligence without ongoing stimulation. Animal research clearly documents that without the experience of problem-solving and novel environments, the deterioration of intelligence in mid- to late life accelerates. Studies with rodents, for instance, have shown that placing them in stimulating environments retards the brain cell death that is characteristic of the aging brain.

Typically, when middle-aged and older people engage in an intellectually stimulating activity, they think in terms of *exposing* themselves to a subject as opposed to actually *mastering* it. The intensity of focus required of young students, who must memorize, analyze, and retain academic material, is lost. The goal for anyone who is serious about developing her mind is to go beyond vague familiarity with new material to *permanent* learning—the basis of intellectual mastery.

On a recent visit with my parents, I witnessed an example of this type of intense learning. My father, now in his seventies, continues to be highly productive in his profession as a physicist and inventor. I happened to see him in his study one morning, an article about the physics of superconductors in one hand and a dictaphone in the other. He explained that he had developed an updated approach to his old favorite study technique. As he read, he would dictate questions about the material into the dictaphone. At the end of the chapter, he would replay the tape and try to answer the questions.

In the days before dictaphones, he would write out his questions by hand. He showed me an old physics textbook of his. Folded between the pages were his handwritten questions on yellow, crumbling paper, written fifty years earlier. I looked at some of the questions:

463. Into what two parts is relativity divided?

464. Define the Galilean frame of reference.

465. Describe the synchronization of clocks in a Galilean system.

And on and on.

If you aren't as self-motivated as my father, seek out organized programs of new learning, to expose yourself to a body of knowledge that you otherwise would never find. Such experiences offer the invaluable benefit of letting you meet other students like yourself, opening up the possibility for long-term relationships that can offer encouragement. So important are organized programs that virtually all professional groups require continuing education in order to maintain credentials.

Another structure for development is to become a teacher yourself. Teaching others requires grappling with ideas at a far higher level of analysis than when you are learning material on your own. If you are still growing in your profession, the process of teaching forces you to jump a level or two in sophistication, for you will quickly become aware of areas where your knowledge is superficial. If you are senior in your area, teaching allows you to review material you may have forgotten and to revisit many old assumptions through the fresh eyes of your students.

Distractions and Procrastination

One woman, Melissa, described how difficult it is for women to find the time required for intense study and productivity. She and her husband were both professors at a small college, but when her teenage children had a crisis—gym clothes forgotten, or an illness at school—it was always she they called, not her husband. She once asked them why.

"It just always seems like Dad is in the middle of something really important," came the answer.

Men have the ability to create an air of importance; doing the same work, women create an air of accessibility. Because of our social nature, we *want* to be accessible, not only to our children but to our spouses, friends, and coworkers. Yet the result is a lifestyle that makes it difficult to focus on work and intellectual development intensely enough to gain real mastery.

Further, in the new age of cyberspace, many women—and men—will increasingly choose to work and study within their homes, relying on the Internet, e-mail, and faxes to do work that once required commuting to a formal office setting. Obviously this offers enormous advantages of convenience. For women who wish to stay at home with children, the ability to maintain some link with the world of work is a wonderful opportunity.

Yet the challenges of working and studying at home in the presence of the distractions of family life are significant, as illustrated by a woman I'll call Meg. I met Meg on a flight into my hometown and was impressed by her brightness and energy. She was a recently divorced mother of three children and was returning from a trip to relocate her children with her ex-husband so they could attend public schools in his state, for the public schools in our state are quite poor and private schools too expensive for her to afford. Until recently, she told me, she had run her business out of her home so that she could be available to drive her children to school and activities and meet their various needs. She had enjoyed working at home since it allowed her so much time to be with her children but her finances had become too shaky to sustain that arrangement.

I was struck by the seeming illogic of what she had described, for she was now *severely* curtailing her time with her children as a result of a lifestyle in which she had been trying to spend *more* time with them. Would it not have made more sense for her to vigorously run her business in a setting in which she was free of constant distractions, earn enough more money to be able to hire someone to drive her children and pay their tuition, and be able to keep them at home with her?

As I listened to Meg, I looked up and saw the little overhead sign that read, *"Parents, please put on oxygen masks before assisting your child."* It is indeed counterintuitive to a mother to save herself before saving her child; yet obviously a mother can help her child only if she is strong herself. Meg was obviously a loving, unselfish mother in her wish to put her career secondary to her children's needs; yet, by not fully investing in herself she ultimately deprived her children.

The process of developing the intellect of achievement is clearly one that requires a high degree of self-discipline: discipline to choose an area of interest, discipline to avoid becoming too distracted by pursuing areas of peripheral interest, and discipline to invest the decade or so of concentrated work that mastery requires. Distancing yourself from the clamor of family demands is yet another form of discipline. Whatever structures or mechanisms you can create for yourself to make this easier are enormously important. Maya Angelou, for instance, never writes at home, finding the pleasures and comforts too distracting. She remarked, "I've never been able to work at home because I try to keep home very pretty, and I can't work in a pretty surrounding. It throws me. It distracts me. So I keep a room in a hotel in downtown Sonoma, and in the morning when Paul goes off to work, I go off to work at 7:15. I go to my hotel, to this tiny room and sit there on the floor, nothing in the room but a bed, which has never been made as far as I know because I've never slept in it. I work till about two, twelve sometimes if it's going badly."

For you to develop the focused intelligence you need to achieve your goals, you may also need to create a "box" for yourself, to minimize your accessibility to the demands of your family or friends and the temptation of the television or the Internet. You can concentrate your mental energy on the goal you have set for yourself, ignoring the call you should return, the desk that needs straightening, even the lure of fresh air on a sunny day. You will be able to maintain your focus and discipline, knowing you will have the rest of the day for more relaxed, undisciplined pursuits; but in the box your goal for the day will be clear.

The activities of your box should be carefully considered, chosen to help you meet your goals over an extended period. If you are a musician, you will be working with your instrument. If you are a writer, you will be sitting at your word processor. If you are a businesswoman, you will be reading the *Wall Street Journal* or analyzing your business reports. If you are a scholar, you will be reading or writing. Whatever your field, you will be focusing intensively on your activity. The stimulation you receive during this period will be absorbed and analyzed unconsciously during the rest of the day—you may have a fresh insight as you open your eyes the next morning or are driving down the highway hours later.

The place where you create your box should ideally be clearly defined as well. Humans, like all animals, are highly responsive to territorial signals; we unconsciously associate certain places with specific activities. Just as you sleep best in your own bed or relax most in your home environment, creating a special place solely for the purpose of personal development is very helpful. Men seem to understand this clearly; it is much more common for homes to have a room designated as "Dad's study" than "Mom's study." Just as it is useful to define a time for your development, designating a place for yourself signals the seriousness of your pursuits to you and to others in the home.

THE CONTRIBUTION OF HOLISTIC HUMAN INTELLIGENCE

Left unchecked, our female tendency to develop diffuse, people-centered intelligence places us at a distinct disadvantage in our technology-driven world. Yet we are beginning to discover the limits of what pure technology can offer, if results are measured in terms of human well-being, at both individual and population levels. Our collective female intelligence has been underutilized in developing systems, programs, and other broad-based efforts to address the limitations of technology in improving human welfare. There are enormous opportunities open to those women who are able to take their intellectual development in hand and develop the skills and specialties needed to translate their human understanding into tangible productivity.

Within the past decade or two, there has been great attention given to encouraging females to become more math- and science-oriented. This attention has helped many women develop in these areas and has drawn women into technology fields as well as broadening the education of women whose major concentration is in human studies. The number of women going into science has increased significantly, and perhaps some day there will be as many female scientists as male.

But even if our gender continues to be more drawn to human rather than technology studies, we will have nothing to apologize for. The notion that math-science-technology intelligence is somehow better than human intelligence is, after all, a distinctly masculine artifact. The particular type of passions that women currently tend to develop are, in fact, uniquely suited to grappling with the most vexing problems faced by humankind.

The list of human needs that beg for human-oriented genius is lengthy. These include preventative health care; crime and violence reduction; substance abuse and mental health treatment; education; cultural development; and on and on. These are problems that desperately need the contributions of the greatest geniuses our society can produce, particularly those who can understand the application of technology in the context of human diversity.

Because of the nature of the most pressing problems of the new century, perhaps millennium, I predict that the coming era will be the age of great female geniuses. Such women will be active in politics, social science, medicine, and education. Their contributions will not necessarily come in the form of a new invention or scientific breakthrough. Rather they will be characterized by women's capacity to grasp the full complexity of social issues and, out of that complexity, find and define worthy and solvable problems.

SHAPING YOUR WORK LIFE

Problem-Fixing or Problem-Finding?

> Galileo formulated the problem of determining the velocity of light, but did not solve it. The formulation of a problem is often more essential than its solution, which may be merely a matter of mathematical or experimental skill. To raise new questions, new problems, to regard old problems from a new angle, requires creative imagination and marks real advances in science.
>
> ALBERT EINSTEIN

WHEN THE PILGRIMS first landed in Massachusetts, they were ecstatic to have reached their destination after sixty-five harrowing days at sea. The men immediately set off in a group to catch their first glimpse of the New World and determine where to situate their historic settlement. It was one of the most extraordinary, exciting moments in American history. Guess what the women did?

They washed the clothes.

This simple vignette, described in the diary of an eleven-year-old girl who sailed on the Mayflower, is a rich illumination of how men and women have divided problem-solving responsibilities throughout history. In the washing of the clothes, the women contributed to the comfort and sanitation of the group, a simple but important task in the service of the survival of the group. Such an activity could be described as problem-*fixing*, responding to a problem that was presented. Yet, as important as such a task is to the group survival, women then as well as now might legitimately ask questions. Is there room for personal expression in problem-fixing? Are my incessant efforts, repeating the same task over and over again, truly noticed or appreciated by anyone? Am I taking on this task to free someone else—such as a male someone else—to find a problem more exciting and challenging, a problem of history-making dimensions—such as locating the first European settlement in the New World?

The legacy of your work, the measure of what you contribute to the world, will be defined by the problems you invest your time and energy in. Given that the world is teeming with an infinite, seemingly exploding number of problems, *which* problems you choose as your own and *how* you define those problems will be pivotally important in determining what you are able to accomplish and contribute. The brilliance, even boldness of the problems you find and define for yourself will set the course for your career development. Simply finding the *right* problem, perhaps even an extraordinarily clever problem that no one else has conceptualized in the way you have, may transform you from a solid worker into a great achiever.

Active, aggressive identification of problems to tackle is a radically new role for women in history. Our traditional role has always been to *fix* the problems that were assigned to us, both at home and in the workplace. The traditional female occupations of nursing, teaching, and secretarial services epitomize the way women's work has been conceived; to strengthen, nurture, and support others. Even today many women remain in roles that involve implementing the visions of others: "junior" associates, "assistant" professors, and so on. If we stay in jobs where we merely perform tasks assigned by others, our names will live on only in the grateful acknowledgments in the footnotes of history. As a group, women simply *must* become more active in finding our own great problems to solve if we are to take our place as thought leaders and visionaries.

The process of actively searching for problems, rather than responding to those assigned to you, results in a higher quality of thought and productivity. A variety of studies have found that children and adults will provide much more creative and numerous solutions to problems they have defined themselves than to problems that have been articulated by others. Is this due to "pride of ownership"? Or is it that people gravitate toward defining a problem for which they have a richer storehouse of possible solutions to begin with? While the answer is not clear, it is observed that humans seem to produce their best creative thought in response to problems of their own choosing.

If finding the best and most interesting problems is important for men, it is doubly important for many women. Women who are mothers have less time for work, so achievement requires extra cleverness in defining problems that are worthy and that will advance their goals. Curiously, however, women often respond in exactly the opposite way, scaling *down* their expectations and seeking problems that are less interesting and important.

What Is Problem-Finding?

Two of the most esteemed researchers in this area, Jacob W. Getzels and Mihaly Csikszentmihalyi, define problem-finding as "the way problems are envisaged, posed, formulated, created." Like creativity, problem-finding is a complex of skills, tendencies, and behaviors. Studies have shown that great problem-finders are capable of looking into phenomena and issues and recognizing gaps of understanding. In the field of art, a problem-finder might experiment with a new medium rather than merely imitating the work of others. In math, she might try to develop a new approach to a type of problem, rather than merely applying old solutions. In business, she might offer a new and innovative service, rather than buying a franchise of an already-successful business.

Problem-finders are sensitive to anomalies in what they observe, and they seize on such observations with curiosity and excitement. Once they see the possibility of a new problem, finders engage in a process of defining and formulating it. As they then work to solve the problem, finders continue to reevaluate their conceptualization of the problem at each step along the way to ensure the originality of the solution, to gauge the feasibility of the solution, and to continually reassess the relevance of the problem itself. In other words, problem-finding occurs not only at the beginning when the problem is identified, but continually throughout the process of solving it.

Studies have confirmed that the capacity for problem-finding is associated with success in a variety of fields. In their seminal study of problem-finding capacity in artists, Getzels and Csikszentmihalyi used as criteria for competent problem-finding a willingness to switch directions when a new approach suggested itself, a continued openness to reformulating the problem, and a tendency to refrain from seeing a work as absolutely finished. The productions of artists who were rated high in these behaviors were judged to be more creative, and a follow-up eighteen years later found they had achieved a higher degree of professional success. Other research has confirmed the link between problem-finding and creativity in student writers. Researchers who compared problem-finding abilities in critically acclaimed vs. professionally competent artists and scientists found that the critically acclaimed group devoted more time and energy to problem-finding. A study of Westinghouse Science Talent Search winners found that those students who were classified as problem-finders were more likely to be involved in research with a mentor years later and had better chances for academic success in their fields.

MEN, WOMEN, AND PROBLEM-FINDING

Problem-finding begins with the capacity to appreciate a broad range of approaches. A certain type of thought, *divergent thinking*, is central to problem-finding; it involves finding numerous associations to the same stimulus and generating a variety of approaches. For example, if an artist takes the time to draw multiple sketches of a planned painting, she is thinking divergently; when she begins to rule out certain approaches, her thinking has begun to converge again. Finding great problems frequently relies on appreciating nontraditional approaches that may be inspired by experiences in nonrelated areas. It may, in fact, be aided by an enjoyment of the exploratory process itself, rather than overemphasis on a quick achievement of a particular goal. While no studies have directly compared problem-finding in men and women, the way women choose to develop their intelligence positions them to bring particular strengths to the problem-finding process.

Earlier I noted that women tend to have a broader range of goals and interests than men do and tend to develop a more diverse set of talents and skills. These traits are a double-edged sword: they threaten to make us overly diffuse, but they also provide us with wonderful strengths that are highly useful in the process of problem-finding. The broadly educated woman is equipped to find superb problems in the overlap between disparate disciplines, such as the arts and psychology, or physical science and social science. She will have exposed herself to concepts in one area that may symbolically or metaphorically suggest how a problem might be formulated in a different area. If she is less unidirectionally focused on a particular goal, she may allow herself greater "play time" in the exploration of a problem. Further, if her goals generally are less money- and prestige-oriented than men's, she can allow herself the pleasure of searching for problems that reflect her humanistic values.

Here's an example that illustrates not only how men and women may find problems differently but the particular challenges a woman may face in her conceptualization of a problem.

Two physicians, Dr. John and Dr. Mary, were assigned to teach a small group of medical students, using a case-based learning format. They were told to use the case of a sixteen-year-old girl with diabetes who refused to comply with her diet and medication regimen and developed complications.

The "problem" that Drs. John and Mary had to find was which of the many aspects of the case were the most important for the students to understand. During his part of the discussion, Dr. John highlighted the biochemistry and pathophysiology of diabetes—the autoimmune mechanisms by which pancreatic cells are destroyed, the processes by which insulin is manufactured, the impact of insulin on cell physiology. All of these, obviously, were essential issues for the young doctors to study.

But Dr. Mary found a different problem. She wanted the students to understand that 50 percent of adolescents with diabetes develop significant emotional problems that limit their compliance with treatment recommendations. She presented the data that two-thirds of diabetic patients do not comply with treatment recommendations and that half of doctors do not perform adequate physical and laboratory exams. Her focus was less on the biochemistry than on the complex web of psychological, social, and economic reasons why the vast medical understanding we have of diabetes is often not translated into improved quality of life for an individual patient.

In the male-dominated world of medicine, John's approach has been traditionally seen as more worthy than Mary's, because it is based on hard science rather than social science, it is easier to conceptualize precisely, and it is certainly easier to obtain grants for, perform research on, and publish scholarly articles about. At this point in history, however, Mary's approach is arguably the more important, for all the knowledge about the pathophysiology of diabetes in the world is meaningless if patients can't afford or don't take their insulin.

Mary's problem-finding orientation faces several challenges. First, in a society that values and rewards the male approach more than the female approach, will she be able to maintain her faith in the value of her point of view? Society rewards technological and scientific breakthroughs. The solutions to *human* problems are less valued, which has limited the contributions women are particularly suited to make. To pursue her particular interests, Mary will need a highly developed sense of internal motivation.

Second, in order for Mary to become a thought leader in the field of diabetes, she will need to devote a great deal of time and energy to the problem she has found. This means she will have less time available for treating individual patients or teaching students; in a medical school, such activities are the ever-present "problems" to be "fixed." Given that the nurturing drive is such a central element of women's psychology, will Mary be able to siphon energy from caring for and treating individuals to invest more fully in exploring abstract issues?

CHARACTERISTICS OF GREAT PROBLEMS

Since the direction in which your productivity develops depends on the problems you choose, it logically follows that recognizing the characteristics of particularly worthy problems is essential. These characteristics include:

- *Originality and ownership:* For a problem to have the potential of leading you to great achievement, it must have unique or original elements. Merely repeating what others have already done well may accomplish certain goals (such as earning you a salary!), but it is unlikely to bring you recognition or establish you as a thought leader. Originality allows you to find a field with less competition; it wins you notice from others; and it allows you to leave a mark on the world that is distinctly your own.

- *Significance:* Optimally, your problem will have broad enough significance that it will be seen as valuable by others. Remember that solving a problem of large scope does not necessarily take more energy than a problem of smaller scope; in my line of work, for instance, it takes me no more time to prepare a radio show for thousands than to give a lecture to a dozen individuals. Significance may be defined in many ways, such as the number of people you reach, the impact of the idea you develop, or the achievements by others your productivity stimulates.

- *Sustainability:* Sustainability refers not only to your practical ability to continue to work on the problem over time but to inherent features of the problem itself that generate new challenges. This issue comes up in research, for instance, when a scientist develops a particular technology that suddenly becomes obsolete when a superior technology emerges; more than one scientist has suddenly found herself bereft of grant money in such a situation. Other aspects of the issue of sustainability include your own genuine interest in the problem and your conviction about the worthiness of your goals.

As you search for your own great problems, you may wish to generate your own list of the characteristics they should include. These characteristics could reflect your value system; your preference for work environments; flexibility to integrate with aspects of your family life; ability to network with others; and so forth. The clarity that guides your thinking will help you not only find some great problems but avoid problems that are not worth your investment.

GETTING STARTED WITH PROBLEM-FINDING

Let's assume that you're sold. You want to find some great problems, but you don't know how to begin. Here are some basic steps to learning to see the world in this new way.

- *Stay on the lookout for problems.* As you go through your day, learn to observe the simplest of phenomena. What are you struggling with repetitively? What walls do you see other people hitting their heads against? Listen to what people talk about, and in particular listen for the emotion in their voices. What are the common frustrations that keep coming up over and over again? What makes people in your life happy, angry, sad, curious, shocked? Example: As I sit at my desk at the university, I have a view of the back entrance of a private doctor's office. Every few minutes, a car drives up and parks. An elderly person gets out of the car, often accompanied by a middle-aged woman—clearly, a daughter taking her elderly parent to the doctor's office. Perhaps she has to take time off from work every two weeks to do this and is using up all her vacation time. Maybe the elderly parent worries about being burdensome. In this simple, repetitive event occurring thousands of time every day in every city of the world, there is a problem to be found. Couldn't an entrepreneur offer to pick up these patients at their home, take them to their appointments, drive them home, and deliver written communication from the doctor to the patient's family about the treatment plan?

Everybody lives in a room with a view, and problem-finding begins with the view that is uniquely yours. An emergency room doctor, Kathy Melaney, started her own business simply by observing a scene she was presented with on a daily basis. She frequently treated visiting tourists who developed minor illnesses for which they would normally see their personal doctors at home. In a strange city, however, they often ended up in the emergency room, for lack of a better alternative. Often they had to wait for hours and were then presented with the large bill that is standard for ER visits. The physician started a company specifically targeted to the health needs of tourists staying in hotels.

Develop the habit of watching, of putting yourself in the role of the people you see who are struggling with everyday problems—problems for which you might have an answer.

- *Find the problems within the problem you are observing. Make a list. Write down all the different hidden problems you can find.* Any problem is actually a *complex* of problems, and this is what makes problem-finding so fascinating. For the elderly patients I see out my window, perhaps the real reason the daughters accompany their parents is to obtain information about the illness and treatment plan—maybe communication between doctors and patients' families, not the transportation, is the real problem. These hidden problems may in fact be much more important than the surface problem.

- *Research the problem.* If I were interested in the problem of elderly patients, the first place to start would be to talk— that is, *listen*—to the patients themselves and to their middle-aged daughters as well. Then I would talk to an unseen group: the middle-aged sons of the patients. I might find out, for instance, that the sons would love to buy their way out of feeling guilty about not participating in their parents' care; maybe they would financially support a service to help their parents. I would call the Council on Aging to determine what other approaches might be tried, and I would check the Net to see what has been tried in other cities. In the process of this research, I might be led to an entirely different problem. I might learn, for instance, that the real reason the daughters accompany their parents has little to do with either transportation or communication. The real reason might be to help their parents manage the anxiety of the doctor's visit and to show loving concern. And so perhaps the daughter might say something like, "I don't really mind the doctor's visits so much. What I could really use help with is running errands for Mother. If there were just a service that could do her grocery shopping for her once a week, that would really lighten my load."

- *Be willing to continually reevaluate and reformulate your problem.* Great problem-finders allow themselves to be deflected from their original path by what they discover in the course of problem-solving. A great problem yields wonderful secrets, which themselves are tantalizing seductions into yet more interesting problems. Allow yourself to surrender to what you find along the way.

Now that you have some sense of how to begin, let's look at some specific problem-finding techniques.

Thinking in the White Space

Great problems do not spring de novo from the head of Zeus. Rather, recognition of them always arises *in response to a stimulus.* The stimulus comes from the moment of looking at something that *is* there and being struck by what *isn't* there.

I call this type of inventive thought process "white space thinking." Think of those carefully crafted drawings in which a black figure defines one picture, while the white space around it defines a very different image, such as two white profiles facing each other that define a goblet. Once one has "seen" the white space, the image is obvious, but until that moment of recognition the image is hidden. You have the "Aha!" experience of suddenly recognizing something that was there all along, whose form was suggested *by the outline* of something already observed.

The broad-based, human-oriented nature of women's intelligence has the potential to open our eyes to the white space that surrounds phenomena in a multidimensional way. An example is the career of Maria Montessori, one of the great twentieth-century thought leaders in the field of education. Montessori, born in 1870, was the first Italian woman to earn a medical degree. Early in her career she worked with children in mental asylums, which allowed her to observe the thinking process of underdeveloped children. She combined her skill base in medicine with her interests in education and underprivileged children to find a novel problem: How do children learn, and how can educational methodology be shaped to reach children for whom traditional approaches don't work? Further, she permitted herself to expand into an area that previously was regarded as outside the boundary of formal education, the preschool years beginning in infancy. Synthesizing her interests and concerns, she developed the renowned Montessori teaching method, which emphasizes the child's freedom and initiative and which remains highly respected and popular to this day.

Learning to think in the white space can be achieved a number of ways. All of those ways, however, begin with the determination to find a wonderful problem and the boldness to synthesize approaches from diverse strategies. The power of that wish must inspire a different way of perceiving the world: studying, observing, questioning, dreaming. Great achievers experience an intensity in their interaction with the world, both animate and inanimate. They allow themselves to be startled by a perception, and they latch on to that perception and fly into space.

Problem Expansion

One way to think in the white space is to recognize the potential value in an undeveloped idea, often one that someone else has already presented. To successfully engage in problem expansion, the most common source of great ideas, you must cultivate your capacity for fascination. Fascination leads to a mental locking on to a simple, sometimes even primitive suggestion of an idea to be explored. You mentally play with the suggestion, much like a child with a new toy, and in the playing come to realize the potential at hand.

One of the greatest women scientists in history, Marie Curie, found her "problem" using the problem-expansion technique. Curie began her studies at the Sorbonne in 1891 and graduated with honors in physical science and mathematics. She married her husband, Pierre, a fellow scientist, in 1895 and soon began her doctoral work. Antoine-Henri Becquerel had just discovered that uranium emitted a mysterious radiation, which fascinated Marie Curie. She expanded his problem, deciding to investigate whether other substances also emitted radiation and in the process discovered a compound a thousand times more radioactive than uranium, consisting of two new elements, polonium and radium. She became the first scientist ever to receive the Nobel Prize twice.

One of the most useful types of problem expansion begins with your observation of your own experience in daily living. This is the process that guided Simone de Beauvoir in writing *The Second Sex,* for much of her writing is indirectly autobiographical. There is little that is unique to any single human life; almost any experience that frustrates you is probably a frustration for many other people as well. You can with some confidence expand your perception of need from yourself to other people as well; any hassle or struggle that you face is a starting point for finding a great problem, and your biggest challenge is to recognize the universal aspects of your experience.

Even more interesting than your struggles with the physical world are your struggles with the world of your inner experience, one of the best places to find great problems. As you search to find answers to the spiritual, emotional, and social issues of daily living, you can safely assume that there are universal themes to these problems. In fact, all great writers, philosophers, and even social scientists begin with the case example they have studied most, themselves. To expand your own experience and insight to speak to others like you requires taking your thoughts seriously and developing the boldness to speak the truth as you perceive it.

Maya Angelou is a wonderful example of the process of finding universal human problems in one's own diverse experiences. From a troubled childhood that included being raped at age seven and having a child at sixteen, Angelou went on to become first the first black woman streetcar conductor in San Francisco; a nightclub dancer, and, briefly, a madam; and later a poet, playwright, memoirist, editor, songwriter, singer, teacher, and director. From this far-reaching mix of experience Angelou was able to synthesize a vision of the lives of blacks and women in American society that has stirred and inspired millions of fans. Angelou commented on the process:

> I hope to look through my life at life. I want to use what has happened to me—what was happening to me—to see what human beings are like, to tell anecdotes so true, to look behind the fact of the anecdote and see what motivated this person in this action, and that person, so that people who have never known blacks—or Americans, for that matter—can read a work of mine and say, you know, that's the truth.

One of the most interesting problems Angelou addresses in her writing is the question of how to face the reality of one's own anger and disappointment without becoming bitter. Her work's breadth of appeal suggests that this is a problem all humans experience, regardless of race or gender.

Recognizing Fallacies

Another approach to finding great problems is to correct fallacies you have perceived.

A historical example: When the sixteenth-century Polish church official Copernicus studied the astronomical principles of his day, he was struck by an oddity in the observation of the planets: namely, at certain points they seemed to follow a retrograde path—in other words, they do a U-turn. He realized that this could only be so if both Earth and the observed planet were in rotation. With relatively crude wooden instruments (telescopes were not yet invented), Copernicus was able to make observations that supported his proposed ordering of the planets revolving around the sun. Once he had taken the risk of disputing current-day thinking, he was able to devise a new set of theories, leading to the development of modern astronomy. His beliefs were so heretical to the Catholic church that decades after Copernicus's death, Galileo was forced to deny his belief in the Copernican theory, and the Dominican friar and philosopher Giordano Bruno was burned at the stake for promoting it. Yet the fundamental truth of Copernicus's idea ultimately survived and stimulated the development of theories of gravity and the motion of bodies in space.

Copernicus is said to have been greater than any scientist in the two thousand years that preceded him. He looked into the same night sky that you, I, and virtually every human being has seen, but *he saw a truth and chose to tell it.* He used the insight he gained through his intellectual risk-taking to find and define one of the most magnificent problems in all of science. Though others must have observed the same unexplained error in theory, it was he who had the character and intellectual integrity to pursue the truth as he observed it.

Listening to Silence

A third technique in problem-finding is listening to silence and noticing what is missing in a given situation. This reflects a phenomenon often observed by psychotherapists. While patients typically talk about issues that are moderately disturbing, they usually avoid altogether issues that are deeply threatening. If a patient talks exclusively about his mother, it may be that his relationship with his father was the more painful one. If he talks only about his difficulties at work, I will begin to wonder what issues at home are being avoided. For this reason, when a patient starts a session by looking blank and saying, "I don't know what to talk about," I will often suggest, "Why don't you start by talking about what you'd least like to discuss?"

Humans choose to think, say, or do things for a reason; they also avoid certain things for a reason. The reasons are often unspoken but powerful, and uncovering those reasons can suddenly illuminate significant problems. For instance, it was not by accident that women and minorities happened to be denied membership or entrance to organizations, such as universities; they were excluded because the experience would make them more competitive with white men.

I recently thumbed through my 1969 high school yearbook for the first time in many years. When I got to the largest section, "Sports," I noticed something I had never observed before. Thirty-two pages were devoted to sports teams—*all* for boys. There was not a single girls' sports team at my school. What amazed me even more, however, was the realization that my friends, our parents, and I hadn't paid much attention to this fact at the time. This is particularly astounding since my family was athletic. But coming up in the school culture of that era, we all took it for granted that the void for girls existed—actually, we didn't even perceive that a void existed. Further, most of us, myself included, eagerly joined in "school spirit" activities. Perhaps cheering for the boys' teams kept us from noticing we had no teams of our own. We were so aware of the "black space" figure—boys' sports—that we never saw the white space problem—the lack of athletics for girls.

A way to approach this type of problem-finding is to study the boundary of an activity or situation. In the case of school sports, the striking boundary was the gender boundary.

Noticing Anachronisms

A fourth technique in problem-finding is to recognize when the standard approach to solving a type of problem has become anachronistic, or outdated. This occurs often when the approach has been determined by a tradition established long ago that has lost its relevance as times have changed.

A recent example of this phenomenon occurred at the Citadel, an all-male military college in Charleston, South Carolina. Under great duress and after years of legal battles, the Citadel was finally required to accept female students. In what could only be interpreted as a combination of rigid obstinacy and hostile intent, the leadership decided that these young women would be subjected to precisely the same level of physical demands as the male students. During the first year, two of the four female cadets developed pelvic stress fractures from lengthy marches with heavy packs. A lawsuit ensued when the women were also subjected to the same bonding rituals that the males apparently delighted in inflicting on each other, including being set on fire. The Citadel, bowing to criticism from the community and even its own alumni, finally declared that it would modify its approach, but only after suffering substantial damage to its public image. Had the leaders of the school "found" the very interesting problem of how to make a male military program meaningful for females, rather than "fixing" the problem by merely stuffing the girls into a dangerously inappropriate model, a good deal of misery for these young women and for the school could have been avoided.

Because the nature of society is changing so fast, we are currently in the midst of countless opportunities for finding great problems that result from anachronisms. The advent of mothers in the labor force, the extraordinary capabilities we now have for instant communication, and the exploding use of the versatile computer—all will undoubtedly lead to many novel ways of running businesses and utilizing personnel. How best to accomplish this is a source of wonderful problems for businesswomen to find.

FINDING SEVERAL PROBLEMS SIMULTANEOUSLY

An essential characteristic of a great problem is that its solution solves several problems simultaneously. Creative and innovative leaders consider numerous problems at once, analyzing how to combine them so that they can be solved together. A typical example is the problem of increasing worker productivity to increase profit margins, while maintaining employee satisfaction and loyalty. Smart companies have begun to address both problems simultaneously by allowing their employees a financial stake in company profits and challenging them to address ways to increase worker productivity for the sake of their own earnings.

Great artistic works are often based on solving several psychological problems simultaneously. In literature this is often accomplished by splitting apart the conflict and assigning each aspect to a different character. Marjie Rynearson, for instance, wrote an award-winning play, *Jenny*, about the meeting and reconciliation of two women: the mother of a murder victim and the mother of the murderer. Within the dialogue between the two characters she sought to resolve two sets of problems: the rage and grief of the victim's mother, and the horror, guilt, and grief of the murderer's mother. She worked on the play for several years, and only when it was finished did she realize that through it she was struggling to resolve her feelings about the suicide of her best friend. Rynearson had simultaneously been, in effect, both the friend of the victim and the friend of the perpetrator of the killing. The power of the work lay in its simultaneous resolution of conflicting problems.

Angie Zealberg won an art contest with a series of abstractions inspired by biblical phrases. Her original artistic problem was fairly simple: to use a blank canvas and a collection of oil paints to create a work of art to submit to a competition. To this she brought an emotional problem: her unresolved anger over a wrong done to her, for which significant compensation would probably never occur. Grappling with this anger, she found herself immersed in a spiritual problem. Although she no longer considered herself to be religious in a formal sense, the teachings of old were nonetheless very much within her, and she remembered the phrase "Vengeance is mine, saith the Lord." The phrase was comforting, for it relieved her of the obligation to find vengeance for herself; she substituted the image of a God who would seek justice for her. In other words, she found three problems—artistic, emotional, and spiritual—that needed simultaneous solution. Her solution was a piece titled *The Avenging Angel*, a magnificent abstraction.

Problem-Solving

After you have found your perfect problem, there remains, of course, the pesky business of actually solving it.

Consider this simple observation about how people solve problems. Ask anyone you know to suggest how to approach a problem you have. It could be any sort of problem—personal, technological, artistic. What you will invariably hear is how that person has approached a similar problem in her own life.

I tested this recently with my teenager as we drove home from the dentist by asking him what I should do to strengthen my aching back. "Mom, you just have to work and work and work at it. It's just like the dentist told me with flossing—you have to do it over and over again until it's just a routine."

When I asked my dean for advice about a program I had to develop, he said, "I recently heard a great talk on that topic in Vermont. Maybe we could take their approach."

A friend asked my father how one could design a more comfortable, lighter-weight bulletproof vest. "Recently I saw a door made of cardboard that had an accordionlike pattern of interfacing fibers, so that there was a parallel lattice of fibers oriented vertically to the surface of the door. Maybe something like that in a special material would be lightweight yet very flexible and strong," he said.

These three answers to disparate problems all recycled solutions from other situations. Further, these solutions had been observed in the very recent past. Constant exposure to new approaches as well as reexposure to time-honored old solutions are clearly both important in creating an internal "solution inventory."

I would suspect that it is virtually impossible to solve any problem without some form of recombination or repurposing of earlier observations or experiences. Often these observations are made quite serendipitously. Velcro, for instance, is said to be based on the inventor's experience with getting prickly plant burrs stuck on his socks. On close examination, he observed tiny half-loops, which he patterned Velcro on. Another example is Post-It notes, which were developed after an inventor for 3-M produced an adhesive that was not sticky enough for the purpose he had in mind.

Given the organizational structure of the brain, perhaps it is not even possible to generate a completely original solution. Your brain is organized in networks of cell clusters that interconnect in specific patterns. Everything you learn stimulates either a strengthening or a weakening of connections between specific clusters of cells. Because of these interconnections, you remember in a multisensory way, recalling the sounds, sights, feel, and smell of an experience. Everything you think, say, feel, or do involves activity in these organized brain circuits. This explains why so many of your thought processes are repetitive and circular. As soon as you stimulate a particular nerve cluster, a reverberating response in other connected cells is triggered.

Thus it seems impossible that the brain could even be *capable* of absolute originality. Rather, individuals vary by how many circuitry connections they establish and the ease with which they can access these circuits. Further, highly creative individuals "cut and paste" parts of ideas derived from disparate experiences. They seem to be able to take seemingly trivial aspects of one experience—such as the sticking of a burr—and cleverly apply it to another use.

Practicing Problem-Solving

When I was a freshman premedical student, I had a great deal of difficulty in general chemistry, and despite earnest efforts I received a C+ during the first semester. This was serious business; I knew I would not get into med school with C's in science courses. My father gave me two words of advice that had life-altering consequences: *Work problems.* I began to work problems like a maniac. If the professor told us to work half the problems at the end of the chapter, I worked every problem twice. From that point on, I had no further difficulties in science. My new approach, which deemphasized learning theory and emphasized repeated exposure to problem-solving strategies, made test-taking relatively straightforward. Almost three decades later, a young listener called me on my radio show with a similar problem. She had failed the math section of the high school graduation exam several times, and without passing it she couldn't go on to college with her friends. The makeup exam was only one week away. *"Work problems!"* I said. "Work problems like the wind!" She did, and called me back some weeks later to say, proudly, that she had passed.

What is an expert? Nothing more than a person who has repetitively solved problems in a specific area. Whether you are talking about art, technology, education, or politics, experts are people with experience who know how to apply their experience to new problems.

The human brain *wants* to become an expert. It hates having to figure entirely new solutions and will always seek to develop patterns of problem-solving. A simple example is learning to drive. When you start out behind the wheel, every movement is a new problem in controlling the car. Soon, however, the process becomes reflexive, and as you drive you negotiate numerous hazards on a second-by-second basis without having to consciously think about them.

Real innovators often surpass their peers by drawing on experience in problem-solving from an area very different from the one where the original problem arose. For example, Martha Ballenger, a brilliant and highly accomplished attorney, told me that the course she found most helpful in developing her legal thinking was a college course in logic, taught by a professor of philosophy. A friend who is a remarkable athlete drew on his knowledge of physics to design optimal exercises for himself. In my work as a psychotherapist, the most helpful source of knowledge for me has been reading literature, especially fiction. The broader the range of fields you expose yourself to, the more creative your problem-solving strategies will be.

Problem-Solving for Non-Geniuses

Obviously, few people are inordinately gifted in solving problems. Let's imagine you have found a great problem, but lack the experience necessary for its solution. There is a simple way to instantly double your access to potential solutions.

You can ask someone for help.

Imagine a hypothetical woman who has just a wee bit of megalomania: She wants to become the most powerful person in the world. She wants her name known by virtually every person on the face of the planet. She wants to have as much control as possible over every major economic and social decision in the United States.

Now let's assume there is one small glitch. She has little experience that would qualify her for that position. In fact, most of the work she has done was at a job that many would consider irrelevant to her goals: she is an actress. Do you think she could pull it off? If she could manage to achieve that power, do you think she could do the job?

Maybe you don't think *she* could, but Ronald Reagan thought *he* could.

Ronald Reagan, as is well known, won his first public office at age fifty-five. Before that, he had appeared in over fifty films. As president of the Screen Actors Guild he built a supportive political structure around himself that helped him become governor of California in 1966. After a whopping two years as governor, so great was his self-confidence that he campaigned briefly in 1968 for president, an office he eventually won twelve years later, at age seventy.

What Reagan was able to do, evidently, was crystallize a vision in a way that excited enough people to elect him to office. Left to his own devices, he could not possibly have had any real idea of how he would accomplish his ideas, for he had no experience in the federal government. But he must have realized that he didn't really need to—all he needed to pull off the governorship and then the presidency was to be able to ask other people to share *their* problem-solving capabilities.

Reagan was known as the Great Communicator. More important, however, is that he "found" problems that resonated with the American public's experience. He also knew how to effectively ask for help from others to achieve his goals. But he had a third quality: he believed in himself.

Problem-Solving Confidence

Once you have found a great problem, will you allow yourself to solve it? The female tendency to underrate ourselves is especially detrimental in this situation. To solve a great problem requires a form of overconfidence; you must believe you can do something that neither you nor anyone else has proved is possible.

Ronald Reagan was not unique in having the hubris to believe that he could be president. How could any person know how to be president before actually assuming the office? I suspect the thought process is not so much, "I know how to do it," as, "Well, if the guys who went before me could figure it out, I can too." It is this confidence in one's ability to figure it out that is so important for women to develop if they wish to achieve fully.

About a decade ago, the "impostor phenomenon" was the subject of many self-help articles. This was the concept that women shun success because they believe they are fakers and fear being found out. I have news. Everyone is an impostor, because none of us can be certain of success until we have succeeded, and even then we always owe much to those who have helped us. Men know they're impostors, too—they just aren't particularly perturbed by it, and they certainly don't feel the need to yodel it from the mountaintops like women sometimes do. Men have always found and solved problems by working hard, getting help, and using their relationships to forge alliances and make progress. They don't have brilliance flowing to them from the ether, either.

Once you begin learning to think in the white space, you will find yourself faced with new challenges you might not anticipate. If you decide to bring your idea to fruition, you will probably need to lead a team of people promoting your idea. How to succeed in the world of competition is the subject of the next chapter.

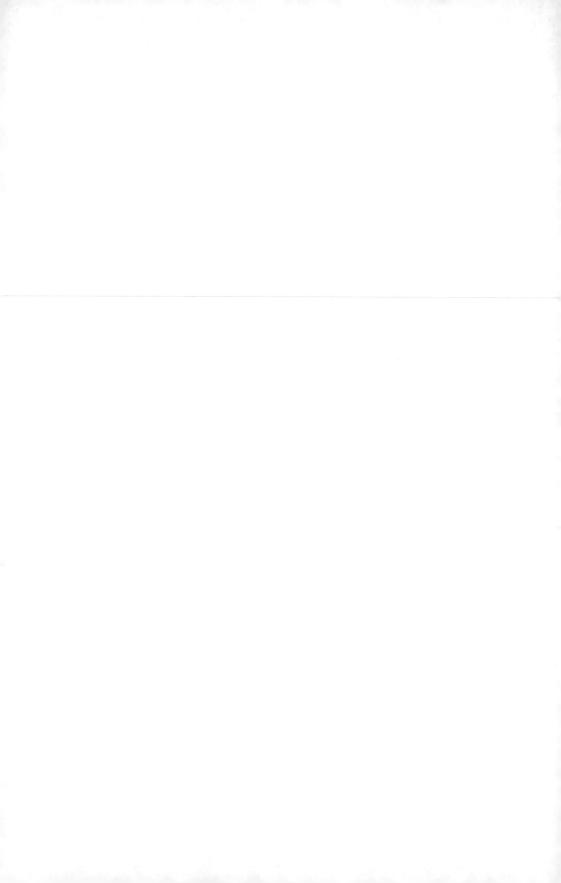

CHOICE 5

COMPETITION

Shaking Pom-Poms or Shooting Hoops?

THE CROWD OF a hundred or so of us waited patiently for the star of the evening to arrive. When Jackie Joyner-Kersee walked into the room, straight, slim, the epitome of womanly grace, not one of us could take our eyes off her. She told her remarkable story with humor, charm, and even a certain shyness.

Joyner-Kersee is one of the greatest female athletes of all time, holder of numerous world titles, including Olympic medals, in track and field events. She has also suffered from chronic asthma, a condition she denied for years until she finally became so ill she had no choice but to take it seriously.

"I had asthma for many years, but I was in total denial. I saw the doctor as the enemy. If something was wrong with me, I'd just think I wasn't in shape. One time in St. Petersburg, Russia, at the Goodwill Games, I knew something was wrong. I had gotten through all the events, and then I had to do the 800. Halfway through the race I could hear myself whistling. By 600 I could hardly breathe. But I was determined to finish the race, even though by the end I could barely jog across the finish line.

My chest was so tight, I started pulling at the straps on my top just to try to get some air in my lungs.

"When I finally got serious about my asthma, I began to think of it in a different way. I always had great respect for my competitors and I *never* underestimated them. Finally, I began to see my asthma as if it were a competitor, the one I had to beat, and my doctor became my coach."

As she continued to speak, it became clear that under the delightful, honest, smiling face was the heart of a fierce competitor. "Whenever we would go to a new country," she said, "I would never go outside the hotel to look around until after the meet was over. I'd just go to my hotel room and rest and concentrate on the race to come. I'd try to visualize myself in the race. I'd see myself as the first one off the starting block. Then I'd see myself, the first one to cross the finish line. I'd imagine myself during the long jump, sailing through the air—I'd just think of myself in the air, never coming down."

This inspiring woman not only could freely express her competitiveness, she'd learned to harness it to vanquish whatever stood in her path—even her asthma. While few of us demonstrate her intensely competitive spirit, there is much to be learned from the way she applied that drive to the overcoming of obstacles. Competitiveness, after all, is a core psychological trait of achievers, for every area of endeavor involves competition of some sort. In any corporate environment, those who are the most competitive are promoted. In the arts and humanities, competition is extraordinarily stiff, and a will of steel is necessary to endure frequent rejection. Even in foundations and charities, competition to attract donations is a fact of life. Further, we have all been educated in highly competitive systems, where the best students are rewarded with more attention, scholarships, prizes, and admission to better schools. To achieve you simply must know how to compete well.

Abundant research, painfully consistent, suggests that women are outcompeted in virtually every area of achievement and that our level of innate competitiveness may be somewhat lower than males'. Males score higher than females on many tests of aggressiveness and competitiveness. In one survey of undergraduates, females were more interested in their future mates' success than their own, while males gave more evidence of competitiveness. In a variety of studies of athletic competitiveness, male athletes express more competitiveness and desire to win than females. But not all females respond in the same way to competitive situation; androgynous females tolerate and enjoy competition more than highly feminine women do. These studies are consistent with Philippe Rushton's study of 573 pairs of twins, which found that females were significantly higher in altruism, empathy, and nurturance than males, while males scored higher than females in aggressiveness and assertiveness.

These data confirm the sorts of comments I frequently hear from men about competitiveness. One patient, a highly successful professional man, said, for instance, "I bill about $250,000 a month, but when my partner bills $300,000 a month it just kills me." Another male executive said, "When I was in school, I didn't care at all about the subject matter. The only thing that drove me was that the competitive thrill of wanting to stomp over everyone on the test." From a pathologist, "I think I'm the best, maybe in the world, in my field because all I think about—when I'm driving, eating, showering—is pathology." Whew! *All* they think about? Evidently so, at least for some men—the men who make it to the top. There seems something troubling, even pathetic about these descriptions of nonstop competitiveness, as if it has completely taken over these men's minds and souls.

It is not that women are not competitive. It is more that, as a group we are not *as* intensely competitive as men, and, I strongly suspect, do not care to be. If the price of success is having to think about one's work endlessly, most women (myself included!) would find that price too high by a mile. Yet we still wish to do well, in fact, very well. Our challenge is to take the significant (though not overwhelming) competitive drive that we have and learn to use it as productively as possible, so that we can achieve our ends without losing our selves in the process. For in fact, we have other traits, in greater abundance than males, that can *also* be used effectively in the service of achievement: namely, collaborativeness and cooperativeness. If we could learn to couple our collaborative strengths with our competitive spirit in a new feminine model of competitive teamwork, I am convinced we could be more effective than we are, fully able to compete in a world shaped by male standards of competitiveness. Later I will describe how this new model might look and how it would work. But first it is important to understand more about the nature of female competitiveness.

Too often innate competitiveness has been corrupted and diverted into meaningless directions. *What* we compete for has too often been prizes of limited intrinsic value that others have dangled before us, rather than our own thoughtfully chosen goals. Further, men, for whom competitiveness is far more permissible and internally accessible, have developed particular competitive strategies that are highly successful for them. The *way* they compete is too often more effective than the way women compete.

THE NATURE OF COMPETITIVENESS

Competition is one of the most basic animal instincts, the legacy of our most primitive animal ancestors. Some might wish to debate whether we, as females, *should* be competitive. It is too late for that discussion, for we just *are*: it is hard-wired into our brain biology through millennia of evolution. Our foremothers survived because they and their offspring got the best mates, the best food, and the safest shelters. They and their offspring survived, and they passed those grabby, pushy, *me-first* genes down to us. We simply would not be here at all if we were not wired for competition.

Competition, like other basic animal drives such as hunger and sex, is not inherently right or wrong but can be channeled in constructive or destructive ways. Eating can be used to sustain survival or to gorge oneself into unhealthy obesity. Sex can be used to express deepest love, or to inflict violence, as in rape. Competitiveness, likewise, can be channeled into work of enormous value or into destructive ruthlessness. It is one of our most powerful and essential drives; it is also one of our most easily corrupted drives.

And like other basic drives, competitiveness, by its nature, is insatiable. If you eat until you pop today, you will be no less likely to get hungry tomorrow. If you have sex today, you're equally likely to want it again tomorrow. And if you achieve a competitive goal today, you will be no less likely to find a new goal tomorrow. As with all drives, the pleasure of satisfying competitiveness is momentary.

These aspects of competitiveness—that it is a *powerful, essential, insatiable,* and *corruptible* drive—make it worthy of special scrutiny as a personality trait of the ambitious woman. As a drive, it is easily deflected into meaningless pursuits. Whether you use your competitiveness to shake pom-poms to incite adulation for others or channel it into going for the slam dunks that will help you achieve your personal goals has definitive impact on your lifetime productivity. Yet because competitiveness is expressed and diffused in such unconscious ways, it is important to understand more about the basic biological drive.

Eyes on the Prize

I am the loving but beleaguered owner of two dogs, Zoey and Sancho. Zoey is a pedigreed German shepherd: high-strung, hyperactive, and untrainable. I thought I was buying a noble beast, one with patrician dignity and refined intelligence; what I got was a dog with the demeanor of a clown school graduate.

Sancho, on the other hand, is a true junkyard dog I rescued from the SPCA. I got Sancho when he was a tiny puppy, thinking Zoey needed a playmate, the same type of thinking that produces most second-born children. As is often the case with their human counterparts, however, happy, idyllic play between these canine siblings has not been the norm. In fact, frequent hostilities, punctuated by breakneck chases up and down the stairs in hot pursuit of the cat, have created a home environment with all the serenity of an aircraft carrier during a World War II battle. Nonetheless, it has been illuminating to watch the two of them as they fight over virtually anything they can find. An object of especially intense competition is an old gardening glove of mine, which for them seems to be a sacred relic. Sancho usually starts the struggle by finding the glove and prancing back and forth in front of Zoey, waiting for her to realize that he has the coveted prize. Zoey then leaps into action, and the two madly dash around the house in figure eights and loop-de-loops until I throw both of them outside.

Occasionally, though, Zoey musters her two or three working neurons in an unusual display of intelligence. She finds another object she thinks Sancho might like—a plastic bone, for instance—and she waits until he lies down with the sacred glove. Then she walks by Sancho, waving the bone in his face. Sancho, of course drops the glove, and in a flash, Zoey gives up the bone and grabs the glove.

This scene is a wonderfully primitive example of how easy it is to corrupt and redirect another's competitiveness. Clearly, for dogs and for people the drive to compete over something, *anything*, is extremely intense. It is because that drive is so powerful and close to the surface that it is possible to divert it in any direction, regardless of how meaningless that new target actually is. Zoey's strategy is fundamentally what advertisers do at the billion-dollar level. The take their plastic bones—in the human case, cars, furniture, jewels—and wave them before our noses. As soon as we see these items in the possession of others, especially beautiful others, we become consumed with a competitive desire to have them ourselves. The glove we drop is money, the medium of exchange for our time and energy.

Women have traditionally been too ready to drop our own sacred gloves for prizes of less value that are waved before us. We have competed to have the tidiest house on the block, as if cleanliness were indeed next to godliness. We compete to be the most beautiful, which makes us more pleasing to men while not challenging them. Often we compete through the accomplishments of our children, which gratifies our husbands and impresses our friends.

The easy corruptibility of our competitiveness is illustrated by a TV show from my childhood, *Queen for a Day*. Four women would be lined up in front of a studio audience, and they would actually compete to see who had the most rotten life. Sick and injured children, husbands, and selves; fire, flood, and pestilence—every form of human misery had afflicted these unfortunate souls. At the end of the recitations, the emcee would majestically hold his hand above each contestant's head in turn, urging the audience to clap hardest for the woman whose story had been most gut-wrenching. The amount of noisy approval was registered on a special Queen-O-Meter, and the victorious victim would burst into racking sobs as she was presented with a crown, a velvet robe, and a Maytag washer.

Female competitiveness has been corrupted—or we have allowed it to be corrupted—in many ways throughout history. Diana, Princess of Wales, is a modern-day case study in how human societies have typically deflected female competitiveness. Diana, as so many women before her, achieved high status not primarily through any accomplishments of her own but through her marriage. Granted, she did some worthwhile things, embracing AIDS patients and campaigning against land mines, but these were newsworthy only because of her title.

Another acceptable form of female competition is through our children. Merely by producing the requisite "heir and a spare" so promptly, Diana secured her exalted position. Her husband might prefer his mistress, but Diana was the mother of a future king of the realm and thus would "not go quietly," as she put it. And the way she broke with British royal precedent to become actively involved in her sons' upbringing, actually hugging them and driving them on outings among commoners, endeared her to those commoners, winning her points in the royal family's ongoing popularity contest.

Yet another form of corrupted competition has been the emphasis on *passive* excellence for women. According to traditional rules, women should avoid the impression of direct, active effort to be the best. For this reason physical beauty has been an area in which women could "excel";

Diana, of course, was a superstar in this area. The image of a determined, goal-directed, highly disciplined woman such as Hillary Rodham Clinton engendered deep distrust during the early years of the Clinton presidency, particularly when she headed the healthcare reform initiative. It was not until the first lady was perceived to be the long-suffering victim of her husband's womanizing—our national Queen for a Day—that her popularity increased.

But if women's competitiveness has been corrupted, men's has been no more noble. In ancient times, men competed on the battlefield to win new territory just because it was there; the history of the world is largely the story of these deadly struggles. Men working in modern corporations have refined this competition over power and domination of others in their work lives. Many midlife crises are triggered by the depressing realization of how utterly meaningless that quest can become. The new directions taken after such a crisis may be better or worse than the original problem.

As a woman working in a male-dominated field, I can attest that it can be enormously seductive to forget one's own vision and make a lunge for the same prizes that men value so highly. Some of these bones truly are worth fighting over, while others have very little intrinsic worth and are merely crazy-making. The realization of how stressful and unsatisfying the never-ending struggle for dominance can be has led many women to rightfully question the value of their entry into the arena.

The challenge for you, as an ambitious woman, is to keep your eye on your own goal, to focus on shooting for the hoops that express your own value system rather than playing to the screams of the crowd. You will gain nothing by abandoning traditional passive, masochistic female behaviors if you merely replace them with the meaningless, ulcer-producing aims of the men around you. Your challenge is to maintain your vision and your values. You might compete, for instance, to be the most creative or innovative. You might compete to be a real leader of great wisdom and insight. You might compete to make the most intelligent contributions. These would be competitions worthy of your deepest ambition.

HOW YOU COMPETE: THE FIVE STAGES

The competitive drive originates deep within the mind in infancy and develops and matures throughout the life cycle. You never fully outgrow the impulses and pleasures of each stage; rather, the succeeding stage is built on it. Even the first stage, the joyous greed of infancy, remains somewhere within you. As you develop, however, your sense of ethics and morality tempers the me-centered competitiveness of your early years. Increasingly you channel competitiveness in ways that reflect your respect for and responsibility to others.

The maturation of competitive energy can be divided into five stages that parallel other stages of child and adult psychological development. With each successive stage, the drive become less and less self-centered and increasingly reflects a connection to others, the ability to delay gratification increases, and the goals that are sought mature in significance and permanence.

Stage One: Gimme!

Beginning in the first year of your life, you displayed the earliest precursor of competition—a joyously primitive grabbiness. As every parent knows, a small child wants what she wants when she wants it—*period*. The adult equivalent of this behavior would be for you to walk up to a friend, yank her new necklace off, and shriek, *"Mine!"* Mind you, it's not that you don't have the urge, occasionally. It's that the feeling is not continually present, and when you do feel that way you muster the wherewithal to undo your envy with a well-phrased compliment.

In the deepest recesses of your unconscious mind, you never fully lose this powerful *gimme* feeling. Of course it's great to be delighted with the pure hedonistic joys of life—a terrific meal at a new restaurant, a new piece of jewelry, or a great vacation. But as you mature, you don't feel the need for constant and continuous gratification, nor do you allow your own satisfaction to come at the expense of depriving others. Rather, the feeling is transformed from *me first, right now* to a recognition that pleasure at times is even deepened by waiting and working toward a goal.

Consider how you would react to this situation: You come home early from work, the first of your family to arrive, and you're ravenous. You open the fridge to survey the possibilities, and your eyes light up. There is *one* piece of that incredible Triple Chocolate Debauchery cake left over from last night. From the dim recesses of your mind, a tiny voice is crying, "Wait! Isn't this your husband's very favorite dessert? Wouldn't someone else in the family like the last piece?" Do you obey that little voice, or do you lunge toward the cake?

Each of us has primitive greed lurking in abundance deep inside. When this early greed becomes a dominant force, an "envy-driven personality" is the result. Psychiatrists believe that failure to modulate this greed originates in an early sense of emotional deprivation. It may have been that the childhood caretakers were emotionally or physically unable to offer sufficient love and attention, or that the child constitutionally was overly needy and demanding. In either case, the child develops an underlying sense of having been cheated of attention. She feels she deserves whatever she can get in order to make up for old wrongs, but simultaneously feels the score can never be really settled.

A patient of mine, Fran, felt eaten alive by her envy. She was an extraordinarily talented businesswoman who had amassed a considerable personal fortune. Yet her life was a personification of the adage "Money can't buy happiness." No matter what she achieved or purchased, she never felt at peace; for she could only plan for the next victory or acquisition. She commented frequently on her envy of me, though I lived a far less lavish lifestyle than she. She assumed that every woman she knew had a better marriage, smarter children, more supportive parents, and an easier lifestyle than she.

People who are consumed by competitive envy often deal with their feelings by making *others* envious of *them*. This accounts for their conspicuous, even bizarre materialistic excesses, as well as their lack of sensitivity toward others of more limited circumstances. No acquisition is ever enough, however, because it is only the act of purchase that temporarily assuages envy.

This was the strategy Fran used. Her shopping splurges were frequent and lavish. For her, buying was a fix: the moment of purchase was the one time when she could temporarily transcend her envy of others. But of course, one never wakes up happier in the morning because one more dress is hanging in an already crowded closet, and Fran would wake up every day to the same gnawing feeling of envy.

As a rule in psychotherapy, the earlier the development phase one has become stuck in, the more difficult it is to dislodge the problem. Envy, as one of the most common but primitive feelings we mortals have, is a real challenge. The easiest way to modify this problem is by attempting to channel that feeling to a higher level of competition.

Stage Two: Pleasing Others

Beginning in the preschool years—ages three, four, five—you began to engage in a different form of competition: pleasing others. Growing up you probably competed with brother and sister to be Mommy or Daddy's favorite. Ratting on your siblings was a way to further your cause, to demonstrate your virtuousness by contrasting it with their criminality. As you began formal schooling, you learned the fine art of pleasing the teacher.

Competition for the approval of others is alive and well in all of us. Marriage, for example, is an institution based on the idea that there *should* be one person in the world for whom you are the ultimate beloved, and it is normal to feel severely threatened if you perceive a rival for your spouse's love. But marriage is a very special compartment for those feelings, and with virtually every other relationship in life it is a sign of psychological health to share love and approval with others.

If you become stuck in this phase, you feel that you spend your life doing back-flips to gain the attention of others. The great psychoanalyst Heinz Kohut coined a wonderful term for those whose self-esteem requires constant feedback from others: "mirror-hungry." Such people demand attention without earning it. You can recognize these people easily. They are the ones who can't refrain from bragging, either obviously or subtly, in order to impress you. They are the ones who seem to yearn for compliments, and when you do praise them they will pretend they didn't hear you so you can say it again. Some seem overly compliant and fawning; others are very demanding of attention.

Those who become stuck in this stage do not necessarily have the same underlying sense of deprivation that Stage One people do. Many Stage Two people do report that the love they received as children felt conditional on conforming to parental expectations. For example, some women who are mirror-hungry have had a close relationship with Mother but felt that Daddy's attention required special effort, such as being pretty, smart, or compliant. Others have had a relationship with their mother in which their role was to shore up her own self-esteem by being a gratifying reflection of her mothering. At the heart of it, Stage Two people feel unseen, unacknowledged, unvalued, and so are continually trying to get a response from others. Since most of us experienced at least glimmers of these dynamics in our early years, a certain amount of mirror-hunger is not unusual.

A common form this type of competition takes is for admiration of one's beauty. A study of five hundred undergraduates revealed that large numbers of the women were critical of other women's looks and concerned about their own in relation to other women's. As noted previously, this is an example of a corruption of innate competitiveness.

A quick scan of women's magazine covers suggests a grand international conspiracy to play to women's mirror-hunger. Virtually every cover features the shining visage of an air-brushed, impossibly gorgeous nymph; the goal of the accompanying advice is to help you look less like you and more like her. Traditional women's homemaking magazines are even more bewildering, featuring cover pictures of a magnificent hunk of gooey chocolate cake and articles that promise ten secrets to slim thighs, a flatter stomach, or a tighter rear.

As if this were not bad enough, the conspiracy has widened to include a new twist for baby boomers: we must appear *young* and beautiful. As Isabel Allende commented in her family memoir, *Paula*, in Latin American countries it has always been considered good form for a middle-aged woman to dress in black, tie a kerchief around her head, let her mustache grow unchecked, and retire from the competition for male admiration. Not here in the United States, however. Mustache, please! We've already been in for electrolysis, and probably Retin-A, liposuction, laser treatments, and plastic surgery.

The anxiety engendered by trying to meet these unrealistic standards of beauty is an enormous obstacle to achievement. Further, it has deadly consequences, which we will see in epidemic numbers in a few decades. The terrible rise in teenage smoking, especially marked in young girls trying to control their weight, is testimony that our gender is so neurotic about our appearance that we are willing to risk our lives for it. It is disturbing that despite decades of feminism we seem to be losing ground in helping our daughters respect their bodies.

Stage Three: Me vs. You

By ages six to eight, children begin to develop yet another layer of competitiveness, the wish to beat each other for the sheer joy of winning. This is, after all, the age of the game, in the family room and on the playing field. Some children also begin to feel competitive about grades, and being the smartest motivates some. Between ages nine and twelve, social competition appears, and children in modern American culture begin to clamor for status symbols such as bikes, clothes, skates, and CDs, looking down on those who lack such possessions.

Stage Three competition is an extraordinarily powerful motivator for success. Consider this description of Michael Jordan from a magazine profile:

> Jordan's teammates came to realize that he was driven by an almost unparalleled desire—or need—to win. All top athletes are driven, some

more than others, but Michael was the most driven of all. He simply hated to lose, on the court in big games, on the court in little games, in practice, even in Monopoly games with friends. (If he fell far behind in Monopoly, he was capable, with one great sweep of his arm, of sending his opponents' hotels and houses crashing to the floor. . . .) In card games and billiards his passion for winning was just as strong—so strong that he sometimes tried to change the rules to fit his circumstances. A pool shot which he had missed did not count because someone had spoken just as he was about to shoot, for instance.

Every competition had the quality of a life-or-death struggle for Jordan.

If you guessed that women are less competitive at the Stage Three level than men, you are right. Most studies of competition look at only this level, doubtless because it's much easier to quantify than the other stages, and they find pretty consistently that in measurable areas of competition such as athletics and in striving for money, men score higher than women. Most social scientists feel this is most likely biologically mediated, for in animals and humans the male hormone testosterone is associated with social dominance behaviors beginning at a very early age.

Because women are less Stage Three–oriented, we are often oblivious to important contests until the race is over and the victor—someone else—is announced. Madeline, a focus group participant, described such an experience at work. Her boss suddenly created a subdivision in her section, and her colleague Dan was appointed head of it. Dan, a manipulative, intensely competitive man, proceeded to undercut the efforts of Madeline and everyone else in this new division in order to claim yet more power for himself. Clearly he was operating in Three, with more than a touch of One greed underlying his motives. Furious, Madeline went to her section chief to complain about what had happened. He shrugged. "I'm sorry it's difficult, Madeline," he said. "But Dan came to me with the idea of creating the subdivision, and then he kept bugging me about it until I told him he could head it. But he has a lot of good qualities, and I'd suggest you work out your issues directly with him."

Had Madeline lobbied first to create the subdivision, she probably could have received the promotion. But she hadn't, because she hadn't been thinking in Three terms. Now her own ability to be productive even in her current position was compromised, and there was little she could do about it.

For many women, competing directly against a colleague for a position of leadership is extremely uncomfortable, directly counter to the cooperative, congenial behavior that we would like to believe is the signature of our gender. But in any complex group, leaders must emerge, and if you shrink from this competition someone else will take charge. It is obviously far better to join the fray and gain the right to assert your own value system than to remain at the mercy of another's priorities. The harsh reality is that regardless of whether you are trying to beat your male colleagues, they assuredly are trying to beat each other *and you.*

Given the intensity of the human competitive spirit, thoughtfully monitoring your behavior is essential. As in all areas of life, compartmentalizing competition in the workplace is essential. In a business, for instance, competing to become the top-producing salesperson may be appropriate, but competition becomes destructive when it spills over into *all* aspects of group function: who dominates meetings, who gets the best office, who spends the most time with the boss. These are activities of Stages One and Two; healthy Three activity is related to actual productivity, with a goal to attain power and autonomy through legitimate competition.

If you are to become a great achiever, at some point "me vs. you" energy becomes experienced as "me vs. me" energy: your motivation will become to surpass your own accomplishments. Some fields lend themselves to this form of competition because the work involved is inherently solitary. Artists, for instance, typically work in isolation and as they mature become increasingly focused on refining a particular artistic approach unique to them. Frequently an artist chooses a particular theme and reworks it numerous times until a sense of mastery is achieved. Musicians and writers likewise frequently work in relative isolation, practicing their craft and aspiring toward personal improvement.

Stage Four: Hierarchical Competition

While me vs. you activities are a fundamental element of competitiveness, in almost all areas of endeavor this strategy is insufficient to achieve goals. Stage Four competition relies on membership in a larger group in which activities can be delegated to specific individuals; the team is thus empowered to compete against other teams. This strategy maximizes each member's specific talent. The group itself becomes a unit of power far greater than any individual member could achieve alone. Within the group is a clearly established order of leadership and authority. An example of Stage Four competition is a basketball team; each member has a carefully delineated role, assigned and guided by the coach, which allows a single player to shoot a hoop—all to the glory of the whole team.

From the basketball courts of childhood arise the complex organizational hierarchies of the corporate world. Alex, a vice president of a major clinical research organization, was in charge of negotiating for and carrying out research protocols for new medications, and he headed up a group of researchers and technicians to accomplish the job. Soon after he started in the position, he told me, he gathered his group together in his conference room. "What I told them was very clear. I told them what the productivity standards were. And I told them that if we met those standards they would all receive large bonuses. If the group failed to achieve those standards, there would be no raises the next year. They thought it was great."

Alex made it very clear who was boss. He communicated that he wielded great power in their lives, but also that if they were loyal to him and worked hard they would be rewarded. It certainly did not occur to him to ask his subordinates for their ideas; *he* was the idea man. There was a baldness, a brashness to his approach, but one that his subordinates found exciting—at least so long as the prospect of a reward was dangled before them.

Of all strategies for competition, the hierarchy is the most powerful—and the most distinctly masculine. Team sports are an early education in subordinating individual will to the needs of the group and displaying strict loyalty and obedience to the coach. The military, of course, is the example par excellence of the hierarchy, for all decisions and communications flow strictly through the chain of command. The high degree of specialization within the hierarchy, directed by the most senior and experienced member, allows the whole of the hierarchy to surpass the sum of its individual members' capabilities. It is testimony to the power of this hierarchy that it creates an ethic that pushes individuals to face terror, pain, and even death to support the goals of the group in the ultimate form of competition—life vs. death.

In a meta-analysis of seventy-six studies comparing the leadership effectiveness of the two genders, the psychologist Alice Eagly and her colleagues found that whether men or women were rated more effective depended on the type of leadership the job demanded. Specifically, when leadership was seen as requiring a high degree of control and direction—a vertical, hierarchical type of leadership—men were rated significantly more effective than women. Men also fared better than women in upper levels of leadership, while women fared better than men in middle levels of management. The military was the strongest example of leadership roles in which men outperformed women.

At an individual level, however, the efficacy of hierarchy comes from the bidirectional flow of power it allows. Alex, for instance, used his position to empower his subordinates to be more successful. But he also drew his own power from his subordinates and their productivity, and that, of course, is why he was so eager to reward them. The fundamental unit of a hierarchy, one leader and one subordinate, is an intensely symbiotic relationship, each person multiplying the power of the other. It is not even necessary that the two *like* each other; it only matters that they *support* each other. This is a difficult concept for many women to grasp, so accustomed are we to thinking of relationships as predicated on affection and intimacy.

Hierarchical competition, in fact, is Mother Nature's greatest strategy for survival in the animal kingdom. Many animal species—birds, fish, mammals, and even some insects—live together in groups. Mammalian groups develop complex power structures with clearly established patterns of leadership and submission. These structures reduce violent confrontations between individuals. Once the dominant animal establishes himself, the impulse for ongoing fighting is reduced.

In primate species the ordering of position within the hierarchy is remarkably clear for males as well as for females. Each animal is well aware of whether it is dominant or submissive to another specific individual. At the top of this hierarchy in most primate species is what anthropologists call the alpha male. (In lemurs, it is the females who are the dominant gender.) The alpha's mating rights supersede those of all other troop members. The alpha leads the troop, defends its members, and may also be generous in sharing food and other resources—provided the proper deference is shown.

While males engage in more fierce and frequent battles over dominance than females do, female primates also establish pecking orders among themselves. A particular individual will become the alpha female, the one who dominates other females. Though dominance behaviors in females are generally not nearly as intense or frequent as among males, females nonetheless also establish a clear pecking order. The alpha female asserts her rights to the best food and the best mates, sometimes through physical fighting and building alliances with others who support her supremacy.

In the past decade, animal researchers have realized that primate hierarchies serve another purpose, one that has significant implications for human group function. Behavioral displays of dominance and submission actually promote affiliation between animals. Among primates, for instance, an aggressive act by a dominant to a subordinate is frequently followed by affectionate behavior between the two animals. This pattern is true for all pairings studied, including male–male, female–female,

male–female, and mother–infant. Further, primates learn to signal these dominance relationships through behavioral rituals such as bobbing and grimacing, rather than outright attacks. Once the relationship has been acknowledged, the dominant animal will often allow the subordinate to share food or other desired commodities.

These fascinating observations force us to reconsider notions of the fundamental nature of affiliation and relationships. Women assume that we are the champions of relationship and that men are relatively deficient in this regard. But this is because we define relationship in a restricted way. We assume that relationship means relative equality; that it is pervaded by good feelings; and that it is characterized by two cherished activities, talking and displaying emotions. But Mother Nature seems to have defined relationship differently. Nature's definition of relationship is an affiliation between two animals, often based on *inequality* in which periodic assertions of power by one over the other actually strengthens bonds of affection and loyalty. Further, it is these unequal relationships that enhance the survival chances of the individual and strengthen the power of the group. And if we were to use Nature's definition, it would be *males* who have the more frequent and intense relationships.

Relative to men, women tend to be uncomfortable with, ambivalent about, or even offended by dominant–subordinant relationships. Many women, in fact, pride themselves on avoiding these relationships, and a portion of feminist rhetoric has been devoted to lambasting the male tendency toward hierarchy. Yet it could be asked: if such relationships are actually wired into our biology as a means to survive, if they have stood the test of time (millions of years) as one of the most important ways to affiliate, might women be too hasty in rejecting the value of hierarchies as a means to compete and thrive?

Stage Five: Altruistic Collaboration

In rejecting Stage Four activities, women often move to Stage Five, altruistic collaboration. In contrast to the vertical ordering of hierarchical relationships, Stage Five activities are horizontal: participants are equal in authority, relying on goodwill and a mutually agreed-upon value system rather than power relationships working toward a common goal. It is here that women shine as leaders. Eagly's meta-analysis found that women are rated as more effective leaders when cooperative approaches to team-building are required; for this reason, women are especially effective leaders in areas such as education and social services.

Is democratic collaboration necessarily a "higher" stage than hierarchical competition? I would argue yes, for it incorporates the logical development of features that mark the progression of stages. Democratic collaboration requires more capacity to delay instant gratification than the previous stages. It is driven by a sense of connection and responsibility to the external world. Often the goals of democratic collaboration are intangible and difficult to measure directly; the energy driving this stage comes only from a sense of knowing what is the right thing to do. It represents the final step of maturation out of a narcissistic, self-absorbed worldview, and even one whereby the needs of one's group are promoted over the needs of other groups.

Because of women's relative aversion to hierarchy coupled with our nurturing instincts, we tend to gravitate to Stage Five, volunteering for community projects, giving unselfishly to our families, and joining social organizations.

Traditional religious structures are an excellent example of how men and women work out of Stages Four and Five. Typically, men become the priests or ministers, the established leaders of the church. They receive the most respect and are acknowledged as the thought leaders and moral voices of the congregation. Their role is to tell everyone else how to live and what to do. As leaders in the church hierarchy, reporting both to denominational authority above them and to their congregants below them, they are working out of Stage Four.

Women, of course, are also essential to the viability of a church and often fill the most pews at services. Women, however, tend to operate out of a spirit of collaborative altruism. When there are cookies to be baked,

flowers to be arranged, or Sunday school classes to be taught, it is more
often the women of the church who fulfill these missions. These activities
are done without regard for hierarchy or authority, and therefore fall into
Stage Five activities.

New Yorker writer Ken Auletta interviewed three dozen female executives from the upper ranks of publishing, advertising, entertainment, and
communications industries for a 1998 article about differences between
male and female leadership styles. Typical of this group of executives was
Amy Pascal, president of Columbia Pictures.

> I manage from a place—how my employees are feeling—and men don't
> do that. We're trained in the art of compromise, and men aren't. We learn
> as girls. I think I am much more attuned to people's feelings. That's a
> good thing and a bad thing. I can read my employees' faces about how
> something has gone down with them. I think I can motivate them and
> talk to them in a more straightforward way. But I probably dwell too
> much in that place. I probably care too much when I should just be
> colder about it.

Anthropologist Helen E. Fisher told Auletta that she believes part of
this difference is biochemical, since the average male carries seven to ten
times as much testosterone as the average female.

According to Auletta, women managers can be characterized as non-
hierarchical, team-oriented, and willing to listen. The approach of the
female leaders he talked to was to inspire employees by making them feel
good about their work, rather than scare them into producing by flaunt-
ing their hierarchical power. Auletta suggested that the female approach
would improve the work environment and productivity. What he did not
point out, though, is that the horizontal management style characteristic
of women wins out only rarely. In the vast majority of cases, the vertical
management style triumphs, as evidenced by the overwhelming prepon-
derance of men at the top of the corporate ladder.

COMPETING IN ORGANIZATIONAL SETTINGS

Men, then, seem to outcompete us at Stage Three, me vs. you, and they are also far more likely than we to engage in Stage Four hierarchical competition. This creates a real dilemma for women, nobly pursuing our Stage Five altruistic collaboration. On the one hand, our Stage Five activities reflect a more mature, loving, and wise value system. On the other hand, operating primarily at this level can diminish our ability to rise within our organizations. While we are contributing to the common good, our male coworkers are competing against us—and winning. It is tempting to argue that we should simply say to hell with the male value system, let's hold on to our ideals and stay in Stage Five. The problem is that this ultimately keeps us from attaining enough power to promote our vision fully.

Here's an example of what happens to women, drawn from my medical school experience. At most universities there are four ranks: instructor, assistant professor, associate professor, and full professor. For each rank, defined criteria cover a dozen or so activities: research, writing papers, teaching, clinical care, committee work, and so forth. It is relatively rare for a woman to achieve the highest rank: about 10 percent of full professors at my university are women; 60 percent of instructors are. In order to achieve the top rank, one must have established national recognition in a specific area. This means publishing scholarly articles in prestigious journals, which in turn depends mostly on guiding research studies to obtain the data to be published.

When this issue was discussed at a meeting of women faculty, the women began to stir, and an undercurrent of frustration was palpable in the room. One woman, a highly competent ob-gyn, spoke up. "I am swamped with my clinical responsibilities," she said. "I'm in the OR several days a week, and then I have clinics in the day. There simply isn't any time allowed me to do research or writing."

Others agreed. "I have responsibility for organizing the medical students' courses. That takes up all my so-called academic time." "I'm spending a day a week extra putting together a clinic in the inner city—my chairman asked me to do it, but you can't get national recognition that way." "I've been asked to head the gender equity program." "I'm in charge of a big piece of the medical student admissions process." One after another, these women described the important contributions they were making that helped the school to function smoothly, but that did not gain them the credentials needed for promotion. And without promotion, their earning capacity as well as power and freedom were limited.

By working in Stage Five, these women were helping others, but they had shortchanged *themselves* by not spending enough energy first in Stages Three and Four. While they were becoming the Earth mothers of their institution, their male colleagues were racking up the publications and honors required for promotion. This phenomenon is by no means unique to academic medicine; in corporations and law firms and industry the vast majority of women play a supportive role and remain outside the power circle. This is common female behavior. The three traditional careers of women—teaching, nursing, and secretarial work—are all based on this concept of devotion to the common good. Men have felt free to leave the altruism to the women and to vigorously and directly compete for their own advancement.

THE FEMININE RESISTANCE TO POWER RELATIONSHIPS

Curious to gauge women's perceptions of the importance of hierarchical relationships, I presented these ideas to several focus groups of professional women who themselves worked at different levels in a variety of organization setting. What would happen if we purposefully decided to compete more vigorously in Stage Four? What does it feel like for a woman to foster relationships of unequal status?

As soon as I began to mention words like "power," "dominant," and "subordinant" I became aware of tension in the room. Several women began to lean forward, excited by the prospect of learning to multiply their personal power. A significant number of women, however, began to look downright hostile. They crossed their arms and stiffened their posture, though they attempted to maintain the look of pleasant interest that is characteristic of our sex. In one such group, a woman pithily expressed the fear that she and her cohorts were experiencing: "Well, I certainly wouldn't want to develop my vertical relationships at the expense of my horizontal relationships." A number of women vigorously nodded their heads in agreement.

The surface content of the anxiety she expressed was not entirely logical. Clearly, her choosing to strengthen her power relationships at work would not force her to dump her friendships at home or even her collegial associations at work. Nor would it mean she and her boss or subordinates would like each other less—in fact, they might like each other more.

But below the surface content, I sensed she was expressing a different anxiety. She was saying, in essence, that she found something vaguely threatening about being a member of a power hierarchy. Something about it didn't seem as, well, *nice* as operating at a Stage Five level. So what, precisely, is it about Stage Four that feels not so nice?

Some women expressed concern about loyalty. "What if the leader is too demanding or doesn't share my vision? Would I lose sight of my own values? Would there be a loss of individual identity?" The simple answer, of course, is that you would leave the hierarchy. Yet the possibility of the loss of identity was frightening to some women.

Others were concerned about changing the relationship to their subordinates. "If I increase the sense of authority I wield, doesn't that deny the value of what subordinates might offer? Mightn't that create a stifling environment?"

Third, "What if I became really caught up in the goals of the group? What if I began to absorb the values of the group, or somehow got carried away with being competitive?" That clearly wouldn't be so nice, either.

Fourth, "What if my team were really successful, able, as a group, to beat the others out?" You would have to learn to tolerate the envy of others and the knowledge that you had surpassed people you like, making them feel bad about themselves. You might have to adjust your self-image and start seeing yourself as a shrewd, politically savvy operator. You might end up feeling isolated by success.

Yet, as we talked further, it began to occur to me that we were not really talking about Stage Four vs. Stage Five. After all, these women could have just as easily fantasized that they'd be inspired by the positive goals of the leader or see that they could use their power to elevate the role of their subordinates. Rather, the innate competitiveness of Stages Three and Four seemed by definition to have a malevolent twist. It was as if naked competition had been defined a priori as bad—certainly off-limits to us as females.

I suspect that the anxiety these women had about competing as part of a hierarchy came from a Stage Two level of functioning—the need to please others, to not rock the boat, to remain in a supportive role. As long as they maintained themselves in a nonthreatening, noncompetitive position, no one could fault them. In fact, everyone would be very pleased to have their unselfishness, their generosity, their helpfulness. They would step on no one's toes. *They would be liked.*

It seems to be part of the female psyche that at the end of the day we are all supposed to hold hands by the firelight and sing "Kumbayah." Obviously our capacity for harmonious connection is a great strength. But the essential question for every woman is clear. Do you have the psychological freedom to take on the Jackie Joyner-Kersee, me vs. you style of competition *when it is necessary* for your advancement? Do you have the emotional discipline required to compete in a hierarchy *when it is essential* to meeting ambitious goals?

A New Competitive Style: The Intelligent Hierarchy

Earlier I commented that our challenge as women is to learn to nurture our competitive drive and integrate it with our great capacity for cooperation and collaboration to create a new model of teamwork. I call this model the intelligent hierarchy, led by an individual who is able to harness the enormous affiliative power of hierarchy but use it to support the smooth functioning of the team and promote the individual development of its members.

Here's an example of how such a leader might lead. Beth, director of a major division of her corporation, had a problem to solve. The company was about to launch a new project, and she had three highly qualified employees who wanted the senior product manager job. All three wanted the promotion intensely, and she was aware that the losers might feel bitter and perhaps seek to transfer out of the division.

She called all three in for an impromptu meeting. "As you know," she said, "we must choose a senior product manager, and we must do it soon. I know that each of you is very qualified for the position, and each of you could do an excellent job. Jane, you have been in our division longest and you have been instrumental in bringing this product to market. Max, you have been a senior product manager of a smaller product in the past, and I know you're ready to move up to something bigger. Sandra, as division chief, you rank highest in the whole section and so you, too, have a very valid claim to the position. So what I would like the three of you to do is to meet together and decide among yourselves who would be the best senior product manager. If you are unable to reach an agreement that is satisfactory, I will make the decision myself. But please be aware that we have little time to decide this; I want your answer soon. Thank you."

Was Beth operating out of Stage Four or Five? Clearly, elements of each were involved. By not making the decision herself, by calling for consensus and making it clear that cooperation was the order of the day, she was demonstrating Stage Five sensibilities. *She preserved her power by not using it.* She invited the three parties involved, the primary stakeholders in the decision, to call the shots.

Yet beneath the democratic surface, Beth's approach was fundamentally hierarchical. She chose her three candidates from within the established power ladder. She supported Sandra's position, the place just one notch down from her own, by not going around her and appointing a subordinate to the slot. By allowing the three employees to privately broker their own power relationships, she was encouraging them to further cement the stability of their own internal hierarchy. Further, Beth recognized that she derived a substantial measure of her own power from the loyalty of her subordinates. By offering them the initial opportunity to resolve the issue themselves she maintained a positive alliance with all three.

As it turned out, Sandra was at a point in her career where she didn't want to take on another big project but was more satisfied to say these words herself than be told by Beth that she was past her prime. Jane was already the one emotionally invested in the project, and Max supported her getting the new position, particularly since he had received the last promotion. Max and Jane even strengthened their alliance in the course of making the deal, with Max pledging to help Jane as second-in-command, and Jane told Beth it was explicitly understood that Max would be product manager for the next big product to come along.

Beth's goal was for the hierarchy to direct its competitive spirit *outward* while strengthening a collaborative spirit *within* the team. Anticipating how divisive the issue could have been, she knew she was taking a bit of a risk in allowing her subordinates to resolve it themselves—but won their appreciation and strengthened affiliation as a result.

A hierarchy is a complex, paradoxical arrangement. Subordinates seem to draw their power from the leader, who protects them. But actually, the leader draws all her power from subordinates. By simultaneously strengthening the power of subordinates and clearly demonstrating one's own leadership, a center of power can be maintained. It is this *affiliative* use of power, drawing strength both from above and below, that women must learn if we are to compete within organizations.

Empowered Mentoring

Mentoring itself has generated a great deal of discussion in academic circles, including institutions such as the NIH, for many believe that women do not advance as fast as men because we lack mentors. Since most senior positions are filled by men, and since men are more likely to offer advice and support to male subordinates than female ones, women fell behind. But some studies on gender aspects of mentoring refute this theory, finding that women are mentored *more* than men. Some studies indicate that the gender of mentors is important, others don't. Some studies even suggest that mentoring in and of itself is not very important for advancement.

I suspect that these contradictory findings can be accounted for by the fact that as typically practiced, mentoring is a toothless exercise. Mentoring usually consists of supporting, teaching, guiding, and critiquing. None of these activities, of course, necessarily result in *good* advice being given or in the advice being actually used. At times mentoring may also include making valuable introductions or securing roles on committees or projects, but these occur only in unusually strong mentoring relationships.

Even so, mentoring, as it is typically practiced, does not involve either the multiplication or the exchange of power. Further, the term implies that the mentor bestows his counsel and wisdom on the protégé in a uni-directional flow of generosity completely dependent on the largess of the mentor, and thus it may be cut off by competing demands on the mentor's time and energy.

I suggest that by reconceptualizing mentoring relationships, women could significantly increase their effectiveness in the workplace. *Empowered mentoring* is far more than quasi-parental guidance, support, and encouragement. Rather, power is multiplied for both mentor and protégé through the optimal use of their respective energy and productivity to support *each other*. Empowered mentoring is symbiotic in nature and derives great strength from this mutual interdependency. The mentor actively supports the protégé within the organization, provides educational and other developmental opportunities, and rewards the protégé financially and in other meaningful ways; meanwhile, all the work of the protégé is "counted" as part of the group productivity of the mentor and everything the protégé accomplishes reflects well on the mentor. The mentor creates too good a deal for the protégé to want to leave, while the protégé is so productive that the mentor is highly motivated to sustain the relationship.

Marla, a division director of a small but highly successful group of computer programmers for a communications firm, commented on the importance of this practice. "The key," she said, "is to pick the best employees and then really give to them. The more you give, the more you get." Each year when she personally received a significant bonus for the productivity of the group, she distributed part of it among all the group members. The money she relinquished was more than made up for by the large raises she received as director of the most successful division in the company.

Earlier I discussed evidence suggesting that women as a group lack the intensity of the I-gotta-win drive that many men describe. But I am convinced that we can more than match the competitive energy of men by an energy that is distinctly feminine: the spirit of collaboration and cooperation, the nurturance and support we instinctively feel and demonstrate toward others of our group. Teaching, advising, and protecting are ancient, natural instincts for us, so we are uniquely well suited to offer empowered mentoring. As we learn to use hierarchies intelligently, to compete as well as to nurture, women can vastly increase their ability to achieve without having to become "more like a man."

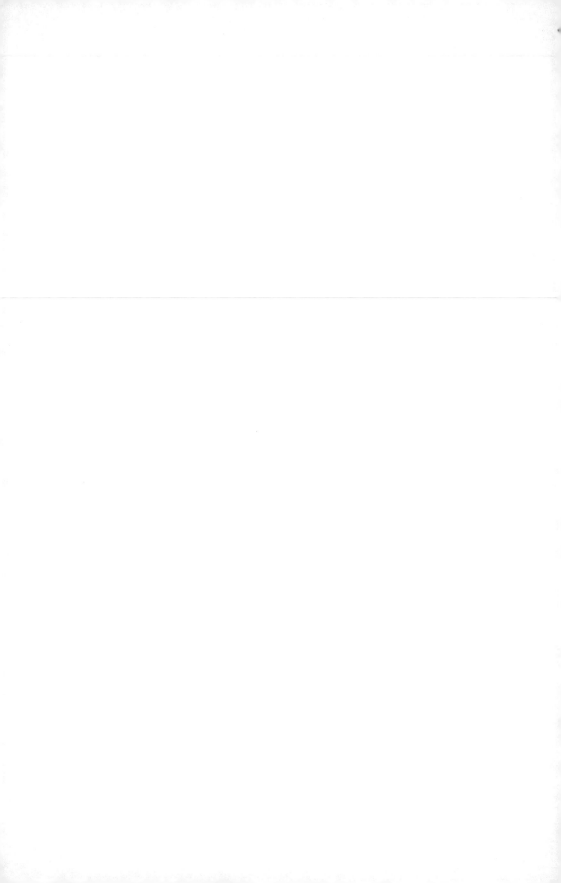

CHOICE

TAR BABIES
IN YOUR PATH

Taking a Swing or Walking On By?

MANY YEARS AGO, I worked with a woman—let's call her May—who was very bright, well organized, and highly disciplined, but so rigid and hostile that she made life difficult for everyone in the division. I discussed May one day with my boss, who made a comment I've never forgotten: "You know, Linda, you will never become an important person unless you can deal with difficult people."

It is often said that it's not what you know, it's who you know. A corollary might be that it is not only who you know, but how you interact with who you know to gain their support, not hindrance. Interacting successfully with others only becomes more important as you ascend in power. The more visible you are, the more you will become a target of envy. The higher your rank in your organizational hierarchy, the more employees you will have to manage. The more successful you are, the greater a threat you will become to some. Your challenge will be to optimally manage your relationships to support your accomplishments and to disarm those who would sabotage you.

It is curious that we receive virtually no formal education in dealing with adversarial relationships, a skill crucial to achievement. Highly gifted people like to think of themselves as orchids, exquisite and exotic specimens deserving of the rarefied conditions of a hothouse. True enough, many of us could be great bloomers if we could work in climate-controlled environments. Your goal, however, should be to become a morning glory, not an orchid, able to flourish and bloom in the most intemperate conditions. You want to be the one who can find the sunshine and nourishment for survival even when others can't.

I have frequently lectured on the topic of dealing with difficult people, and I always begin my talk by asking my audience, "How many of you know a difficult person?" Everyone immediately raises her hand, and some even raise both hands. The question energizes the group, and there are usually jokes and comments. Then I ask a second question: "How many of *you* are difficult people?" The hands all come down. How remarkable, I comment, that in a world so filled with difficult people, I have managed to gather an audience of several hundred without a single one!

The obvious point is that *nobody* experiences herself as unreasonable, particularly not in the heat of a conflict. Yet the heart of what makes another person seem difficult is her capacity to stir up unpleasant feelings within *you*: anger, frustration, impatience, boredom, or envy. In other words, difficult people are those who bring to your awareness the worst parts of *yourself*, though you project the responsibility for this back onto them. But you will never change another person, of course, you can only work on yourself. The challenge is clear: *In order to manage difficult people, you must learn to manage yourself.*

Baiting

The Uncle Remus story of Brer Rabbit and the tar baby illustrates how *not* to manage oneself with difficult people. Brer Fox decided one day to set a trap for Brer Rabbit. He made a little doll out of hot tar and set it beside the road where he knew Brer Rabbit would pass. Sure enough, along came Brer Rabbit, and he hollered out to the tar baby. The tar baby, of course, was silent. Irritated that he was being ignored, Brer Rabbit yelled out again to the tar baby, who still remained quiet. Feeling his dander rise, Brer Rabbit angrily demanded why the tar baby just sat there grinning at him. When the tar baby *still* remained silent, Brer Rabbit could contain himself no longer. He walked up to the tar baby and socked him. Immediately his paw was stuck in the hot, soft tar. Enraged, he took a second swing at the tar baby, and became even more stuck. Now he put both of his hind legs up against the tar baby, and of course he was stuck fast. Brer Fox whooped with delight and claimed his victim.

The moral of the story is clear: When you pass a tar baby in the road, walk on by. It may be going too far to say that there is *never* an entanglement with a difficult person that is worth your time and energy, but it is almost always the case. Yet steering clear is easier said than done. In most of your life you probably do walk on by one tar baby after another but nonetheless find yourself taking a swing from time to time that hinders you from attaining the goals that are most meaningful to you.

The tar baby story is relevant for women because of gender-specific behavior in a form of interaction I'll call *baiting*. Baiting is the way one person throws out some enticing tidbit—a comment, a behavior, a style of interaction—*in order to make you behave in ways you otherwise would not*. A shift in your emotional equilibrium signals you that you have taken the bait: you might feel angry, hurt, embarrassed, or envious. Your challenge is to monitor and control the response that has been provoked—not to have your behavior determined by the bait thrown at you.

At its heart, baiting is a power play, usually covert in nature. An older child baits a younger sibling for the sadism-tinged joy of watching the younger child fall for the trap. "Susie, you play basketball just like a girl." A coworker may bait another with derogatory comments in order to gain a competitive advantage. "Jane, you did well for someone so inexperienced." A boss may bait an employee in order to assert domination. At times, an employee may bait a boss to equalize power and control. Because women are so new to equality and perceive our hold on power as tenuous, we react strongly to being baited; we feel threatened by what we perceive as the provocateur's attempt to diminish our newly won stature. Like Brer Rabbit, we may be tempted to respond with a show of force, only to find that the entanglement has resulted in a total loss of power.

Most baiting occurs unconsciously. Gloria, for example, had to teach a course with a colleague whose area of expertise was more relevant than hers to the course. In addition, he had a very dominating personality, so for much of the time, Gloria sat quietly while he led the discussion. When the subject matter turned to her area of expertise, however, her colleague interrupted her frequently with extraneous, even silly comments that destroyed the flow of conversation. When she confronted him, he insisted he was only trying be light and humorous, for he was consciously oblivious to his intense competitiveness with his female colleague. Gloria decided to simply persevere in trying to be a good teacher. Later, several students commented on the inappropriateness of her colleague's behavior.

If baiting is conceptualized as a power challenge, it becomes clear that your goal will be to have maintained or increased your power once the dust has settled. Because each baiting situation has its own unique elements, exactly how you respond will vary from situation to situation. In fact, a characteristic of a great leader is the capacity to choose flexibly from an array of responses to power challenges. In one setting it may be wise to ignore your provocateur; in another setting to use humor; in yet another, you may need to use a show of force to defeat your challenger. But while the fine points of your behavior may change, your guiding image should be maintaining your stance as an alpha female, a leader of women and men.

Responding Like an Alpha

In Chapter 5 I described dominance hierarchies in primate groups. "Leaders of the pack" also emerge among humans. If you were asked to describe an alpha male, you might cite a particular political leader, or business tycoon, or military officer. He might be unselfish or mercenary, generous or withholding, but he would always be a *leader*, asserting his vision and his will. Power and strength are held up to boys as the masculine ideal.

Occasional alpha females have emerged in human history—for example, Queen Elizabeth I, Catherine the Great, and Golda Meir. But because female leaders have been rare in history, women have only a vague idea of how alpha women behave, and often this idea has been shaped by unflattering media treatment of them. Margaret Thatcher and Hillary Clinton are recent examples. Our society provides us with very few positive role models of heroic women. In America, for instance, we have never elected a woman president, female senior executives are rare, and we even lack images of great female lawyers with national reputations for dominance in the courtroom.

This lack of clear images of the alpha female means you must articulate such an image for yourself. If your goal is to become an alpha yourself, you will use this image to guide your behavior and decisions in many areas. In particular, your alpha image will shape the way you respond to difficult people, because your goal will be to respond to provocation from a position of strength and dignity, rather than hurt and defensiveness.

Many qualities of the alpha female are identical to those of an alpha male, including strength, vision, and the willingness to lead. For the male, however, being a leader is often in some respects a hyper-*masculinity*—the alpha male is generally even more powerful, decisive, and courageous than most men. For the female, hyper-*femininity* is enfeebling; particularly in situations with difficult people, such traits are interpreted as weakness and vulnerability. The alpha woman's psychological task is to separate her self-image and behavior from society's gender stereotype. She needs the flexibility to respond to difficult people in a way very different from what they anticipate, and often different from what her spontaneous reaction would be. This requires the psychological capacity for nonreactivity, particularly in response to gender stereotypes in action, for much baiting of women is for the express purpose of undermining their sense of authority and leadership.

FOUR STEREOTYPES

While the specifics of interactions with difficult people are as variable as snowflakes in a storm, issues that are unique for women often spring from particular female caricatures. The format of these interactions is consistent. The feminine caricature is dangled before a woman, and the enticement to conform to the caricature is communicated. While the specifics of the caricature may vary, the underlying theme is some form of devaluation. The woman then has the opportunity either to take the bait by assuming the traits of the caricature, or she may project back a very different image of herself in order to realign the relationship. Four stereotypes of women illustrate this process.

"You Sweet Little Thing"

There may well be no woman who has made her way up the ranks of high achievement untouched by some form of sexual baiting. One form is calling attention to the woman's physical appearance. Baiting may involve a trivialization of the woman through terms such as "young lady" or "honey," or a reference to her hormonal status.

This problem has been particularly noticed and discussed by women attorneys. Women's entrance into the field of law was a hard-fought battle, and even today women lawyers are exposed to belittling courtroom comments by judges or opposing attorneys. These comments are infuriating not only because they are insulting, but because they can undermine the woman's stature in the eyes of the jury and jeopardize her client's case. One law review article commented:

> Some female attorneys, when confronted with biased remarks or conduct in the courtroom "swallow their pride" and suffer in silence. This

approach stems from their belief that their clients' interests are paramount, and that attention should not be diverted in order to respond to insults which are the result of gender bias. Other female attorneys, however, take a direct approach and confront biased remarks immediately when they occur. Still other female attorneys address the issue in a low-key, professional manner, usually after the case has been concluded. Conversely, certain women do not view gender bias as a pressing problem and maintain that gender bias, if it exists, can be used to their advantage. For example, at Jill Wine-Banks' first trial, the defense counsel persisted in referring to her as "young lady" and she chose to ignore it. She later realized that she had made a good choice because this condescension antagonized the jury toward the defense counsel. When the same tactic was used against her during the Watergate trials, however, Wine-Banks put a stop to it because she realized the tactic was achieving its desired effect of demeaning her before the jury.

This passage reflects the spectrum of how a woman attorney can position herself within the dominance hierarchy. This positioning establishes the way the woman experiences the exchange and conveys it to the jury. Take, for instance, the response of a hypothetical woman lawyer who has chosen to "suffer in silence" or "swallow her pride." A male who prefers to remain silent in response to such belittlement would not be likely to characterize his non-reactiveness with such words. If, through body language, facial expression, and verbal cues, the woman attorney communicates the role of the masochistic, put-down, long-suffering woman, how can she hope to be taken seriously by the jury or her client?

By contrast, attorney Jill Wine-Banks displayed characteristics of an alpha female in the manner in which she chose to handle the offending remark. At her first trial, she perceived that the jury would interpret the remarks in a fashion sympathetic to her cause; she maintained her dignity by ignoring the defense counsel's baiting, and prevailed. In the Watergate trial, when she perceived this strategy was not working she had the flexibility to change course and shift the dynamics in her favor by challenging the put-down. Her overt behavior appeared superficially different in these two situations, but the principle that guided her in both was to maintain control.

Another wonderful example of an alpha woman lawyer's response to baiting was the response of attorney Flo Kennedy to a judge who had scolded her for wearing pants in the courtroom. Kennedy looked at the male judge, attired in a flowing black gown, and quipped, "I won't talk about what you're wearing, Your Honor, if you won't talk about what I'm wearing."

The Idiot Mother

Another female stereotype used to bait women arises from teenagers' portrayal of their mothers as a lower form of animal life. Hannah, an internist on the faculty of a medical school, told me about a problem she was having at work, where her duties included supervising the residents who were on call for the emergency room, a task that fifteen years in private practice had not prepared her for. Her confidence was being undermined by the attitude of some of the young male residents.

"These young kids are such a bunch of know-it-alls!" she fumed. "The other night we were in the emergency room with a sick lady. The resident really didn't want to admit her—probably because it would have been a lot of work for him. I really thought we should admit, just to watch the woman overnight. We argued and argued about it. The resident was so bullheaded about it that we ended up not admitting the woman, and she ended up doing well, so of course he interpreted that to mean that he was right and I was wrong. It was so infuriating."

I asked Hannah why she had not stuck to her guns. "Well, that's a good question," she said. "I think I'm intimidated because with their fresh training they're more up on the literature than I am—they're always quoting this study and that study."

"But that can never make up for the many years of experience you have taking care of sick patients," I commented. "You must really have a feel for what's safe and what isn't; you have a feel for which family members can watch a loved one adequately and which can't." Hannah agreed.

"Here's what I think," I said. "You're the faculty person; they're the trainees. You in fact know much more than they do, and you have the ultimate responsibility. Let them know that you are happy to engage in discussions in deference to their training needs, but not true debates that they might win if you disagree. Reassert your authority, and let them stew in their juices if they don't like it."

A couple of years later, I ran into Hannah again. She related how much better things were going since she had assumed genuine, unshakable authority with her residents. The arguments with the residents had stopped, and she felt much more confident.

It is not uncommon for a midlife woman to fall into a dynamic with young subordinates that is strikingly like a mother's with her teenagers. After all, it is the time-honored role of juveniles to challenge the leaders of the troop. Just as teenagers are quick to sense any weakness in their mother and exploit it to gain dominance, in work settings juniors are prone to challenge their senior bosses if they sense timidity. This challenge is of course at times directed toward male bosses as well, though this occurs much less frequently than toward women. Male bosses routinely respond with a verbal cuff that sends the young pups sprawling and often resolves the issue. Much as we do with our teenagers at home, women often fall into the trap of trying to placate the rebellious juvenile associate with kindness, which only inflames their defiance.

A good alpha will do most of her leading by offering rewards, praise, and modeling good behavior. But a good alpha also has the ability to withhold praise or criticize when necessary. She is capable of disciplining the juveniles of the troop when necessary. She makes clear what behavior is necessary to stay in her good graces.

At times women, whether in their role as mothers or bosses, will express reluctance to become stricter because of not wanting to appear "inconsistent." Men, I've noticed, never worry much about being inconsistent. More important than the question "Am I being consistent?" is the question "Is my approach effective?" If your approach isn't working, you will in fact display stronger leadership by correcting it.

There is an understandable tendency for women (and men) to extend their approach to family living into the workplace. The traditional role for women at home is to monitor and regulate family emotions. Mom hears the baby cry and seeks to soothe the wailing infant. Mom is sensitive to Dad's moods and accommodates herself and the children, making home life pleasanter for him. She intuitively senses her children's issues and needs and is ready to offer her services as nurse, therapist, teacher, or cheerleader to reestablish her children's equilibrium. The motherly approach to emotional regulation of the family is making nice, the nicer the better.

Life in the workplace mimics many aspects of family life, and subordinates often unconsciously ask their bosses to help them regulate their self-esteem. With most employees this dynamic does not become problematic. Occasionally, however, if a subordinate has had a troubling relationship in the past with a dominant female (such as her mother or a teacher) these issues may be reenacted with a female boss. (Occasionally dynamics that originated with the father may also be reenacted with a female boss.) This, I suspect, was the dynamic that Hannah was experiencing with her male residents. Residency itself is a painfully prolonged professional adolescence, and the residents evidently experienced Hannah as a frustrating, weak mother. As Hannah took on a more masculine style with the residents, they related to her less as a mother and more as a professional supervisor worthy of respect. The more she let go of her need to make the residents "feel good," the freer she felt to simply do her job.

The Bullied Weakling

One focus group participant, Dell, told a story of a particular boss known for his hot temper and his occasional anti-female statements: "One time he said, 'You know, Dell, we men just don't feel comfortable with women around. You can have a bunch of guys sitting around a conference table, feeling perfectly fine. Then the door opens and a woman walks in, and you can just feel the tension in the air.' Of course, what he was really talking about was his own discomfort with women.

"Another time, I had had a problem with one of my subordinates, a man, who had behaved in a recklessly irresponsible way and had seriously jeopardized an important project. It was the first time I have ever raised my voice at work, but I did with him—he was insufferably arrogant, and he richly deserved a dressing-down. He, in turn, went and complained to my boss, who called me in—and dressed *me* down! I'll never forget what he said: 'You know, Dell, you just have to learn to be sweet.' *Sweet!* He was the least sweet person in our whole corporation. In fact, he was a real bully. He had the worst temper of anyone I've ever worked with, and he'd vent his spleen when he felt he could get away with it."

Someone asked how she had dealt with the situation. "Well, I just endured for a couple of years, and then he was actually promoted. I couldn't believe it, but he was a smart guy and evidently knew how to look good for the upper guys. Then I heard he alienated several of his coworkers, some men this time, so I don't anticipate he'll last too long there, either. He's tolerated, at least for now, but he's on a dead-end track."

When men such as Dell's boss vent their hostility on women, it often takes a woman-baiting form, with obnoxious, sexist comments, for that's where they perceive our Achilles' heel to be. But the personality pathology of these men is an equal opportunity offender—with other men they can be harsh, critical, and overly competitive.

With such men, it is counterproductive to try to address the misogyny of their words and behavior, for it is not as if just clearing up that one little problem area will cure their meanness and get the relationship on track. Misogynists typically have personality problems that pervade *all* their relationships—with men, women, and children, at work and at home. In fact, addressing the issue from a gender perspective may only make things worse, for now you have alerted them to an area that is sensitive for you.

Your goal should be merely to limit and structure your relationship with the bully as much as you are able. If it is possible to transfer out of his division or to limit any projects you must collaborate on, consider the option. If you must continue your interaction, limit the amount of time you spend together; control the range of conversation you will engage in by subtly changing topics when he attempts to pull you off-track; when possible, meet with that person only in group settings. Above all, do not give him the satisfaction of taking his ill will to heart, and do not waste your time brooding over the sexist aspects of your situation. It's really not worth it, and certainly not befitting your stature as an alpha female.

The Shut-Out Little Sister

Women sometimes describe a phenomenon akin to the childhood experience of arriving at the clubhouse door to find a *"No Girlz— Allowed. Keep Out"* sign. Geraldine Laybourne, then president of Disney/ABC Cable Networks, described to *New Yorker* reporter Ken Auletta an experience she had at a retreat in rural Connecticut for ABC executives to talk about branding. Laybourne found herself on one side of the discussion, while all the men seemed lined up on the other.

> "[Each time I spoke] I felt I was just not being heard." The branding discussion continued as if she weren't there, and she was angry. That evening, when everyone got together for pre-dinner cocktails, Laybourne marched into the room where drinks were being served and said, "Am I just the biggest ass in the world?" No, no, her colleagues protested. It was great that she persisted, they declared, even if they didn't necessarily agree with her position. . . . [A]t the conclusion of the retreat, Robert Iger, the president of ABC, whom Laybourne is close to, appointed her to lead one of the two branding task forces."

Laybourne, clearly an alpha female, sensed a shut-out but persisted to speak her views. She even went one step further and boldly confronted the situation. But I suspect it was her friendship with her boss rather than her challenging her colleagues that got her the task force appointment.

Gender-based clustering is a natural way of forming alliances within a large group setting. In social settings, for instance, males cluster with males and females with females. The human tendency for such clustering is easily observable in children, who may actively and strenuously resist cross-gender mingling.

Clustering occurs across lines other than gender, of course. If you place a group of people of both sexes but from different cultures in the same room, you will see clustering according to culture, not gender. If you place a group of people from the same culture but different social classes together, they are likely to cluster on the basis of class, not gender. Put a group of doctors and nurses together, and the women doctors will cluster with the male doctors, not with the female nurses. The clustering phenomenon results from a subliminal seeking of the most important commonalities to strengthen an affiliation.

If you view clustering as a natural behavior, rather than a malicious conspiracy to exclude, you'll see that a persistent and friendly effort to break into the boys' club is the most appropriate choice for a woman who is rising in the ranks. To respond to a sense of exclusion with anger only deepens the schism. To express hurt invites male scorn. Given the still-skewed male–female ratio in the higher levels of achievement, most women achievers will sooner or later find themselves knocking at the door of the boys' club. One gains entry by establishing friendships, not by storming the walls.

How does an alpha female go about establishing these friendships with men? With a measure of outreach that might be more active than when building a friendship with a woman. You go out of your way to invite a male colleague to have lunch at the cafeteria; you invite him and his wife to your home for a meal, or treat them to a restaurant meal; you make it a point to walk out with him after the committee meeting is over. Above all, you do not take the male clustering personally, and you begin with the assumption that you are welcome in the group.

Yet even gaining admittance to the boys' club may not wholly solve the problem of being shut out of important activities. Several women I interviewed commented that despite having formed good friendships with male coworkers, they continued to be excluded from projects and committees. There is really one way to address this problem. *Ask* to be included, not just once, but as many times as it takes until you are automatically thought of as one of the gang. Further, don't wait several years to see if you have been included. From the beginning, make it clear that you want to be considered for interesting projects and positions.

One woman executive complained, "I just feel so isolated in my position. I'm the only female at my level, and there's just no one I feel close to." If a woman working in a large group of men is unable to find even a single man to be friends with, she would do well to examine her own behavior. It is less likely that the group lacks a single simpatico man than that she has stereotyped all men as being unsuitable for friendship and is projecting aloofness. In any event, it is far easier for her to change her own behavior than to change a group of men's, and it is, after all, her own interests that are at stake.

Common Elements

The types of difficult people and the dynamics of disturbing interpersonal conflicts are seemingly infinitely diverse. Are there elements in how alpha women deal with such situations? To review:

Expected to respond to sexual patronizing by becoming flustered and angry, the alpha woman responds by instantly analyzing how to use the inappropriate comment to her own advantage.

Expected to respond to dismissive treatment by junior associates by becoming yet more obsequious, the alpha woman responds with a show of competence and authority.

Expected to feel hurt and angry after a mean-spirited insult, the alpha woman refuses to engage emotionally and allows her adversary to hang himself with his own noose.

Expected to wait outside the clubhouse door, the alpha woman invites herself in, takes her seat, and assumes she is welcome.

The common element defining the best response to all these diverse situations is this: the alpha female, assigned a role to play that diminishes her position, does not respond as her saboteur expects her to. Rather than reacting in a way that would confirm her status as inferior—hurt, angry, intimidated, or embarrassed—she artfully reshapes her role and reconfigures the form of the interaction.

To understand this process more clearly, a brief review of the psychology of interpersonal interactions is in order.

TEMPLATES

Over the last century, a considerable body of work has explored the unconscious ways that each human being seeks to structure her interactions in predictable ways. It is, after all, the nature of intelligence to draw conclusions from limited experience and generalize one's observations to future experiences. A child only has to burn her fingers once in a flame to learn that fire is hot. Likewise she begins at an early age to form generalized expectations of how she and others are likely to interact and to assume that future encounters will conform to those early experiences.

These generalizations become codified in the unconscious mind in the form of "templates" of interactions. Think of a template as the unconscious assumptions you bring to any interaction. Your template will consist of an expectation of how the other person is likely to behave. It includes an expectation of the role you will play in the interaction. Finally, your template will be colored by the feelings and emotions that the interaction will stir up within you.

For example, in Hannah's situation the young male resident clearly was operating out of a particular template—for the sake of discussion, let's assume it was based on his relationship with his mother (though it could have been derived from another source, such as his father, or from an amalgamation of experiences with teachers). This template caused his perception of Hannah to be something like, "She is a woman with power and control over me which she will use to make me feel belittled. In fact, she is unreliable, knows little, and cannot to be trusted to lead." His role might be described as, "I am the young male, ready to take my place as an alpha male. I am being unfairly dominated by an aging, incompetent female who must be challenged if I am to assume my rightful place." The feeling coloring his template is one of arrogance and contempt.

Hannah, on the receiving end, has a template of her own that is being activated. Hers might be something like, "As a male, he is a dominating, know-it-all who is seeking to humiliate me by making me appear incompetent. I feel like the idiot mother who is feebly trying to assert my authority, but am frightened that he will expose my weakness." The emotional coloration for Hannah is anxiety and vulnerability, and if she conveys this she will have validated the resident's perceptions.

It is one thing for Hannah to experience her own reactive template, but quite another to play it out. Her challenge, which she successfully met, was to psychologically sit still long enough to observe the interaction and to consciously, willfully, choose to alter it. She based this template on identifying with old images of wise and trusted caretakers, assigning the resident the role of the juvenile who was expected to follow her lead.

The story of Flo Kennedy is a terrific example of how one can instantly deflate an attack that come from a pathological template. By making a comment about her pants, the judge was assigning her a role in his template: "I, the mighty male judge, have the authority to embarrass you, the lowly female lawyer, about your attire. Your role, now, is to feel put down. If you react with anger, embarrassment, or defensiveness, you will display your emotional vulnerability to me." With her humorous response, Kennedy immediately rejected that role.

Dell's interactions with her misogynist boss is more complicated. His style of interaction, which compelled him to repetitively assert his domination by humiliating and devaluing others whom he perceived as weaker than he, had a sadistic element. To accept the role of the shamed subordinate would not only make Dell feel terrible, but would also invite future contemptuous treatment. But to attempt to reverse roles by asserting herself as more competent and savvy than he would only further inflame his need to dominate. The only recourse was to be a nonplayer, businesslike and aloof, and attempt to keep interactions on neutral territory.

All of us, in fact, have templates with negative characteristics that are activated from time to time. With most difficult people your task is to reconfigure the interaction. In most cases, your difficult person will be relieved to find the interaction more comfortable. But when personality pathology is pervasive, as it was with Dell's boss, the difficult person will actively resist your effort to realign the relationship. A level of hostility will always be present in the relationship, impervious to your attempts at establishing good will and mutual support. It may be that your adversary is simply unable to function in any way other than the pathologic dynamic you are experiencing—and he or she exhibits the same behavior with virtually everyone.

There are two other explanations for an inability to dislodge a particularly unpleasant template. It may be that *you* are the one who is having a pathologic aspect of your own personality triggered by your adversary; in other words, the area of conflict is occurring in an aspect of your own unconscious emotional life. Or it may be that you and your adversary happen to have *complementary* areas of psychopathology, such that you connect with each other like a key fitting into a lock. Perhaps your need to take charge is inflamed by her need to be independent; your need for admiration from others is frustrated by his emotional stinginess. In such situations, you have an opportunity presented to you: Instead of trying to change the other person, *you can set a goal of changing yourself.*

WORK LIFE AS AN OPPORTUNITY FOR GROWTH AND CHANGE

It is a tenet of some branches of psychology that basic personality patterns are established in childhood and are fairly resistant to change. But in my clinical work I have repeatedly been impressed by patients' ability to achieve personality growth and change throughout adulthood. What happens is that while huge areas of the personality do remain stable, small changes occur that can have an enormous impact.

The analogy that comes to mind is two ships that are setting sail from New York to England. Although the ships might be identical in virtually every way, a tiny alteration in one—let's say a minute resetting of a compass, or a slight deflection of a rudder—might result in the two ships' reaching very different destinations. Likewise, identifying and changing small aspects of personality function can have an enormous impact on what you are able to accomplish in your life.

In the course of several decades of work life, you will interact with hundreds of personalities making demands of you in countless ways. Inevitably, you will interact with people who are able to reveal *your* islands of personality weakness. With introspection and honesty, you may resist the temptation of merely blaming the other party and instead view your interaction as an opportunity to master and resolve significant issues for yourself. This is, however, a process requiring the discipline and willpower *not* to react spontaneously. Your task is to sit still with your feelings, observe the impulses that are stirred up within you, and make a conscious decision to behave in a way consistent with your goals in life—in other words, to act like an alpha female.

This, obviously, is easier said than done. But, life is a patient teacher, inviting us back over and over again to learn lessons we have not fully mastered. The form of that invitation is in the experience of *failure*, for failure, the subject of the next chapter, is a powerful opportunity for personal growth.

CHOICE 7

LOSING LIKE
A WOMAN

Retreat or Rebound?

ONE LAZY SPRING DAY during my junior year of college, several girl-friends and I went to a nearby river to swim and sunbathe. Out of the forest stepped a man who unzipped his pants and displayed his manly charms. I was the first to notice.

"Ladies," I hissed. "I believe we have a visitor."

We convened a hasty conference. I proposed taking the traditional female approach and bolting. Marcia, however, would have none of that. She stood up and shouted, "Is that all you've got?" The man, of course, disappeared immediately. Marcia wasn't about to give up her lazy afternoon, and not much has stood in her way since then.

In that instant, Marcia demonstrated a trait that is utterly essential for the woman of achievement: the capacity to persevere toward a goal despite a variety of forces that might throw one off course. Consider, for instance, the statistics on female achievement. If roughly only 10 percent of top positions in any field are held by women—rather than the 50 percent that would represent our proportion of the population—simple arithmetic suggests that *four out of five* women who could become top achievers become deflected somewhere along their path. Four out of five of the potential female presidents, executive, deans, judges, professors, and CEOs become derailed or stall out, relinquishing their positions to men.

It might be argued that at times a woman's decision not to seek advancement is a legitimate choice reflecting her personal value system. I suspect, however, that for every woman for whom this might be the case, there are many more who never get a shot at making such a conscious decision. Rather, the accumulation of internal and external acts of sabotage creates such a mountain of defeat that they may not even be able to visualize what might be on the other side.

CONFRONTING DISCRIMINATION

Despite the progress in opportunities won by feminists of the past several decades, in many settings achievement remains considerably further out of reach for women than for men. Sexist discrimination still exists—it is just less blatant than in the past, when discrimination could be measured in terms of "deeds done," such as openly verbalized policies of gender exclusion. Now discrimination takes the form of "deeds undone"—collaborations not offered, acknowledgments unvoiced, introductions not made, opportunities withheld. Because these are omissions rather than commissions, they go unnoticed. Further, gender-based discrimination is a spotty phenomenon; even within a single organization (my own is an example) some departments are supportive of women, others aren't.

Thus it is crucial for any ambitious woman to periodically stop and review her career, perhaps even to compare her progress with that of her colleagues. This monitoring may alert her to a subtle derailing of her progress that may require active steps to remedy. A useful way to self-evaluate is to exchange progress notes with a trusted female colleague.

A group of women academicians at MIT recently demonstrated the value of such shared monitoring. When three tenured women professors in the School of Science casually shared experiences with each other one day, they found themselves remarking on perceptions of gender-based discrimination that had previously gone undiscussed. All sixteen tenured women on the faculty organized to study the issue and prepare a report. The dean of the School of Science subsequently admitted that discriminatory policies had indeed existed, and instituted policy reforms.

Some of the MIT women's observations are doubtless applicable to the situation of many women. The report commented, for instance, that the women had previously not recognized the gender discrimination because it did not "look like" what they had always thought of as civil rights violations. Research indicates that *most* women do not consider themselves to have been victims of gender discrimination. Rather, the MIT women's experience was one of quiet marginalization combined with policies that worked to the disadvantage of women, such as the inequitable distribution of laboratory space and equipment. Previously, each woman had experienced her own problems with advancement as an individual and had accepted the attitude that she was responsible for her own problems.

The report also noted that the junior (untenured) women faculty denied experiencing gender bias; it was the senior, successful women who were most aware of the problem. This confirms comments I have heard repeatedly from successful senior women that younger women just don't "get it." But if not, why not?

First, the power pyramid increasingly squeezes women as they work their way up. As competition for fewer spots of authority increases, the personal and political challenges from male colleagues intensify. Second, junior women are often in a particular honeymoon period of their professional development. Being in the minority as a young woman in a preponderantly male environment can be fun. The friendly sexual dynamics of that environment can be flattering and easy to mistake for true opportunities for career advancement. As the woman matures out of the ingenue role, the reality of gender-based marginalization becomes clearer and more disturbing.

Air Wars and Ground Wars

The MIT women banded together to create a highly effective protest against gender discrimination that resulted in tangible gains. Their example should inspire women suffering from gender discrimination in other organizations, for it reminds us that the problem continues to exist and that a group effort is often more effective than an individual one.

Even where group protests succeed in creating a more level playing field, each individual woman must still battle her own way to secure her position. An organized protest might be thought of as similar to an air attack in a war, potentially useful to dismantle the adversary's defenses. Yet, as Colin Powell once commented, a war is ultimately won with ground troops, the soldiers who go in and actually occupy the embattled territory. As a woman seeking advancement, you may well encounter situations where you must engage in your own individual struggle in order to secure your position. In order to win those skirmishes, you will need a significant amount of courage and fortitude, as well as the capacity to analyze how to compensate for your weaknesses and capitalize on your strengths.

Psychological Causes of Failure

One of the most important determinants of personality is the set of identifications with your mother and father you developed in childhood. Their attitudes toward achievement, success, and failure all created powerful subliminal ideas about these issues within you. Because all children identify most strongly with the same-sex parent, women's primary identification is with our mothers. For women whose mothers were raised in an era when equality for women was at best a theory, breaking free of their mothers' attitudes toward achievement can feel like an act of disloyalty: "If I adopt a completely different lifestyle from my mother, it's as if I'm saying all that she sacrificed for me didn't matter."

But it isn't only identification with her mother that affects a woman's capacity to succeed. Her relationship with her father also has an influence.

My patient Sarah was a very bright woman who never fulfilled her career potential, remaining in the same clerical position for her entire working life. Married to a well-to-do professional man and childless, she really did have the opportunity to seek more education and take work risks. Her father, however, had been a very cold and withholding man who criticized Sarah and her mother incessantly and belittled Sarah's childhood achievements. She then went on to marry a carbon copy of her father: her husband also demeaned her. Clearly, her self-esteem was never established well enough in her developmental years to allow her to consider her intelligence and talents worth developing.

Although it is possible to generalize about the sorts of dynamic conflicts that women experience regarding success and failure, such generalities can never take the place of an individual woman understanding her own very specific life story. As a therapist, I've come to realize that the devil is always in the details. Women often begin therapy saying, "Oh, I had a happy childhood, and a good mother and father." But beneath this high-gloss summary may lurk some unresolved conflicts. What specifically were the messages you received about achievement? What were the models you had for success or failure within your own family? What were the roles you played with your mother, father, brother, or sister? What were the ideas you absorbed as you watched your parents respond to the achievements of your siblings? When you failed, did your parents work with you to try to understand the problem, did they berate you, or were they so self-absorbed they never even noticed? When you succeeded, were they there in the audience applauding for you, did they hog your glory, or did they tell you not to become conceited? Every day of your life you received images and messages about what it meant to succeed and what it meant to fail, and all of those created your own unique psychology of achievement. An example:

Dina was the youngest of four children and the only girl. Her parents were hardworking, decent people who nonetheless were usually too overwhelmed by the demands of their rambunctious family to exert as much control as would have been helpful. While not actually abusive, Dina's three older brothers took great delight in joining together to play practical jokes on her. On a daily basis she was the butt of teasing and ridicule. Fortunately, she was endowed with a bright intellect and a feisty spirit that sustained her; yet the incessant chipping away at her sense of childhood dignity understandably left a deep wound within her. As an adult she was intensely ambivalent about men, experiencing both the anger she had once felt toward her brothers and her yearning to be accepted by them as an equal.

Following the predictable human pattern of orchestrating adult life to repeat childhood dynamics, Dina chose to become an operating room nurse. The doctors—most of them men—had to depend on her and respect her. Yet her work environment neatly recapitulated her childhood. In the OR, the nurses are always subordinate to the doctors. Further, the OR is a setting where temper outbursts, inappropriate humor, and other displays of dominance by doctors are permissible. For years Dina chafed under the humiliations of a work environment that repeated many aspects of her childhood.

Dina, however, had determination and a will of steel. Eventually she was promoted up the ranks and became senior nurse administrator of the OR. Then there was a change of administration within the hospital, and the new chief of nursing pushed for greater power and control by nurses. Dina was given administrative control not only of the OR but of all surgical clinical services.

As her power grew, the lifelong anger she had felt toward men became more and more overt. She instituted a series of administrative changes that empowered the nursing staff and disempowered the doctors, all with the support of the chief administrator. Predictably, of course, this came to an abrupt end when the doctors joined together and demanded her dismissal.

Just as Dina was reenacting her own childhood dynamics, the male doctors were undoubtedly replaying their respective childhoods as well. Each of them was once a little boy with a mother, aunts, sisters, and teachers who controlled them, disciplined them, criticized them, or possibly even abused them. Dina, of course, couldn't know their individual stories, nor could they know hers, as they butted heads over control issues in the OR. Neither Dina nor the doctors were consciously aware of the impact of their unresolved psychological themes on their decisions and responses. They only knew they were angry and frustrated by the behavior of the other, and in almost complete denial about the workings of their own dynamics.

As a psychiatrist, I have learned that when controversial events occur within work settings that superficially are explained on the basis of policy or competence, there is always a subterranean layer of psychological forces that is at least as influential in determining these events. Further, these forces are multidirectional. All parties involved are acting out their ancient issues on one another. All the education, intelligence, and boldness one brings to career development can be self-sabotaged by unresolved psychological issues. Dina's situation is a particularly dramatic example of this. Subtler issues can divert the trajectory of a career in less obvious ways that may have enormous consequences over a lifetime.

You can begin the process of analyzing such issues yourself. You may be aware of the dynamics of your family of origin and their impact on you. You are probably most aware of how those dynamics affect your relationships in your marriage family. Take the next step, and consider how you replay those issues with your workmates. If you begin to suspect that you may be limiting yourself by repeating childhood issues at work, a course of exploratory psychotherapy may be the best investment of time and money you may ever make for your career.

Whether or not you have the luxury of being in psychotherapy at some point in your life, you can do much of the work of analysis on your own by keeping a journal. By taking the time to write only about yourself, on a daily, weekly, or intermittent basis, you will begin to see certain themes emerge over time. You will notice that in moments of conflict, the players may change, the situations will be different, but your feelings and responses will be highly repetitive.

The Defect of Your Virtues

While Dina's case is an example of very specific dynamics being repeated in the workplace, at a more general level your personality traits have an enormous impact on the unfolding of your career. Always remember that your very best traits are also your very worst traits; that is, a given trait that serves you beautifully in many situations may be counterproductive in certain other circumstances. Your goal should be to become consciously aware and in control of how, where, when, and why you exercise your most prominent traits in order to achieve your goals.

Laura was a teacher who sought my advice because of a very troubling problem at school. She and a number of her colleagues had successfully applied for a federal grant. By explicit agreement with the principal, the funds were to be used to hire additional teachers in order to reduce class size, but when the money arrived, the principal decided to use it to establish a Head Start program at the school instead—meaning that Laura and the other teachers would remain as overwhelmed as ever by large classes.

Laura and her colleagues were furious. This betrayal was only the last straw in a series of altercations with the principal, whose support they'd felt was lacking all along. Laura was considering leading a full-scale revolt of the teachers against the principal and wanted my advice.

What was at stake for Laura, personally? I wondered. The stakes were actually high, she explained. She had been working hard to get her master's and wanted to become a principal herself. If she led a revolt against the principal, she risked damaging her reputation with the county school administration and losing her shot at becoming a principal.

My advice to Laura was clear, though not entirely unambivalent: *Get back in line.* I admired her fighting spirit, her leadership of the teachers, and her determination to be dealt with honestly. Further, it was clear that her finest qualities—her insistence on excellence in the classroom, her vision, her sense of fairness and commitment to a democratic process— were now the very qualities that made it painful for her to sit passively and accept the high-handed behavior of the principal.

But in the bigger picture, there was so much more to be lost than gained by following through on her urge to seek justice. She clearly would make a wonderful principal and could contribute so much more by becoming a leader herself than by becoming a victim of someone else's poor leadership. Laura's beef with the principal was a sideshow; her career was the main event. Caught up as she was in the passions of the moment, she couldn't fully appreciate the importance of focusing her energy on her quest for promotion.

For women, the interpersonal culture in a work environment can feel so intense that it is easy to lose sight of the main event. We then end up judging our career satisfaction in terms of how daily life at work *feels* rather than what is objectively occurring. In Laura's case, the sideshow was a negative event. Far more commonly, however, the sideshow can actually be a *positive* interaction, which nonetheless can distract one from larger goals.

Helen's story is another illustration of how a woman's best traits can negatively affect her career growth in hidden ways. Helen was an exceptionally bright woman who had dropped out of college and married because of an unplanned pregnancy. Eventually her marriage fell apart, and she entered the workforce as an administrative assistant. Although she lacked a college degree, she had such superb interpersonal and administrative skills that she eventually rose to become the assistant of a foundation executive. Her boss was good to her, giving her solid raises and a supportive work environment. But her lack of a degree meant she could never move beyond the level of support staff, and therefore her earnings and achievement potential were capped, despite working very long hours.

Because her work environment felt so good, it was hard for Helen to appreciate that the wonderful relationship with her boss was a sideshow—it had become, in fact, the main event. Had she bitten the proverbial bullet, finished her college degree, and perhaps received advanced training, Helen could have used her innate intelligence and interpersonal skills to be as influential as her boss was. Among Helen's best personality traits were the high value she placed on loyalty, her capacity to form deep interpersonal connections, as with her boss, and her ability to contribute to and enjoy working as part of a team. Yet because these traits were so very strong within her, she was *too* successful in quieting the little voice within her that told her that she could be doing more with her career.

My viewpoint on Helen's story can be challenged. "Don't we need the Helens of the world? Does everyone have to be a high achiever? If Helen is financially comfortable and content with her life, isn't that good enough?"

I would answer, of course it is good enough in the sense that Helen is living a meaningful, worthy life. And of course Helen's value as a human being is no less than her boss's. The disquieting question, however, is, given that Helen was working long hard hours anyway, had she short-changed herself by restricting her ability to move to a position in which she could have actualized *her own* vision, rather than supporting that of her boss? After all, one never hears those who have moved to positions of leadership (usually men) lament that they had not stayed in supportive roles, or regret that they had achieved too much power, made too great an impact on the world, or had too many interesting experiences.

The Defects of Traditionally Feminine Virtues

Our collective feminine identity makes us particularly susceptible to particular defects. How could it be otherwise? The masculine gender identity renders men vulnerable to particular problems. We must be alert to situations where our capacity for nurturance makes it difficult to set limits with subordinates; our preference for collaboration weakens our capacity to compete; our loyalty limits our ability to safeguard our self-interest.

Nurturance, collaboration, and loyalty are all examples of wonderful traits that serve us very well in *most* environments. The experience of failure, however, provides us with personal examples of how our greatest strengths may also be our greatest weakness. Our goal should be to increase conscious control over what might otherwise be unconscious behaviors and to cultivate our ability to flexibly choose to act in such a way as to optimize our chances for success.

RESPONDING TO FAILURE

In the course of a long career, it is inevitable that you won't win 'em all. If you never experience failure, it is probably because you are not taking on big enough challenges. Defeat can occur for many reasons, ranging from the personal limitations just described to sabotage from adversaries. Yet it is precisely because achievement may be harder to attain for women than for men that it is essential to learn as much as possible about yourself from every failure you experience. Every setback in your life contains seeds of information about ways you can change and grow that will help you avoid a similar defeat in the future. Your future success depends on your ability to extract that information and use it productively.

The issue of scrutinizing one's own behavior as part of an analysis of failure is emotionally charged, for good reason. Too often women have used such analysis in a self-defeating way, as if to say, "They were right—I really don't belong here. If my failure was at all my fault, I really ought to fold my tent and give up." It is tempting to slip into an either-or thought process—my fault-or-theirs—and feminists rightfully protest the "blaming the victim" explanation of why women fail to progress. The problem with this approach is that feeling like either a helpless victim or a total failure can lead to a paralysis of will that's difficult to shake off. It is both more helpful and usually more accurate to begin with the assumption that you are a person with strengths and weaknesses working in a competitive and challenging environment. It is how you interact with those challenging forces that determines the outcome, and your goal is to optimize that interaction.

A good deal of research has explored possible differences between how men and women respond to success and failure. In 1968, M. S. Horner speculated that an underlying fear of success is more pronounced in women and is related to gender-role socialization. Later, an opposite but related dynamic, fear of failure, was described. Still later, P. R. Clance and S. A. Imes described the "impostor phenomenon," theorizing that women were more likely than men to feel that they were not as genuinely competent and gifted as their achievements might suggest.

A review of studies on how males and females feel about and respond to failure reveals inconsistent findings. Failure causes both men and women shame, discouragement, and great loss of self-esteem; both genders employ a mixture of responses to the experience of failure, including denial, self-blame, and even depression. For each study showing a tantalizing bit of difference in the emotional response of males vs. females, another study indicates the opposite.

Yet most of these studies have an inherent methodological limitation: the majority have been conducted either in the laboratory, using artificial situations in which to fail or succeed, or in the classroom, where the life experience of the subjects and the size of the stakes remain relatively low compared to those in the work world. Outside the lab and the classroom, an age-old concept is as alive and well today as it doubtless was centuries, even millennia ago, the notion that there is a way to "lose like a man," a code my teenage son could sum up for me in three simple words: "You don't whine."

The Male Code

From early childhood, boys establish daily, intense competitions of winning and losing. The psychiatrist Lenore Terr, studying the childhood games of boys, notes the nature of competitive games is that they are often structured so that everyone gets a turn at being a winner and being a loser. In the repetition of this experience, males establish a code of losing with honor. One is gracious, congratulates the victor, and is neither angry, sullen, nor defensive. The young boy learns to accept defeat as part and parcel of a game played fairly.

Throughout history, men have established concrete rules of winning and losing fairly. In war, an internationally accepted code of military conduct spells out the rules for victory and defeat. Rules of conduct for prisoner of war as well as for soldiers in occupied territory are delineated. In bygone eras, rules were also established for one-to-one combat, such as the jousting of knights of the medieval period and duels in more recent centuries. In Japanese warrior culture, personal honor could be maintained in the face of defeat by comporting oneself stoically while performing hara-kiri, ritual suicide by self-disembowelment.

Thus males have invested great energy in developing an agreement about what it is to "lose like a man," but no similar concept of what it is to "lose like a woman" exists. The reason for this lack is obvious. Historically, women weren't in the game to begin with. How could one lose like a woman, with honor, if there was no real opportunity to win like a woman?

Toward a Female Code

While the male code of combat sets a standard of stoicism and suppression of outward displays of emotion in defeat, many high-achieving women I interviewed said they felt comfortable about openly expressing rage, pain, or shock following a defeat or failure. The fact, of course, that feelings may be *expressed* differently does not necessarily mean that they are internally *experienced* differently. It may simply be that women are less ashamed of their feelings.

If you consider the gender differences in emotional resilience described in Chapter 1, however, it should come as no surprise that the two genders might react to defeat differently. Jack Block's work on male resilience would predict that men might indeed respond to failure by a suppression of emotional response and a studied attempt to conform to the established code of respectful, dignified stoicism. For women, however, submitting gracefully to defeat might come perilously close to the traditional norms of feminine submissiveness that have served us so poorly in the past. The resilient woman, with her capacity for spontaneous emotional reaction and her determination not to be overly compliant, would be predicted to respond defiantly to defeat, to shake her fist at failure with a sense of personal outrage.

Outrage, in fact, can be an enormously useful response to failure if it is eventually channeled constructively. Outrage can reflect a variety of feelings: perception of injustice if gender discrimination was an issue; disappointment with oneself for having fallen short of expectations; competitive fury at having lost; or frustration about being denied an expected reward. The value of outrage is that it is a hyperenergized state. If that heightened energy can be eventually transformed into a powerful determination to do things differently next time, it can provide an enormous source of motivation.

Interested in learning more about the female "code," I gave a questionnaire to 74 women from the South Carolina Women Lawyer's Association that asked them to reflect on major defeats in the courtroom. Their responses indicated that "losing like a woman" is indeed an emotionally charged experience. Thirty-three of them had expressed anger to colleagues, and 46 to friends or family. Thirty-nine became tearful or cried: 6 with colleagues, 23 with friends or family, 29 alone. Thirty-four felt they were somewhat to blame for the failure; for 20 of them, this was the predominant feeling. Twenty-eight had thoughts that they were not cut out for law, and for 10 women this was the predominant feeling. Thirty-nine became at least mildly depressed, and 5 became significantly depressed after a defeat. When asked "How long was it before you were able to put the experience behind you and move on?" 13 said "hours"; 36 said "days"; 17 said "weeks"; and 8 said "months." One woman said she had still not recovered eighteen months later.

Of the respondents, 60 (81 percent) rationally analyzed what they could have done differently; 20 (27 percent) felt they had learned nothing important from their failures—even though they were specifically asked about their most significant defeats. Thirty (40 percent) did not seek critical advice from a colleagues—from whom they might have gained useful insights.

Certainly, this group of women took failure hard; most expressed anger, cried, blamed themselves, or felt a loss of self-confidence for days, weeks, or months. And a sizable group nonetheless learned little from the experience. An even larger group did not seek objective advice that might have helped them in the future.

This small survey of one profession says little about how women as a group respond to failure. But it does reflect the intensity and protracted duration of pain that women experience after a defeat, even women who willfully choose a field where defeat is to be expected. It also suggests that the process of responding to that pain by seeking objective, critical analysis is exceedingly difficult and often avoided. Yet the question must be asked: What is the point of failure if one learns nothing from the experience?

Transforming Failure

The transformation of emotionality into productive energy is particularly important at points of major failure. Invariably in the heat of the moment defeat feels catastrophic, though in retrospect it may prove to be enormously helpful. Stop, for a moment, and review your own life. You will probably notice that many of the most significant surges of growth followed from your being forced to make a change in response to a dramatic failure.

Many different types of failure may precipitate an emotional crisis: a breakup, a flunked exam, a rejected application. Sometimes those events are genuinely tragic, such as getting a divorce or being fired. They are the moments when the world seems to stop for a moment as you gasp for the air that was knocked out of you.

Such moments are the time to work on optimizing your capacity for *enlightened* resilience—as opposed to retreat or directionless rebound. To achieve this, you will want to extract as much new knowledge about your own strengths and weaknesses as possible from the situation to guide you in a new direction. That new direction may consist of a shift in approach to your regular responsibilities, or it may be a change of career direction. Your challenge is to use the setback to foster new development, much as a gardener carefully prunes a tree after the ravages of winter to stimulate exuberant growth in the spring.

Seek out an objective, critical analysis of your failure from someone who has more experience that you. If your failure was a significant one, it is likely that you did indeed give the matter your best shot. Merely reiterating the thought process that has already proved unsuccessful will get you nowhere. You need a fresh view from a different perspective. The person you choose to consult should be someone who is likely to have a genuine interest in seeing you succeed and who is easy to share painful truths with.

How do you go about finding this feedback? You can request it periodically from those around you over the course of your career. You can wait until a failure has made you so miserable that you are willing to ask a mentor or supervisor for advice. You can set up regular evaluations with your boss and discipline yourself to ask for, and accept, criticism. There are also some excellent evaluation services you can hire that will provide you with detailed evaluation forms to distribute to peers, bosses, and subordinates; these services will then score you and provide you with detailed feedback.

To begin to analyze a failure, study the elements that determined the outcome. If you've been fired, the obvious question is whether you were productive enough. If you failed in a competition, analyze why your effort was judged not as good as the winner's. If a relationship has collapsed, the tough but essential questions are of course about the dynamics of the relationship—not only through your eyes, but also through the eyes of the other.

The next level of analysis is to look at the *environment* in which the failure occurred. In large organizations, the political environment may have caused the failure: someone with more power than you wanted a bigger share of the pie and without much ado grabbed yours away from you. It may be that you lost in a competition—say, to make a sale, get a case, or win a grant—because of unseen political alliances that gave your competitor the edge. Though painful, by analyzing your environment you may become more insightful and shrewd about living in the politicized world of your workplace. In a failed relationship, the most common "environmental" cause is a third party who has moved into your territory. While it may be too late to undo the sabotage that has been committed against you, there are invaluable lessons to be learned from the catastrophe that will help you in the future.

But the ultimate level, and the one that is most relevant for you as a woman who wants to find out what's holding you back, consists of the *psychological* forces within you that contributed to your defeat. You bring your own characteristic psychological response to every adversity you encounter, and it is your psychology, far more than the event itself, that shapes the nature of the experience. The projects you work on will vary, the environment you work in will change, but your own psychology is something you take with you wherever you go. For that reason it is imperative that you learn to analyze, as dispassionately as possible, whatever contributions you may have made to your own defeat and to your perceptions of the experience. The goal of this analysis is to change, so as not to bring the same self-defeating dynamics with you wherever you go.

The value of failure is its capacity to reveal elements of yourself that you never see at other times. After all, anyone can function well when the work environment is supportive, when the project is successful, and when rewards are clearly on their way. It is when the going gets tough that your emotional weak spots become most evident. Losing to an adversary may reveal gaps in your interpersonal skills. Reworking a rejected proposal confronts you with the flaws in your approach. Experiences of defeat test your capacity to persevere.

The process of learning takes place in steps, each of which contributes to the transformation of your failure from lemon to lemonade.

Although I will describe these steps as if they occur in a neat order, in truth you will often go to the next stage before completing the previous one, only to return at some time to finish the work you left undone.

Step One: Regrouping

The dictionary defines *regrouping* as: "to come back together in tactical formation, as after a dispersal in a retreat; to reorganize for renewed effort, as after a temporary setback." After a setback, your regrouping must occur at several levels, but the first is a reestablishment of your self-esteem. The process is indeed analogous to a military effort. Some of your "ego troops" have been shot down. Your intact troops must gather together and help the wounded before considering another charge. Without taking time to regroup, your next effort will be fragmented and weak.

Karen, a patient of mine, was distraught after failing the bar exam. The feelings she described were typical of someone who has suffered a severe blow. For the first few days, she was confused, saying, "I just don't know what to think, what to do, or where to turn." She then became depressed for a few weeks, with crying spells and insomnia. During this period she could hardly concentrate, much less formulate a plan. It was only after she had been able to talk about her devastation—to me, to her boyfriend, parents, and fellow law students—that she was able to put her experience in perspective. During her "convalescence" she drew strength from the love of those close to her. They told her story after story of their own defeats, stories she had never heard before. Repeatedly they encouraged her to persevere. After a couple of months, she formulated a new plan for studying for the bar, and the second time she passed. It was not until she was able to reclaim her self-esteem that she could even think clearly enough to know how to proceed.

Investing the effort, time, and energy that meaningful endeavors require creates an internal state in which your work feels like your self. The operant word, of course is *feel*, for eventually your sense of self does heal after a blow. But the process of healing takes time and an energy of its own.

How your mind responds to a devastating loss of self-esteem—a psychological trauma—parallels what survivors of physical trauma experience. Early on, images of the trauma will bombard your awareness in a very painful way. In response, you will try to retreat from those images through withdrawal and avoidance of reminders.

Your natural tendency is to try to limit the bombardment by building a firewall around the experience, to block it from your awareness so that it can no longer cause you pain. The problem is that by walling off the experience, your ability to learn from it is lost. Your sense of self, already shaken, is further diminished because keeping the wall up requires a fair amount of mental energy and may eventually unconsciously contribute to the sense of being an impostor. And, the experience remains alive and well behind the wall, ready to hurt you all over again the next time you fail.

In cases of potentially serious post-traumatic stress disorder, psychotherapists try to counter this withdrawal by gently helping the victim reexperience the trauma in the setting of a safe and secure relationship. Therapists treating PTSD have learned that talking about the experience, reexperiencing the trauma in a context of love and concern, is the best way to restore self-esteem. A caring, understanding, and supportive listener can help your fallen ego soldiers pick themselves up, brush themselves off, and trudge back to camp headquarters.

Step Two: Reassessment

While regrouping is an emotional process, reassessment is a cognitive, intellectual one. It is only when your sense of self begins to be reestablished that you can think rationally about the defeat. After the red-hot shock of your failure and the slow cooling-down process of regrouping, reassessment is an ice-cold, crystal-clear analysis of what went wrong, where your own choices might have made things turn out differently, and how you plan to get back on track.

Think of reassessment as similar to having to file a report about an incident you were involved in. You retrace your steps (thought patterns) that guided your behavior as the incident occurred. You also think through the behavior and reactions of the other people who were involved in the incident. You try to remember exactly what you had once predicted, and you compare it to what transpired. Then you ask yourself: "At the points where I made critical errors in judgment, why did that happen? Was I overly optimistic, and is denying obvious problems a personal shortcoming of mine? Did I begin the project with enthusiasm, only to fail to follow through on what the complete project required? Did I underestimate my competition, or overestimate the support of my boss or colleagues? Am I (shudder) not quite as smart as I think I am, and does that mean I have to go back and prepare more intensely for my next try? Did I do well on the creative parts of the project, but neglect the grunt work that was required for a big success?"

Remember, for this process to be productive you must disentangle it from your badly bruised self-esteem. Reassessment does not involve kicking yourself or engaging in an orgy of self-blame. Its purpose is to teach you as much as possible about how you failed. The opportunity for growth from failure often goes unrecognized for a very simple reason: the pain of the wound you have experienced feels so devastating. To avoid the pain, you will be tempted to abort the learning process before it has begun by minimizing your own responsibility for the course of events. Recognition is itself a painful process, and your very human mind will try to avoid the added pain in unique and creative ways.

If your setback has been obvious and dramatic, you may have little difficulty recognizing you have a problem. Often, though, failure is a more insidious, gradual process; in such situations the capacity to recognize one's own weaknesses may be extremely limited, for your mind will want to avoid the truth. This avoidance often involves a two-step mechanism. The first step is the process of *denial*, whereby you unconsciously attempt to trivialize your own contribution to your failure. The second step is *projection*, meaning that you will not only blame others for your misfortune, you may even accuse others of the very issues that you yourself are unconsciously struggling with. Both men and women use denial and projection, but there are some gender-specific variations.

A colleague told a story illustrating this issue. Her role at her university was to help academic women gain faculty promotions. One late-middle-aged woman was denied a promotion. Incensed, she claimed sex discrimination. But, my colleague commented, there was more to the story than met the eye—or perhaps a significant part of the story was actually what *did* meet the eye! The woman wore extremely short skirts and tight sweaters to work, often appearing provocative and inappropriate. Unconsciously she comported herself as if she did not take herself seriously as a professional, though consciously she would have denied this. She projected this dynamic in her accusation that "they" did not take her seriously. *Of course* appearance shouldn't have anything to do with promotions; but *of course*, in reality, it does, for humans are visual creatures who respond to images and cues. While the vast majority of women conduct themselves appropriately at work, a small but visible minority continue to sabotage themselves by soliciting the sexual responses they profess to be indignant about. It was a tragedy that this issue affected the course of this woman's career and that she had never sought advice—or perhaps no one dared to tell her the truth—that might have made a difference.

More than the overtly sexual presentation is the way women undermine themselves with reflexive, stereotypically feminine behaviors. Nadia, a journalist, reflected on this issue in her own history: "I think that an enormous problem for me was that I always made my way at work as the young ingenue looking up admiringly at my big, powerful male bosses. I was always there, ready to do their bidding, to make their projects turn out well, to support their dreams. But in playing the role of the ingenue I didn't require them to take me seriously as an independent thinker. I was never aggressive about pushing my own agenda."

When behavior is used as a means to express issues it is particularly easy to remain oblivious to the self-perceptions underlying the behavior.

As a young woman, Nadia was in denial about her self-doubts about her own competence; she consciously perceived herself as effective, even though she behaved ineffectively by not initiating her own projects. When her bosses then failed to promote her, she projected her own self-criticism on them, and was angry that she was unappreciated.

Step Three: Rebounding

Rebounding is the process of springing back after a defeat. The engine that drives rebounding is the capacity to persevere, to hold on to the absolute determination to succeed and achieve.

If I were to weight the personality attributes most important for success, I would give perseverance a value of at least 50 percent, maybe 70 percent. Because failure is such a vital ingredient of ultimate success, the capacity to persevere despite failure is utterly essential. I have never met a high-achieving person who was not a bulldog of perseverance, nor have I ever met someone with great perseverance who did not ultimately succeed.

Generally, following a setback high-achieving people neither go off in entirely new directions, nor do they merely repeat their drive to the original, unmodified goal. Rather, they use the process of reassessment to reformulate their goal as well as the approaches they take in their effort. They hold on to the elements of what worked well, and they build and expand on them. They abandon the aspects of their effort that did not work well, and may make dramatic alterations in those areas.

In other words, you should never, *ever* lose sight of your strengths. Real achievement is always a long, slow developmental process that depends on the accumulation of years of experience. Build on all that you have already invested, which includes your knowledge, your skills, and your network of personal contacts. However, in the process of reassessment you can hopefully identify some area of weakness that needs correction. Perhaps you are talented, but the field of competition is too crowded; your new goals should address that problem, perhaps by developing a more specialized area of expertise in which you are unique. Perhaps you failed because you were politically naive; your rebound should be informed by a more sophisticated appreciation of the dynamics of your world and a determination to strengthen your position within your organization. Perhaps you failed because of personality problems that led to self-sabotage; by all means, find the best psychotherapist in your town and make a commitment to really change your approach.

BROKERING POWER

Diffused or Directed?

THROUGHOUT the psychological literature on gender differences, one theme appears in a thousand disguises. That theme is the female tendency to connect with the world through relationships, emotional sharing, and nurturance, as contrasted with the male tendency to connect through dominance hierarchies and competition. These tendencies are seen in genetic studies of male and female personality traits; they emerge in studies of children's play; they are reflected in Deborah Tannen's sociolinguistic studies; and they are described by the psychologist Carol Gilligan in her studies of male and female moral decision-making.

It should come as no surprise, therefore, that these tendencies distinguish the way women and men aspire to the ultimate currency in any organization: *power*. Interestingly no differences have been found in the intensity of the psychological need and wish for power that males and females experience. A review of twenty-seven studies found that men scored higher in need for power in fourteen studies, women in thirteen. Further, this need has been shown to be important for both genders; upper-level managers of both sexes have been found to express a need for power twice as often as lower-level managers.

Where differences emerge is in how the two genders conceptualize power itself. Men tend to experience power through assertive behavior— having *power over* another. Women tend to express power by building up their resources in order to have more to give to others—having *power to* support, protect, or enable another.

To study this issue, the psychologists Ruth Jacobs and David McClelland gave a group of almost four hundred male and female entry-level managers a well-known psychological test called the Thematic Apperception Test (TAT) and studied individuals' responses to pictures that were selected to gauge motivation to achieve power. The managers' responses clustered around three themes: "resourceful power," used to help, support, inspire, or protect another; "reactive power," used in an assertive or aggressive act against someone, especially someone in authority; and powerlessness. They contacted the managers eight to thirteen years later to determine whether the tests accurately predicted their advancement. The results:

- 76 percent of women who became upper-level managers had previously scored high in resourceful-power imagery, compared to 32 percent of upper-level men and only 14 percent of lower-level women.

- 79 percent of men who eventually became upper-level managers had scored high in reactive-power imagery, compared to a mere 10 percent of upper level women, and 33 percent of lower-level men.

- Only 4 percent of upper-level men and 7 percent of upper-level women had scored high on powerlessness, compared to 52 percent and 56 percent of lower-level men and women, respectively.

These findings demonstrate distinct patterns of gender-based power motivations that are highly associated with career attainment. Males and females with high motivation to achieve power advanced, while those whose psychology reflected a sense of helplessness did not. Further, males and females have distinctly different motives for desiring power, but both ways were highly associated with career success.

Women's preferred power style, I am convinced, is derived from the deepest and most ancient levels of our feminine biology. It can be channeled in ways that give us explosive energy to achieve, or in ways that absolutely squelch our ambition.

THE PREFERENCE FOR RESOURCEFUL POWER

The ultimate source of any particular psychological trait lies within our biological wiring. The data for this sweeping statement come from studies of biological vs. environmental contributions to personality traits, intelligence, and even mental disorders. Studying 573 sets of adult twins, Philippe Rushton measured the heritability (determination by genes) of a variety of traits. He found the genetic contribution in determining personality to be 56 percent for altruism; 68 percent for empathy; 70 percent for nurturance; 72 percent for aggression; and 64 percent for assertiveness. Males scored higher than females on aggressiveness and assertiveness; females scored higher on empathy and nurturance; and the two sexes were roughly equal on altruism. Further, Rushton and his colleagues have shown that genetic traits tend to be reinforced by the environment. For example, aggressive children provoke aggression from others, while nurturing children elicit nurturance from others.

Those two traits women score so high on—empathy and nurturance—have everything to do with our need for resourceful power. They are traits that have dominated the female psyche since before we were human, as hominid females joined together in communal groups. They are traits that can be observed in young girls who are far more interested in their younger siblings than their brothers are. They are traits that shape girls' intellectual preference for humanistic subjects and motivate them to choose careers in which they help others.

And clearly, also, the power of those traits can be harnessed and directed in the service of great achievement. Think of the women I have described in this book: Hildegard of Bingen and Heather Paul; Anne Darby Parker, Marjie Rynearson, Florence Nightingale, and Harriet Tubman. All these women directed their resourceful power toward uplifting the lives of others. Their work expressed their intense need for connection to other humans.

But for every Heather, Marjie, or Bobbi, there are many more women who do not direct their inner energy to developing resourceful power. Why not?

The words of women themselves as they reflect on the quality of their daily lives tell the tale of the fate of this abundant wish to help others. Political scientist Roberta Sigel surveyed 650 men and women from New Jersey in 1985 to learn how ordinary women themselves understood the progress that women in general have made in achieving equal opportunity. Although Sigel's purpose was to study how the two genders conceptualized political aspects of gender equality, she soon found herself hearing different types of stories about the brokering of power within American families.

Asking the women whether they felt they personally experienced discrimination, Sigel observed what she came to call the "not-me" syndrome: a significant majority (ranging from 58 to 86 percent) thought that women in general received a poorer deal than men on a variety of items, but the majority of the women surveyed denied ever having been significantly personally discriminated against at work. A significant majority of the women respondents denied feeling like an outsider at work, and most felt their opinion was valued as much as or more than men's at work. Only 16 percent described encountering the problem of discrimination daily or often; 34 percent encountered discrimination once in a while; 47 percent never encountered discrimination.

In a fascinating paradox, however, 80 percent of the women surveyed also attributed the failure of women in general to advance to men's holding them back. The picture emerged that women had the deepest emotional reactions not to inequality in the workplace but at home:

One topic, housework, commanded an extraordinary amount of their attention. Much of the women's groups' two hours together was devoted to complaining about the unfair division of labor at home, especially the lack of cooperation they receive from their partners. . . . I realized what a central role these everyday activities played in the formation of their gendered perspectives. . . . Many women of all ages in these groups are dissatisfied with their current domestic arrangements. Younger women especially tend to view the "second shift" as a forceful indication that women have not yet achieved true equality.

Although 53 percent of these women viewed heavy domestic responsibilities as a significant factor holding them back, I suspect that the actual contribution of this factor is far higher, for Sigel noted that most women seemed resigned, if somewhat bitterly, to this burden. Fully 89 percent of them described themselves as carrying the lion's share of household responsibilities.

The fact that women do far more housework than men is hardly latebreaking news and has been documented in numerous studies. One of the largest of these studies, which examined the sex segregation of housework in three thousand couples, found that the average American woman devoted thirty-three or more hours each week to housework, compared to less than fifteen hours a week for men. What is less discussed, however, is the typical female response to this inequity: resentment coupled with passive resignation. Women in one 1992 study, for instance, typically responded to the lack of assistance with domestic responsibilities by "crying alone" or "holding it in." The desire for relationships and intimacy so characteristic of women also makes many of us not to want to disturb domestic tranquillity even when we are suffering.

A study by researcher Marianne Frankenhaeuser and colleagues of work activity in 1,200 men and women who were employed full time found that women reported higher levels of work overload, stress, and conflict than men, which increased significantly with the number of children at home. In another study, Frankenhaeuser compared blood pressure and norepinephrine levels throughout the day in male and female managers, choosing nor-epinephrine because it reflects moment-by-moment stress levels. She found that the male managers' blood pressure and stress-hormone levels dropped sharply at five P.M., while the women's blood pressure remained high and stress-hormone levels actually *increased* after work. Similarly, researcher Linda Luecken and her colleagues studied work strain and the excretion of stress hormones in employed mothers and childless women. Those who had children at home excreted more of the stress hormone cortisol and reported more home strain—though not work strain.

The stress experienced by working women who have heavy domestic responsibilities takes its toll on physical as well as mental health. Chronic elevation of blood pressure caused by norepinephrine secretion, for exam-ple, is a significant risk factor for heart disease, the number one killer of women. The Framingham Heart Study, for instance, found employment was not a risk factor for heart disease for women, but having three or more children or being married to a blue-collar husband increased the risk of ill-ness two- to threefold.

In fact, study after study consistently documents that working moth-ers experience more stress and depression than working fathers do. This phenomenon is often trumpeted by the popular media, but curiously, the cause of the stress is frequently misattributed. It is often implied that employment is causing women stress and depression and that the rem-edy is staying home. A study of 3,800 men and women concluded that paid employment is associated with reduced depression among both husbands and wives, while time spent in housework is associated with increased depression for both genders, regardless of other roles. These data suggest that the fact that the average American wife spends twice as much time each week on housework as her husband does may contribute to the finding that depression is twice as common in women as in men.

And what is the male response to this issue? Roberta Sigel commented:

> Listening to the focus group men discuss the topic, one suspects that women's complaints have merit. The men we observed were not particu-

larly empathic with the dual responsibility thrust upon wives as they are working two shifts, one at home and one at work. In the focus groups, men simply ignored the subject, as though it were quite natural to expect women to work two shifts, perhaps assuming that they could do it with as much ease as they might add a weekly aerobics class. If they mentioned it at all—as a few blue-collar men did—they did so to complain about demands their working wives are beginning to make on them, especially with respect to help in the house. . . . In the female focus groups . . . men's lack of cooperation in the domestic sphere carried at least as much, if not more, emotional baggage as any other gender-based inequity about which they complained.

Clearly, the responsibilities of home life significantly drain women's capacity to achieve. A number of studies have documented the high association between female singlehood and high achievement. For example, Dean Keith Simonton notes that women who are cited in *Who's Who* are four times more likely than equally distinguished men to be unmarried, and successful married women are three times more likely to be childless than equally accomplished men. A study of 236 eminent men and 81 eminent women found that the eminent women had a higher rate of divorce and unconventional lifestyles, and another comparing matched male and female managers found that the women were less likely to be married and had fewer children than the men. Although these studies seem to suggest that high achievement and heavy domestic responsibilities do not mix, they do not clarify the direction of causality in this association. I asked women I interviewed to talk about this issue.

Mia, a business executive, observed: "I'm so amazed sometimes when I travel with my male colleagues at the differences in their lifestyles and mine. I see it in little things—like one guy might good-naturedly complain that his wife had packed too many shirts for him, or another might say that his wife had forgotten to get him his cash. I can't imagine how easy my life would be if I had someone to pack for me or run to the ATM—to say nothing of the millions of household jobs I'm responsible for. For them, being home is a time to kick back and relax, while for me it's the beginning of my responsibilities to my kids and husband. No wonder my male colleagues seem to be able to have energy and focus for work."

Mia's comments suggest what the studies on stress hormones and illness related to domestic responsibilities confirm. High stress at home takes an enormous toll on a woman; of course this will be reflected her work performance. If she depletes her mental and physical energy by performing more than her share of domestic activities, little may be left for career advancement.

Another explanation for the association of singlehood with achievement is that single women may experience a greater financial urgency to support themselves. Trina, a computer analyst and single mother of one child, commented: "In the seven years since my divorce my career has really taken off. For me, the divorce was a real wake-up call. I sat down one day and realized that unless I got a raise, I would never be able to afford a vacation. If I didn't get promoted, I couldn't afford excellent child care, or private school when the time came. Always before that time I'd been pretty complacent, because my salary was seen as icing on the cake. I didn't take my work seriously. I think it was becoming the financial head of a household that put the fire in my belly to go as far as I could. I started looking around at the men at work—men who were no smarter than I—and I realized they were all supporting themselves better than I was. That really got me revved up."

Obviously the most fundamental reason to work is to support oneself; the greater the need to do that, the more willing people are to work hard. But Trina's comments also reflect a profound *psychological* status change. She began to take herself seriously for the first time.

Even in this era, boys and girls are raised with different expectations of what will be required of them as adults. All children are now generally raised to believe they will need to support themselves. For middle-class boys, the expectation that they will need to support themselves and probably a family as well is quite unambivalent. For girls, there is always the possibility, at least, of a safety net, that marriage may eventually mean the income they earn will be secondary. The reality, of course, is that for many women the safety net either fails to materialize or eventually disappears. At that point, women like Trina may become as unambivalent about their desire to succeed as their male counterparts.

But could attributes associated with high achievement also be associated with difficulty sustaining marriage and a greater willingness to divorce? Lil, a divorced executive, commented, "Maybe the fact that high-achieving women often divorce just reflects that they and their husbands have the means to end an unhappy marriage if they choose." Studies indicate that financial and social independence in women are, indeed, associated with a high divorce rate. Throughout the world, and in cultures on every continent, the less dependent men and women are on each other, the more likely they are to divorce. In the United States, divorce rates climbed steadily as women's earning increased until 1981 and have remained stable since 1986. The anthropologist Helen Fisher puts it simply: when people can divorce, they will. But divorce is a phenomenon of the young, peaking between ages twenty and twenty-four for both men and women. Further, rates are also highest in the first few years of marriage and decline steadily thereafter. In the United States, divorce rates are highest between the second and third years of marriage and are two and a half times higher than during the tenth year. These data suggest that divorce is not associated with achievement per se, for it commonly occurs long before the age of peak achievement. But it may still be associated with women's recognition of their capacity to live independently.

How Women Wield Power

Studies of how women attain and wield power in the workplace suggest that we do relatively well there. Some studies have focused on two aspects of power: leadership and negotiation.

Judy Rosener, professor in the graduate school of management at the University of California, Irvine, and a leading writer in the area of gender-based leadership differences, observed in an article in the *Harvard Business*

Review that women managers are more comfortable with ambiguity than men are and favor a collaborative style that leads to an increased sense of empowerment among subordinates. Rosener has written that it is their "second shift" responsibility and women's tendency to speak "in a different voice" (as Carol Gilligan put it) that have led to the depressing statistic that only 10 percent or less of top business executives are women.

Rosener's view is confirmed by a number of studies. In the late 1970s and early '80s, an in depth study by Bell Telephone of 344 managers found that women had advantages in administrative ability, interpersonal skills, sensitivity, written communication skills, energy, and inner work standards. Men had advantages in company loyalty, motivation to advance, and awareness of power structures. Overall, however, no gender differences in managerial potential were perceived. Several large meta-analyses also found no overall gender differences in leader effectiveness, although they confirmed the observation that women are more effective as democratic leaders while men are more effective in hierarchical structures. Carol Watson's studies of negotiation have led her to conclude that most apparent gender-based differences in negotiating style result from the typical power differential between men and women, rather than from gender per se.

If we're so skillful at wielding resourceful power at work, why do we fare so poorly at home? Surely the answer lies in the basic traits that distinguish male from female psychology. Because men since ancient times have tended to organize themselves in hierarchies, they expect Papa to be the "alpha" of the family unit, with all the special privileges that status entails. Many women acquiesce to this expectation in order to promote domestic harmony. And women's intense drive to connect, to nurture, and to support leads them to be relatively more willing than men are to sacrifice their time and energy for the welfare of the family, particularly if the alternative is an ongoing state of conflict and discord over these issues.

Not only do our efforts on our family's behalf deplete the energy we could be putting toward career advancement, they may result in our having *less* power *at home.* It is often observed that whoever is *less* invested in a relationship is likely to exert the *most* power. In relationships characterized by unequal power, it is more likely to be the man who has more of it, and also the man who is less emotionally invested. Further, the most common way that men maintain their power is by withdrawing—a response that is particularly disturbing for women and extremely difficult to respond to effectively.

Throughout this book I have looked to the sphere of evolutionary and individual biology as the ultimate explanatory source of *why* we do *what* we do. Yet if we humans were solely driven by our biology, civilization would not have developed as it has. The mark of a healthy individual as well as of a thriving, productive culture is in the capacity to control, direct, and harness biological impulses, whether they be sex, aggression, eating, or seizing others' property, in the service of important aims.

Similarly, the development of an individual psychology of achievement depends on the ability to channel your fundamental biological drive to affiliate. Without purposeful direction, this drive can easily become diffused in myriad directions, leaving you exhausted, depressed—and bewildered. We know we are working hard, often terribly hard, and yet are angry that as a group we lack status and financial power. We perceive the intensity of our efforts to give to others, yet realize how unappreciated those efforts seem to be. We realize our efforts have been the foundation of civilization, and yet we have been left out of the pages of written history.

"I'M NOT A FEMINIST, BUT" FEMINISM

Numerous scholars and observers of women's issues have noted that many everyday women express discomfort with the feminist movement, even as they acknowledge the importance of women's greater access to power that the movement has brought. Two issues are frequently cited: the fear that the movement has antagonized men, and resentment that because of "second shift" issues, women are now working harder than ever.

Jackie, a thirty-five-year-old retailer, expressed the anxiety women feel that openly endorsing feminist aims might limit their ability to sustain a relationship with a man. "Men are just sick of hearing about these women's issues. They get really irritated when it comes up—they think we're whining or something. I think the feminist movement in some ways has gone too far, because it's produced a lot more conflict between men and women. I agree with a lot of things that the women's movement has accomplished— like the chance to get an education and not be discriminated against at work. But I don't really say too much about those things around men, because it creates so much tension."

Bessie, a seventy-three-year-old woman who had worked for thirty years as a grade school teacher, expressed the second source of ambivalence. "I often wonder why women of my generation settled for so little. I look at the young girls of today—they're getting their Ph.D.s, they're doctors and lawyers—and I just have to wonder, Why did it never dawn on us that we might have those things, too?" Yet later in the conversation, Bessie also commented, "I think the younger generation of women has it pretty hard. They seem to be working so hard all the time. They're running themselves ragged, and really aren't much better off than we were." Those two very different sets of feelings, coming from the same person, are testimony to the confusion that many women feel—wanting equality and opportunity, yet feeling that the more opportunity women get, the harder our lives becomes. Not infrequently this confusion turns into resentment toward feminism and feminists. Yes, the women's movement has achieved many gains, but why do many of us seem to be losing ground?

It may well be that the "I'm not a feminist, but" feminists have the hardest time of all women. Wanting equality in the workplace, they shoulder their workload and rise to positions of responsibility. Unwilling or unable to insist on equality at home, they are drained and demoralized by the second shift. Frustrated, they point the finger of blame at the women's movement: Why has it failed to deliver on its promise of a better life for women? Yet this resentment ignores a painful reality. The resolution of these issues in the domestic realm is outside the reach of political ideology; the feminist movement stops at the front door of the home. Private power relations can only be negotiated by an individual woman relating to an individual man. It is here that the toughest issues of feminism arise, and it is here that the real fate of feminism will ultimately be determined. And it is small wonder that so many women back off from pursuing a feminist agenda in the home, for the issues and consequences are personally painful and complex, far more difficult than the resolution of the public issues proved to be.

One of the feminist movement's inspirations was the fight for equal rights and opportunities by black activists. Like African Americans, women historically were denied civil liberties, such as the right to vote or to own property. Like African Americans, women were denied equal access to education and were freely discriminated against by employers. As they did with African Americans, the dominant group often openly devalued women's talents and capabilities.

Also like African Americans, women were ready to seek access to full liberties and opportunities long before the dominant group cared to share them. Prejudice, as Daniela Gioseffi has written, is always a matter of the more powerful group attempting to maintain their economic and political privilege by excluding other competing interests. Whites as a group lagged far behind blacks in believing that all races should have equal opportunity, and began to change their thinking only after a great deal of struggle, pressure, and, occasionally, violence. And males would lag behind females in thinking that women should have equal power at home and at work, and this gap continues to exist.

Although many parallels can be drawn between the struggles of African Americans and women for equality, one enormous difference exists. For the most part, blacks were not married to whites. But women loved, wedded, and lived with men, the very group whose power we wished to share. When we returned home from work seething with feelings about the difficulties of living as women in a man's world, we went to bed with the gender who had the privileges we longed for. As we desperately juggled family and work, in pursuit of our own dreams, we observed the lives of our own husbands, who were able to sustain a much narrower focus.

Further, while women were vigorously struggling to redefine gender roles, no such parallel struggle occurred to any significant degree for men—*they* certainly weren't fighting for a change in status! While the women of my generation were meeting in our dorm rooms to talk of our dreams for our careers, our male counterparts across campus were hardly talking about their excitement in learning to change diapers. While our teachers and professors were encouraging us, while the females of my generation were gradually being prepared for opportunities in the traditionally male world of work, no one was suggesting that our brothers learn to perform traditionally female domestic tasks They anticipated a home life very much like what they had witnessed as children. We took them by surprise and were in turn surprised to often find ourselves married to men who seemed to be from another era.

The story of Betsy, a hospital administrator, illustrates some of the difficulties arising from these issues. "My marriage broke up after close to twenty years. One of the complaints that Will had about me was that he saw me as an angry feminist. In the early years of our marriage, I would come home from work fit to be tied about the sexist experiences I had had. Remember, that was back in the seventies, and hospitals were still extremely male-dominated institutions. I was angry a lot, and for good reason. But our marriage was really good for about the first ten years or so, and Will was sympathetic about the problems I had.

"Then things started to change. Our twins were born. My career was stalling, but Will's business was taking off. So I took a couple of years off to take care of the boys, and Will was spending longer and longer hours at work. I was really frustrated and eventually went back to work, but by then a lot of tension had been built up between us. I think he was getting frustrated that I wasn't content just staying with the boys, and I was resentful that his life choices and ability to work without guilt made his life so much more straightforward than mine. I think also that he was angry that he felt powerless to make things right for me. He seemed to take my frustration about feminist issues so personally—if I complained about a sexist issue, he seemed to think I was complaining about *him*. His first affair was with a woman who was a very successful attorney—she didn't have children, and I think he was attracted to her because she was a lot like him, hard-driving and without the internal conflicts that I had."

Many high-achieving women find their marriage is easy enough in the early years, particularly if they postpone having children. Both partners can pursue their respective interests, and each has relatively plenty of energy for the relationship. With the coming of children, however, the marital dynamic shifts dramatically. The children become a focus, taking energy away from the intense focus on each other. For many couples, romance and sex takes a distant second place to meeting the needs of a baby. What feels like a temporary reordering of daily priorities becomes a way of life that dilutes the intimacy of the marriage.

It is easy enough during the early years to espouse principles of equal responsibility in the home, generosity and flexibility in resolving conflicts, and working as a team to meet the goals of each partner. What happens, though, when the husband begins to realize that if he does not work long hours at the office he will not make partner? What happens when the wife gladly steps back from her career for a few years, only to observe that her devotion to the family is not appreciated? If resentment on both sides builds, the marriage may eventually fail.

Further, the issue is complicated by that which can never be minimized or ignored: the children. If marriage becomes a protracted battle the offspring become the helpless victims. It is, after all, the children whose emotional lives may be derailed during the developmental years if there is constant tension in the home; it is the children who will lose active relationships with both parents if the marriage ends in divorce. And like one of the two women who brought the baby to Solomon, it is the parent who cares most about the welfare of the child who is often willing to make personal sacrifices for the sake of the child.

If there were easy answers to these problems they would not be as widespread as they are. Obviously the best solution is for a woman of ambition to find a mate who is as dedicated to equality in the marriage as she is. Not surprisingly, research documents that a husband's capacity to be nurturant and expressive is the most important indicator of marital satisfaction for working wives with young children. For those financially able, "buying out" of responsibility-related conflicts by hiring domestic surrogates is helpful. One of the most common solutions, of course, is for the woman to accept an imbalanced share of domestic responsibilities and postpone her years of work-related achievement.

If this is not the golden age of harmony and stability in heterosexual unions, we should not be amazed. Perhaps it is even a wonder that we have all managed as well as we have, and we should be more impressed by couples who do make it through this difficult era than critical of those who don't. There is room for compassion for our men, many of whom are struggling to adapt to roles for which they were not trained and may not have desired. There is obvious need for compassion for ourselves as women, as we expand our own roles and values without benefit of models who have gone before us; of course we may at time be frazzled and confused. Both genders are in transition, and the progress we all make in the evolution of our respective gender cultures will make life that much easier for our sons and daughters.

DIVERSITY

I have repeatedly emphasized that women who are able to acknowledge ambition are indeed a brave lot, for they are challenged to develop an individuated sense of identity. Yet women who devote themselves to supporting their families also show great strength of character, for the enormous sacrifices they make are often unnoticed and unsung. As we work our way through the morass of complex issues and choices that face us, each woman will be called upon to wrestle with her particular issues as she sees fit, and undoubtedly we will witness an increasing diversification of arrangements for women—and for men. After all, we will have gained very little from the feminist revolution if we merely straitjacket ourselves into another set of rigid role expectations. To expect all women, at all points of their adult lives, to maintain a single-minded focus on career is every bit as enslaving as expecting all women to have no career and stay home full time with their children. Diversification would allow each individual woman to create a life in which work and family life can shift in variable, individual priorities throughout the life cycle. We will know, however, that feminism has reached the kitchen and the bedroom when we observe that men, also, can comfortably shift between a variety of roles.

While this transitional era is marked by increasing diversity of choice, we have yet to reach the time when these choices are made comfortably. Our decisions remain colored by two competing, conflicting sets of expectations. First, many people remain uncertain about what "good mothering" really is. The opinions of experts about the importance of a primary caretaker continue to swing back and forth. Most recently, findings about the relative importance of genetics in shaping personality have led to a louder voice from those who minimize the role of parents; this in turn inspired a cry of protest from experts on the other side of the debate. While much more research is needed to understand the interaction of genes and environment, such decisions will always need to be based on individual wisdom, and our collective opinion must always bow to the highly variable choices that parents will make.

Second, current corporate culture has yet to evolve to support diverse lifestyle choices. Broader options for work life certainly exist at the lower levels of organizations than previously, manifested by on-site child care and flexible hours. At upper levels, however, it remains very difficult to succeed without the commitment of long hours. Coexisting with this reality is the expectation that career ascendance should occur by midlife; women who do not enter the workforce until their forties are given fewer opportunities for promotion.

To achieve a new feminine psychology of achievement, the diversity we are seeing in women's choices must be matched by an increasing appreciation by individual women for diversity of wishes, goals, and talents within themselves. Our collective psychology continues to be dominated by stereotypes that tell us a woman can be a great mother or have a great career, but not both; like the women psychiatric residents I teach, too many women give up dreams of great accomplishment once they make the choice to have families. We must actively teach young women to anticipate that their interests and priorities will evolve over the decades of their lives. We must mentor them and encourage them to make early educational and career choices that will enhance their professional options later in life.

As the collective psychology of women evolves, we must pay more attention to the necessity for growth in the collective psychology of men. It is unlikely that women will ever be wholly comfortable with the range of diversity we require until men, also, have achieved psychological and social freedom to make diverse choices. Men will not fully respect women who enter the workforce in midlife until both sexes respect men who do so as well. It is unlikely that men will perceive their responsibility to contribute fully to the home until they have learned to respect women's equal need to achieve, just as women have always respected that need in men.

The first feminists were driven by a hefty dose of anger. All revolutions, in fact, need the energy of anger to ignite a fire bright enough to illuminate the urgency of the issues. As women of this transitional era raise their sons, however, it will be not through anger but through love that they will create a society that embraces women's need for diversity. Beneath all the social-science jargon that describes what motivates women—words like "resourceful power," "affiliative needs," and "nurturing drives"—the emotion that inspires women is simple love, and it is in love that we will raise the next generation of achievers. Our boys, after all, will grow to maturity with very different images of their fathers, images that will allow them far more freedom and flexibility. They, and our girls, will live lives that make us far more appreciative of the similarity of our hopes and ambitions than resentful of our differences. Our commonality of values and ambitions may well make it easier to build lives of accomplishment as well as loving relationships, with deeper appreciation of our shared humanity.

NOTES

CHOICE ONE. MOTIVATION:
DERAILED BY ANXIETY OR INSPIRED BY MEANING?

page

2 Hildegard: Sabina Flangan, *Hildegard of Bingen, 1098–1179: A Visionary Life*, 2nd ed. (New York: Routledge, 1998). See also Andrea Hopkins, "Hildegard of Bingen," in *Heroines: Remarkable and Inspiring Women*, ed. Sara Hunt (New York: Crescent Books, 1995).

4 Florence Nightingale: *Heroines*, pp. 24–26.

7 "[A]ll of the women": S. M. Reis, "Older Women's Reflections on Eminence: Obstacles and Opportunities," *Roeper Review* 18 (1): 66–72 (1995).

8 Jacquelynn Eccles: J. S. Eccles, "Understanding Women's Educational and Occupational Choices: Applying the Eccles et al. Model of Achievement-Related Choices," *Psychology of Women Quarterly* 18 (4): 585–609 (1994). See also J. S. Eccles, E. Janis Jacobs, and R. D. Harold, "Gender Role Stereotypes, Expectancy Effects, and Parents' Socialization of Gender Differences," *Journal of Social Issues* 46 (2): 183–201 (1990). A body of literature explores this issue within the context of achievement motivation. See, for example, H. S. Farmer, "Women's Motivation Related to Mastery, Career Salience, and Career Aspiration: A Multivariate Model Focusing on the Effect of Sex Role Socialization," *Journal of Career Assessment* 5 (4): 355–81 (1997).

8 Specific values: D. M. Jozefowicz, B. L. Barber, and J. S. Eccles, "Adolescent Work-Related Values and Beliefs: Gender Differences and Relation to Occupational Aspirations" (Paper presented at biennial meeting of the Society for Research on Child Development, New Orleans, 1993).

8 high school seniors: A. M. Beutel, Marini, and M. Mooney, "Gender and Values," *American Sociological Review* 60 (3): 436–48 (1995). See also B. Hardcastle, "Midlife Themes of Invisible Citizens: An Exploration into How Ordinary People Make Sense of Their Lives," *Journal of Humanistic Psychology* 25 (2): 45–63a (1985). Although a small study, it confirms that women's sense of meaning is derived from relational events, while men's is derived from public or personal events. Another interesting study had college-age grandchildren ask their grandparents to tell them stories that explained the meaning of life. Grandmothers spoke longer and about family; grandfathers talked about their youth and morals. See J. F. Nussbaum and L. M. Bettini, "Shared Stories of the Grandparent-Gandchild Relation-

ship," *International Journal of Aging & Human Development* 39 (1): 67–80 (1994).

8 Women limiting careers: See, for example, B. A. Kerr, *Smart Girls, Gifted Women* (Dayton: Ohio Psychology Publishing, 1985).

9 Terman study: P. S. Sears, "The Terman Genetic Study of Genius, 1922–1972," in *The Gifted and the Talented: Their Education and Development, The Seventy-eighth Yearbook of the National Society of the Study of Education*, ed. A. H. Passow (Chicago: University of Chicago Press, 1979).

9 Nancy J. Chodorow, "Family Structure and Feminine Personality," in *Woman, Culture and Society*, ed. M. Z. Rosaldo and L. Lamphere (Palo Alto, Calif.: Stanford University Press, 1974), pp. 43–44. See also Chodorow, "Gender, Relation, and Difference in Psychoanalytic Perspective," in *Essential Papers on the Psychology of Women*, ed. Claudia Zanardi et al. (New York: New York University Press, 1990), pp. 420–36.

9 Jean Baker Miller, *Toward a New Psychology of Women* (Boston: Beacon Press, 1976), p. 83.

10 "[G]irls are preoccupied": E. S. Person, "Women Working: Fears of Failure, Deviance, and Success," *Journal of the American Academy of Psychoanalysis* 10 (1): 67–84 (1982). On fear of failure, see also C. C. Nadelson, M. Norman, and M. B. Bennett, "Success or Failure: Psychotherapeutic Considerations for Women in Conflict," *American Journal of Psychiatry* 13: 1092–96 (1978). The concept of fear of success was popularized my M. Horner, "Toward an Understanding of Achievement-Related Conflicts in Women," *Journal of Social Issues* 28: 157–76 (1972).

17 Intellectual stimulation: One study of 934 female human service workers found that the single best predictor of job satisfaction for this group was whether work was perceived as dull or stimulating. R. L. McNeely, "Job Satisfaction Differences Among Three Age Groups of Female Human Service Workers," *Journal of Aging Studies* 2 (2): 109–20 (1988).

17 Hedonism: I. Yalom, *Existential Psychotherapy* (New York: Basic Books, 1980) p. 437.

20 The Female Paradox: Jo Phelan, "The Paradox of the Contented Female Worker: An Assessment of Alternative Explanations," *Psychology Quarterly* 57 (2): 95–107 (June 1994).

21 Women and emotional resilience: J. Block and A. M. Kremen, 1996, "IQ and Ego-Resiliency: Conceptual and Empirical Connections and Separate-

ness," *Journal of Personality and Social Psychology* 70 (2): 349–61 (1996).

22 Study of multiethnic girls: L. A. Bell, "Something's Wrong Here and It's Not Me: Challenging the Dilemmas that Block Girls' Success," *Journal for the Education of the Gifted* 12: 118–30 (1989).

24 Breadth of interests: G. Baruch, R. Barnett, and C. Rivers, *Life Prints* (New York: McGraw-Hill, 1983). D. R. Maines, "A Theory of Informal Barriers for Women in Mathematics" (Paper presented at the annual meeting of the American Educational Research Association, Montreal, 1983).

24 Study of married grad students: J. S. Eccles, "Understanding Women's Educational and Occupational Choices," *Psychology of Women Quarterly* 18: 585–609 (1994).

CHOICE TWO. INVESTING YOUR ENERGY:
NEST-BUILDING OR RISK-TAKING?

page

35 Female aversion to bodily harm: J. H. Block, "Differential Premises Arising from Differential Socialization of the Sexes: Some Conjectures," *Child Development* 54: 1335–54 (1983). See also E. L. "Evidence of Neuroandrogenic Etiology of Sex Roles from a Combined Analysis of Human and Nonhuman Primates and Nonprimate Mammalian Studies," *Personality and Individual Differences*, 7: 19–552 (1986).

35 Men, women, and health risks: L. D. McNair, J. A. Carter, M. K. Williams, "Self-esteem, Gender, and Alcohol Use: Relationships with HIV Risk Perception and Behaviors in College Students," *Journal of Sex & Marital Therapy* 24 (1): 29–36 (1998). N. D. Collins and L. N. Janet, "Co-Occurrence of Health-Risk Behaviors Among Adolescents in the United States," *Journal of Adolescent Health* 22 (3): 209–13 (1998).

35 Boys and girls: E. Jelalian, A. Spirito, D. Rasile, L. Vinnick, C. Rohrbeck, and M. Arrigan, "Risk Taking, Reported Injury, and Perception of Future Injury Among Adolescents," *Journal of Pediatric Psychology* 22 (4): 513–31 (1997). B. A. Morrongiello and H. Rennie. "Why Do Boys Engage in More Risk Taking than Girls? The Role of Attributions, Beliefs, and Risk Appraisals," *Journal of Pediatric Psychology* 23 (1): 33–43 (1998). J. H. Kerr and J. Vlaminkx, "Gender Differences in the Experience of Risk," *Personality and Individual Differences* 22 (2): 293–95 (1997).

35 Taking risks in cyberspace: G. A. Hudgens and L.T. Fatkin. "Sex Differ-

Notes

Introduction: Breaking the Psychological Glass Ceiling

page

xiii 10 percent of top-level jobs: N. Neft and A. D. Levine, *Where Women Stand* (New York: Random House, 1997), p. 457.

xx Survey of 186 indigenous cultures: T. S. Weisner and R. Gallimore, "My Brother's Keeper: Child and Sibling Caretaking," *Current Anthropology* 18: 169–70 (1977). For an extensive review of the storm of philosophical and political issues that has swirled around research on child care by surrogates, see H. McGurk, M. Kaplan, E. Hennessy, and P. Moss, "Controversy, Theory and Social Context in Contemporary Day Care Research," *Journal of Child Psychology and Psychiatry* 34: 3–23 (1992).

xx "The woman's day": Neft and Levine, *Where Women Stand*, p. 26.

xxi marrying well: For a fascinating description of the lives of women in preindustrial Europe, see Olwen, Hufton, *The Prospect Before Her: A History of Women in Western Europe 1500–1800* (New York: Knopf, 1996).

xxv "In the diverse histories": D. K. Simonton, *Greatness: Who Makes History and Why* (New York: Guilford Press, 1994), pp. 33–34.

CHOICE ONE. MOTIVATION:
DERAILED BY ANXIETY OR INSPIRED BY MEANING?

page

2 Hildegard: Sabina Flangan, *Hildegard of Bingen, 1098–1179: A Visionary Life*, 2nd ed. (New York: Routledge, 1998). See also Andrea Hopkins, "Hildegard of Bingen," in *Heroines: Remarkable and Inspiring Women*, ed. Sara Hunt (New York: Crescent Books, 1995).

4 Florence Nightingale: *Heroines*, pp. 24–26.

7 "[A]ll of the women": S. M. Reis, "Older Women's Reflections on Eminence: Obstacles and Opportunities," *Roeper Review* 18 (1): 66–72 (1995).

8 Jacquelynn Eccles: J. S. Eccles, "Understanding Women's Educational and Occupational Choices: Applying the Eccles et al. Model of Achievement-Related Choices," *Psychology of Women Quarterly* 18 (4): 585–609 (1994). See also J. S. Eccles, E. Janis Jacobs, and R. D. Harold, "Gender Role Stereotypes, Expectancy Effects, and Parents' Socialization of Gender Differences," *Journal of Social Issues* 46 (2): 183–201 (1990). A body of literature explores this issue within the context of achievement motivation. See, for example, H. S. Farmer, "Women's Motivation Related to Mastery, Career Salience, and Career Aspiration: A Multivariate Model Focusing on the Effect of Sex Role Socialization," *Journal of Career Assessment* 5 (4): 355–81 (1997).

8 Specific values: D. M. Jozefowicz, B. L. Barber, and J. S. Eccles, "Adolescent Work-Related Values and Beliefs: Gender Differences and Relation to Occupational Aspirations" (Paper presented at biennial meeting of the Society for Research on Child Development, New Orleans, 1993).

8 high school seniors: A. M. Beutel, Marini, and M. Mooney, "Gender and Values," *American Sociological Review* 60 (3): 436–48 (1995). See also B. Hardcastle, "Midlife Themes of Invisible Citizens: An Exploration into How Ordinary People Make Sense of Their Lives," *Journal of Humanistic Psychology* 25 (2): 45–63a (1985). Although a small study, it confirms that women's sense of meaning is derived from relational events, while men's is derived from public or personal events. Another interesting study had college-age grandchildren ask their grandparents to tell them stories that explained the meaning of life. Grandmothers spoke longer and about family; grandfathers talked about their youth and morals. See J. F. Nussbaum and L. M. Bettini, "Shared Stories of the Grandparent-Gandchild Relation-

ences in Risk Taking: Repeated Sessions on a Computer-Simulated Task," *Journal of Psychology* 119 (3): 197–206 (1985).

35 E. C. Arch, "Risk-Taking: A Motivational Basis for Sex Differences," *Psychological Reports* 73: 3–11 (1993).

35 Deborah Tannen, *You Just Don't Understand* (New York: Ballantine, 1990), pp. 87–95.

35 Women and Evaluation: E. C. Arch, "Differential Responses of Females and Males to Evaluative Stress: Anxiety, Self-Esteem, Efficacy and Willingness to Participate," in *Advances in Test Anxiety Research*. Vol 5., ed. R. Schwarzer, H. van der Ploeg, and C. D. Spielberger (Lisse, The Netherlands: Swets & Zeitlinger, 1987), pp. 97–106.

36 Gambling studies: J. L. Derevensky, R. Gupta, and G. D. Cioppa, "A Developmental Perspective of Gambling Behavior in Children and Adolescents," *Journal of Gambling Studies* 12 (1): 49–66 (1996). I. P. Levin, M. A. Snyder, and D. P. Chapman, "The Interaction of Experiential and Situational Factors and Gender in a Simulated Risky Decision-Making Task." *Journal of Psychology* 122 (2): 173–81 (1988).

36 Real-life gambling: A. C. Bruce and J. E. V. Johnson, "Male and Female Betting Behaviour: New Perspectives," *Journal of Gambling Studies* 10 (2): 183–98 (1994). R. M. Buchta, "Gambling Among Adolescents," *Clinical Pediatrics* 34 (7): 346–48 (1995). D. A. Abbot and S. L. Cramer, "Gambling Attitudes and Participation: A Midwestern Survey," *Journal of Gambling Studies* 9 (3): 247–63 (1993). A. K. Wolfgang, "Gambling as a Function of Gender and Sensation Seeking," *Journal of Gambling Behavior* 4 (2): 71–77 (1988).

36 Women-owned businesses: N. Neft, A. D. Levine. *Where Women Stand* (New York: Random House, 1997), p. 459.

36 Marvin Zuckerman's research on sensation-seeking: M. Zuckerman, M. S. Buchsbaum, and D. L. Murphy, "Sensation Seeking and Its Biological Correlates," *Psychological Bulletin* 88: 187–214 (1980).

37 Knowledgeable about current affairs: K. F. Slevin and D. P. Aday, "Gender Differences in Self-Evaluations of Information About Current Affairs," *Sex Roles* 29 (11–12): 817–28 (1993).

37 Teachers: H. A. Kalaian and D. J. Freeman, "Gender Differences in Self-Confidence and Educational Beliefs Among Secondary Teacher Candidates," *Teaching and Teacher Education* 10 (6): 647–58 (1994).

37 Athletes: V. Krane, J. M. Williams, "Cognitive Anxiety, Somatic Anxiety, and Confidence in Track and Field Athletes: The Impact of Gender, Competitive Level and Task Characteristics," *International Journal of Sport Psychology* 25 (2): 203–17 (1994).

37 Financial analysts: R. L. Webster and T. Ellis, "Men's and Women's Self-Confidence in Performing Financial Analysis," *Psychological Reports* 79 (3, pt. 2): 1251–54 (1996).

37 Late-adolescent students: A. Stables and S. Stables, "Gender Differences in Students' Approaches to A-Level Subject Choices and Perceptions of A-Level Subjects: A Study of First-Year A-Level Students in a Tertiary College," *Educational Research* 37 (1): 39–51 (1995). P. E. Yarab, C. C. Sensibaugh, and E. R. Allgeier, "Over-Confidence and Under-Performance: Men's Perceived Accuracy and Actual Performance in a Course," Psychological Reports 81 (1): 76–78 (1997).

38 Westinghouse winners: J. R. Campbell, "The Roots of Gender Inequity in Technical Areas," *Journal of Research in Science Teaching* 28 (3): 251–56 (1991).

39 Females and external locus of control: K. Kunhikrishnan and K. Manikandan, "Sex Difference in Locus of Control: An Analysis Based on Calicut L.O.C. Scale," *Psychological Studies* 37 (2–3): 121–25 (1995). T. J. Wade, "An Examination of Locus of Control/Fatalism for Blacks, Whites, Boys, and Girls over a Two-Year Period of Adolescence," *Social Behavior and Personality* 24 (93): 239–48 (1996). B. de Brabander and C. Boone, "Sex Differences in Perceived Locus of Control," *Journal of Social Psychology* 130 (2): 271–72 (1990).

39 Study of 4,500 managers: P. B. Smith, S. Dugan, and F. Trompenaars, "Locus of Control and Affectivity by Gender and Occupational Status: A 14-Nation Study," *Sex Roles* 36 (1–2): 51–57 (1997).

44 "I had not yet settled": Simone de Beauvoir, Introduction to the Vintage Edition, *The Second Sex* (New York: Random House, Vintage Books, 1989), p. x.

49 Women and competitive challenge: E. C. Arch, "Differential Responses of Females and Males to Evaluative Stress." J. H. Block, "Differential Premises Arising from Differential Socialization of the Sexes: Some Conjectures," *Child Development* 54: 1335–54 (1983). N. R. Goldberger, B. M. Clinchy, M. F. Belenky, and J. M. Tarule, "Women's Ways of Knowing: On Gaining a

Voice," in *Sex and Gender*, ed. P. Shaver and C. Hendrick (Newbury Park, Calif.: Sage, 1987).

55 "The defensive use of reality": Inderbitzin developed this concept in the context of psychoanalytic treatment, when the patient uses reality issues unconsciously to avoid exploring anxiety-provoking issues. See L. B. Inderbitzin, S. T. Levy, "On Grist for the Mill: External Reality as Defense," *Journal of the American Psychoanalytic Association* 42 (3): 763–88 (1994).

Choice Three. Focusing Your Intelligence: Scattered Light or Piercing Laser?

page

61 emotional intelligence: D. Goleman, *Working with Emotional Intelligence* (New York: Bantam Books, 1998), pp. 15–23.

62 Nineteenth-century debate: S. S. Mosedale, "Science Corrupted: Victorian Biologists Consider 'The Woman Question,'" *Journal of the History of Biology* 11: 1–55 (1978).

63 Test score variability: N. Eisenberg, C. L. Martin, R. A. Fabes, "Gender Development and Gender Effects." In *Handbook of Educational Psychology*, ed. David C. Berliner and Robert E. Calfee (New York: Macmillan, 1996), pp. 369–71.

63 "There are essentially no": J. T. E. Richardson, "Conclusions from the Study of Human Differences in Cognition," in *Gender Differences in Human Cognition*, ed. P. J. Caplan, M. Crawford, J. S. Hyde, and J. T. E. Richardson (New York: Oxford University Press, 1997), pp. 131–32.

67 "One of the most celebrated": D. Lubinski, C. P. Benbow, and C. E. Sanders, "Reconceptualizing Gender Differences in Achievement Among the Gifted," In *International Handbook of Research and Development of Giftedness and Talent*, ed. K. A. Heller et al. (Great Britain: Pergamon Press, 1993), pp. 693–707. Also see D. Lubinski and L. G. Humphreys, "A Broadly Based Analysis of Mathematical Giftedness," *Intelligence* 14: 327–55 (1990), and L. H. Fox, S. R. Pasternak, and N. L. Peiser, "Career-Related Interests of Adolescent Boys and Girls," In *Intellectual Talent: Research and Development*, ed. D. P. Keating (Baltimore: Johns Hopkins University Press, 1976), pp. 242–61.

70 Duke study: John Wilson et al., "Gender Differences in Motivations for

Course Selection: Academically Talented Students in an Intensive Summer Program," *Sex Roles* 31 (5–6): 349–67 (1994).

70 Formative years: This issue is considered by some to be a significant obstacle to girls' achieving their full potential. See V. S. Garrison, J. H. Stronge, and C. R. Smith, "Are Gifted Girls Encouraged to Achieve Their Occupational Potential?" *Roeper Review* 9 (2): 101–104 (1986).

70 Patricia W. Lunneborg and Clifford E. Lunneborg, "Nontraditional and Traditional Female College Graduates: What Separates Them from the Men?" *Journal of College Student Personnel* 26 (1): 33–35 (1985).

70 Housework: S. L. Blair and D. T. Lichter, "Measuring the Division of Household Labor: Gender Segregation of Housework Among American Couples," *Journal of Family Issues* 12 (1): 91–113 (1991).

73 Herbert Simon and chess: H. A. Simon and W. G. Chase, "Skill in Chess," *American Scientist* 61: 394–403 (1973).

74 Peak years: Dean Keith Simonton, *Greatness: Who Makes History and Why* (New York: Guilford Press, 1994), pp. 181–87.

77 The aging brain: M. C. Diamond, "An Optimistic View of the Aging Brain," *Generations* 17 (1): 31–33 (1993). Idem, "Morphological Cortical Changes as a Consequence of Learning and Experience," in *Neurobiology of Higher Cognitive Function*, ed. Arnold B. Scheibel, Adam F. Wechsler et al. *UCLA Forum in Medical Sciences* 29 (New York: Guilford Press, 1990), p. xiv.

80 Maya Angelou: Walter Blum, "Listening to Maya Angelou," *California Living*, 14 December 1975, 12–23, cited in *Conversations with Maya Angelou*, ed. J. M. Elliot (Jackson, University Press of Mississippi).

CHOICE FOUR: SHAPING YOUR WORK LIFE:
PROBLEM-FIXING OR PROBLEM-FINDING?

page

85 "Galileo formulated": A. Einstein and L. Infeld, *The Evolution of Physics* (New York: Simon & Schuster, 1938).

85 Pilgrims: K. Lasby, *A Journey to the New World: The Diary of Remember Patience Whipple* (New York: Scholastic, 1996).

87 Two types of tasks: M. A. Runco and I. Chand, "Problem Finding, Evaluative Thinking, and Creativity," in *Problem Finding, Problem Solving, and Creativity*, ed. M. A. Runco (Norwood, N.J.: Ablex, 1994), pp. 40–76.

87 "The way problems": J. W. Getzels and M. Csikszentmihalyi, *The Creative*

Vision: A Longitudinal Study of *Problem Finding in Art* (New York: Wiley, 1976), p. 5.

87 Gaps of understanding: M. Wertheimer, *Productive Thinking* (Westport, Conn.: Greenwood Press, 1945). M. Henle, "The Snail Beneath the Shell," in *Essays in Creativity*, ed. S. Rosner and L. E. Alit (Croton-on-Hudson, N.Y.: North Riner Press, 1974).

88 The problem-finding process: Runco and Chand, "Problem Finding, Evaluative Thinking and Creativity."

88 Eighteen-year artists study: M. Csikszentmihalyi, "The Domain of Creativity," in *Theories of Creativity*, ed. M. A. Runco (Newbury Park, Calif.: Sage, 1990), pp. 190–212.

88 Writers study: M. T. Moore, "The Relationship Between the Originality of Essays and Variables in the Problem Discovery Process: A Study of Creative and Non-Creative Middle School Students," *Research in the Teaching of English* 19 (1): 84–95 (1985).

88 Artists and scientists study: S. Rostan, "Problem Finding, Problem Solving, and Cognitive Controls: An Empirical Investigation of Critically Acclaimed Professional Productivity," *Creativity Research Journal* 7 (2): 97–110 (1994).

88 Westinghouse study: R. F. Subotnik, "Factors from the Structure of Intellect Model Associated with Gifted Adolescents' Problem Finding in Science: Research with Westinghouse Science Talent Search Winners," *Journal of Creative Behavior* 22: 42–54 (1984).

89 Divergent thinking: Runco and Chand, "Problem Finding, Evaluative Thinking and Creativity."

96 Montessori: R. Kramer, *Maria Montessori: A Biography.* (New York: Putnam, 1976).

96 Curie: Eve Curie, *Madame Curie: A Biography* (Garden City, N.Y.: Doubleday, Doran, 1937).

97 "I hope to look": *California Living*, 14 December 1975, 12–23, cited in *Conversations with Maya Angelou*, ed. J. M. Elliot (Jackson: University Press of Mississippi, 1989), p. 74.

98 Copernicus: A. Armitage, *The World of Copernicus* (New York: New American Library, 1952).

107 Impostor phenomenon: P. R. Clance, "The Impostor Phenomenon," *New Woman* 15 (7): 40–43 (1985).

CHOICE FIVE: COMPETITION:
SHAKING POM-POMS OR SHOOTING HOOPS?

page

110 Tests of aggressiveness: B. A. Glaude and J. M. Bailey, "Aggressiveness, Competitiveness, and Human Sexual Orientation," *Psychoneuroendocrinology* 20 (5): 475–85 (1995).

111 Survey of undergraduates: D. Thiessen and M. Ross, "The Use of a Sociobiological Questionnaire (WQ) for the Assessment of Sexual Diomorphism," *Behavior Genetics* 20 (2): 297–305 (1988). D. L. Gill, "Gender Differences in Competitive Orientation and Sport Participation," *International Journal of Sport Psychology* 19 (2): 145–59 (1988).

111 Androgynous females: C. C. Weisfeld, "Female Behavior in Mixed-Sex Competition: A Review of the Literature," *Developmental Review* 6 (3): 278–99 (1986). A. Swain and G. Jones, "Gender Role Endorsement and Competitive Anxiety," *International Journal of Sport Psychology* 22 (1): 50–65 (1991).

117 Stages of development: For a delightful, timeless description of the stages of young children's psychological development, see Selma E. Fraiberg, *The Magic Years: Understanding and Handling the Problems of Early Childhood* (New York: Scribner, 1959).

118 "Envy-driven personality": For a fuller discussion of primitive envy in the narcissistic personality, see Otto F. Kernberg, "Pathological Narcissism and Narcissistic Personality Disorder: Theoretical Background and Diagnostic Classification," in *Disorders of Narcissism: Diagnostic, Clinical, and Empirical Implications*, ed. E. F. Ronningstam et al. (Washington, D.C.: American Psychiatric Press, 1998), pp. 29–51.

120 Mirror hunger: For a fuller discussion of this issue, see the writings of Heinz Kohut, including: H. Kohut and E. S. Wolf, "The Disorders of the Self and Their Treatment," in *Individualism Reconsidered: Readings Bearing on the Endangered Self in Modern Society*, ed. D. Capps et al. (Princeton, N.J.: Princeton Theological Seminary, 1992), pp. 315–32. H. Kohut, "The Endangered Self," in ibid., pp. 307–14. H. Kohut, "The Psychoanalytic Treatment of Narcissistic Personality Disorders," in *Handbook of Character Studies: Psychoanalytic Explorations*, ed. Kets de Vries et al. (Madison, Conn.: International Universities Press, 1991), pp. 529–56.

120 Study of undergraduates: R. Joseph, "Competition Between Women," *Psy-*

chology: A Quarterly Journal of Human Behavior 22 (3–4): 1–12 (1985).

121 Isabel Allende, *Paula* (New York: Harper Perennial, 1995), p. 258.

122 "Jordan's teammates": David Halberstam, "Becoming Michael Jordan," *Vanity Fair*, October 1998, p. 143.

122 Studies of competition: B. A. Gladue and J. M. Bailey, "Aggressiveness, Competitiveness, and Human Sexual Orientation," R. Lynn, "Sex Differences in Competitiveness and the Valuation of Money in Twenty Countries." *Journal of Social Psychology* 133 (4): 507–11. Thiessen and Ross, "Competitive Orientation Among Intercollegiate Athletes."

125 Meta-analysis of leadership studies: A. H. Eagly, S. J. Karau, M. G. Makhijani, "Gender and the Effectiveness of Leaders: A Meta-Analysis," *Psychological Bulletin* 117 (1): 125–45 (1995).

126 Lemurs: P. M. Kappeler, "Female Dominance in Lemur Catta: More than Just Female Feeding Priority?" *Folia Primatologica* 55 (2): 92–95 (1990).

126 Affiliation: F. De Waal, "The Integration of Dominance and Social Bonding in Primates," *Quarterly Review of Biology* 61 (4): 459–79 (1986).

129 Ken Auletta, "In the Company of Women," *New Yorker*, 20 April 1998, pp. 72–78.

136 Mentoring studies: For a review of studies on mentoring, see S. Merriam, "Mentors and Protégés: A Critical Review of the Literature," *Adult Education Quarterly* 33 (3): 161–73 (1983). See also G. F. Dreher and R. A. Ash, "A Comparative Study of Mentoring Among Men and Women in Managerial, Professional, and Technical Positions," *Journal of Applied Psychology* 75 (5): 539–46 (1990).

CHOICE SIX: TAR BABIES IN YOUR PATH:
TAKING A SWING OR WALKING ON BY?

page

145 "Some female attorneys": D. R. Round, "Gender Bias in the Judicial System," *Southern California Law Review* 2193 (September 1988).

146 "I won't talk": K. H. Jamieson, *Beyond the Double Bind* (New York: Oxford University Press, 1995), back cover.

150 Geraldine Laybourne: Ken Auletta, "In the Company of Women," pp. 72–73.

153 Templates: The concept of templates has dominated a prominent school of psychoanalytic theorists. See, for instance, Otto Kernberg, *Borderline Con-*

ditions and Pathological Narcissism (New York: Jason Aronson, 1975) and
J. F. Masterson and R. Klein, eds. *Psychotherapy of the Disorders of the Self:
The Masterson Approach* (New York: Brunner Mazel, 1989).

Choice Seven: Losing Like a Woman: Retreat or Rebound ?

page

160 MIT women: Members of the First and Second Committees, "A Study on the Status of Women Faculty in Science at MIT," *MIT Faculty Newsletter* XI #4 (March 1999).

160 Most women do not consider themselves discrimination victims: R. Sigel, *Ambition & Accommodation: How Women View Gender Relations* (Chicago: University of Chicago Press, 1996), pp. 43–68.

168 Fear of success: M. S. Horner, "Sex Differences in Achievement Motivation and Performance in Competitive and Noncompetitive Situations," 1968, *Dissertation Abstracts International* 30, 407B. (University Microfilms No. 69–12, 135.) Idem, "Toward an Understanding of Achievement-Related Conflicts in Women," *Journal of Social Issues* 28 (2): 157–76.

168 Fear of failure: A. J. Horner, *The Wish for Power and the Fear of Having It* (New York: Jason Aronson, 1989).

168 P. R. Clance, "The Impostor Phenomenon," *New Woman* 15 (7): 40–43.

168 A review of studies: See, for instance M. A. Paludi "Psychometric Properties and Underlying Assumptions of Four Objective Measures of Fear of Success," *Sex Roles* 10 (9/10): 765–81 (1984); M. Lewis, M. Alessandri, and M. W. Sullivan, "Differences in Shame and Pride as a Function of Children's Gender and Task Difficulty," *Child Development* 63 (3): 630–38 (1992); and S. Fried-Buchalter, "Fear of Success, Fear of Failure, and the Imposter Phenomenon Among Male and Female Marketing Managers," *Sex Roles* 37 (11–12): 847–59.

168 L. Terr, *Beyond Love and Work* (New York: Scribner, 1999).

Choice Eight. Brokering Power: Diffused or Directed?

page

181 A review of twenty-seven studies: D. G. Winter, "The Power Motive in Women and Men," *Journal of Personality and Social Psychology* 54 (3): 10–19 (1988).

182 This need has been shown: R. L. Jacobs and D. C. McClelland, "Moving Up the Corporate Ladder: A Longitudinal Study of the Leadership Motive Pattern and Managerial Success in Women and Men," *Consulting Psychology Journal* (Winter): 32–41 (1994).

183 Rushton and his colleagues: J. P. Rushton, D. W. Fulker, M. C. Neale, D. K. B. Nias, and H. J. Eysenck, "Altruism and Aggression: The Heritability of Individual Differences," *Journal of Personality and Social Psychology* 50 (6): 1192–98 (1986).

185 "Younger women": R. S. Sigel, *Ambition and Accommodation: How Women View Gender Relations*, (Chicago: University of Chicago Press, 1996), pp. 90–121.

185 One of the largest of these studies: S. L. Blair, T. Lichter, and T. Daniel, "Measuring the Division of Household Labor: Gender Segregation of Housework Among American Couples," *Journal of Family Issues* 12 (1): 91–113 (1991).

185 "Holding it in": A. I. Meleis and P. E. Stevens, "Women in Clerical Jobs: Spousal Role Satisfaction, Stress, and Coping," *Women & Health* 18 (1): 23–40 (1992).

186 Duke reseacher L. Luecken: L. J. Leucken, E. C. Suarez, C. M. Kuhn, J. C. Barefoot et al., "Stress in Employed Women: Impact of Marital Status and Children at Home on Neurohormone Output and Home Strain," *Psychosomatic Medicine* 59 (4): 352–59 (1997) and T. M. Pollard, G. Ungpakorn, Harrison, and K. R. Parkes, "Epinephrine and Cortisol Responses to Work: A Test of the Models of Frankenhaeuser and Karasek," *Annals of Behavioral Medicine* 18 (4): 229–37 (1996).

186 Framingham heart study: S. G. Haynes and M. Feinleib, "Women, Work, and Coronary Heart Disease: Results from the Framingham 10-Year Follow-Up Study," in *Women: A Developmental Perspective*, eds. P. Berman and E. Ramey (Publication No. 82–2298), (Bethesda, Md.: National Institutes of Health, 1982), pp. 79–101.

186 More stress and depression: S. Bullers, "Women's Roles and Health: The Mediating Effect of Perceived Control," *Women & Health.* 22, (2): 11–30 (1994) and I. Waldron and J. Herold, "Employment, Attitudes Toward Employment, and Women's Health," *Women & Health* 11 (1): 79–98 (1986).

186 "The remedy is staying home": See, for instance, Friedman and Rosenman in their acclaimed book on Type A behavior: "Most American women, at

least in the immediate past, have remained in their homes, and although they have had many chores to do, relatively few were constrained to work under conditions whose essence consisted of deadlines and competition and hostility. The mother of growing children of course does suffer many anxieties, but the effects are clearly less pernicious" in M. Friedman and R. H. Rosenman, *Type A Behavior and Your Heart* (New York: Knopf, 1974), p. 74.

186 Study of 3,800 men and women: J. Glass and T. Fujimoto, "Housework, Paid Work, and Depression Among Husbands and Wives," *Journal of Health & Social Behavior* 35 (2): 179–91 (1994).

186 Average American wife and housework: S. L. Blair and D. T. Lichter, "Measuring the Division of Household Labor: Gender Segregation of Housework Among American Couples," *Journal of Family Issues* 12 (1): 91–113 (1991).

186 depression twice as common in women: For a full discussion of this issue, see A. R. Hochschild with A. MacHung, *The Second Shift* (New York: Avon, 1997).

186 See, for instance, R. Reviere and I. W. Eberstein, "Work, Marital Status, and Heart Disease," *Health Care for Women International* 13 (4): 393–99 (1992); S. Jennings, C. Mazaik, and S. McKinlay, "Women and Work: An Investigation of the Association between Health and Employment Status in Middle-Aged Women." Eighth International Conference on the Social Sciences and Medicine, *Social Science & Medicine* 19 (4): 423–31 (1984); P. K. Adelmann, T. C. Antonucci, S. E. Crohan, and L. M. Coleman, "Empty Nest, Cohort, and Employment in the Well-being of Midlife Women, *Sex Roles* 20 (3–4): 173–89 (1989); O. Anson and J. Anson, "Women's Health and Labour Force Status: An Enquiry Using a Multi-Point Measure of Labour Force Participation," *Social Science & Medicine* 25 (1): 57–63 (1987).

187 "About which they complained": R. S. Sigel, pp. 167–68.

187 Simonton notes: D. K. Simonton, *Greatness: Who Makes History and Why* (New York: Guilford Press, 1994), p. 36.

187 Study of 236 men: R. M. Kelly, "Sex and Becoming Eminent as a Political/ Organizational Leader," *Sex Roles* (9): 1073–90 (1983).

187 Fewer children than the males: L. Larwood , L. M. Radford, and D. Berger, "Do Job Tactics Predict Success? A Comparison of Female with Male

Executives in 14 Corporations," *Academy of Management Proceedings* (Detroit, Mich.: Academy of Management, 1980), pp. 386–90.

189 two and a half times higher: H. Fisher, *Anatomy of Love: A Natural History of Mating, Marriage, and Why We Stray* (New York: W.W. Norton, 1992), p. 113.

190 Rosener has written: J. B. Rosener, "Ways Women Lead," *Harvard Business Review,* (November–December): 119–25 (1990) and J. B.Rosener, "Leadership and the Paradox of Gender," in *Women, Men, and Gender: Ongoing Debates,* ed. M. R. Walsh (New Haven, Conn.: Yale University Press, 1997), pp. 294–97.

190 hierarchical organizational studies: A. H. Eagly and B. T. Johnson, "Gender and Leadership Style: A Meta-Analysis," *Psychological Bulletin* 108: 233–56 (1990). See also A. H. Eagly, "Sex Differences in Human Social Behavior: Meta-Analytic Studies of Social Psychological Research," in *The Development of Sex Differences and Similarities in Behavior,* eds. M. Haug, R. E. Whalen, C. Aron, and K. L. Olsen (Dordrecht, The Netherlands: Kluwer Academic, 1993) and A. H. Eagly, S. J. Karau, and J. B. Johnson, "Gender and the Effectiveness of Leaders: A Meta-Analysis," *Psychological Bulletin* 117: 125–45 (1995).

190 Rather than to gender per se: C. Watson, "Gender versus Power as a Predictor of Negotiation Behavior and Outcomes," in *Women, Men, and Gender,* ed. M. R.Walsh (New Haven, Conn.: Yale University Press, 1997), pp. 145–52.

191 Less invested in a relationship: S. Sprecher and D. Felmlee, "The Balance of Power in Romantic Heterosexual Couples Over Time from 'His' and 'Her' Perspectives," *Sex Roles* 37 (5–6): 361–79 (1997).

191 Respond to affectively: P. Noller, "Gender and Emotional Communication in Marriage: Different Cultures or Differential Social Power?" *Journal of Language & Social Psychology* 12 (1–2): 132–52 (1993).

193 Prejudice: D. Gioseffi, ed., *On Prejudice: A Global Perspective* (New York, Anchor, 1993), pp. xi–l.

196 Working wives with young children: K. Cooper, L. Chassin, S. Braver, and A. Zeiss, "Correlates of Mood and Marital Satisfaction Among Dual-Worker and Single-Worker Couples," *Social Psychology Quarterly 49* (4): 322–29 (1986).

ACKNOWLEDGMENTS

I OWE MY INTEREST in achievement to many people who mentored and inspired me beginning in early childhood. My parents, Robert and Elpidia Smith, were deeply involved in my at-home learning and were constant sources of encouragement. A remarkable childhood friend, Dr. Jane Binger Bernstein, began coaching me about achievement when I was eleven and she was twelve, teaching me how to set and methodically work toward important goals. Jane is still a great friend and advisor to me, thirty-five years later. She has had an enormous impact on my life.

I have been blessed since those early years with wonderful teachers and role models, male and female. Dr. Larry Inderbitzin, a psychoanalyst and academic psychiatrist, was my greatest teacher and mentor during my Georgetown residency and in the years since, giving me the foundation of my understanding of mental life. I would also like to thank another psychiatrist, Dr. Layton McCurdy, Dean of the College of Medicine at MUSC, for his great support and direct encouragement in the writing of this book. Psychiatry has offered me contact with a number of inspirational women who have been pioneers in women's issues, particularly Drs. Carol Nadelson and Carolyn Robinowitz.

A number of women offered me their personal stories and own ideas about achievement, which are incorporated in this book. Special thanks go to Martha Ballenger, Leeda Marting, Linda Godleski, Susan Hull, Anne Darby Parker, Angie Zealberg, Zyra DeFries, Judy Barker, Heather Paul, Kathy Malaney, Marjie Rynearson, Bobbi Conner, and especially my sister, Barbara Bisel. I appreciate the male perspective offered to me by my good friends Joe Zealberg, Michael Scardato, Jeb Hallett, Bob Rynearson, and Charlie Kellner. I am deeply grateful to Page Morahan and Rosalyn Richman, co-directors of the Hedwig van Ameringen Executive Leadership in Academic Medicine, and to its benfactor, Ms. Pat Kind, for the superb experience I had in that program. The thirty-five women in my fellowship class offered me great support and encouragement; I extend special thanks to Drs. Barb Bayer, Rose Goldstein, Lynda Powell, Sarah Kilpatrick, and Debra Schwinn for many stimulating conversations.

Many patients and focus group members' stories appear in this book, significantly disguised to protect their confidentiality; thanks to all for letting me share your wisdom with others. I am also indebted to Katherine Husted, the producer of my radio show and program coordinator of the Office of Public Education at MUSC, and to Hollie Watson and Paula DiCenzo, my assistants, who helped with numerous trips to the library to locate research materials.

This book consumed much of my free time for almost two years. To my children, Stephanie and Matt, thanks so much for your patience with this process.

Most importantly, I would like to thank Lois Morris, who helped from the beginning with the conceptualization, editing, and structuring of the book; to my agent, Barbara Lowenstein, for her enthusiasm for this project; and to Jo Ann Miller, my editor at Basic Books, who offered superb critical analysis of the approach and key concepts in this book.

Index

sense of meaning and, 1–4
strategic plan, 25–29
women's value systems and, 13–21
Mozart, Wolfgang Amadeus, 73
Multidimensionality, 24–25
Musical intelligence, 63, 76–77

National Merit Scholarship, 68
National Safe Kids Campaign, 64–65, 66
Negotiation, 189–191
Nest-building, vs. risk-taking, 42–43, 54–55, 60
Networking, 58–59
New Yorker, The, 129, 150
Nightingale, Florence, 1, 4, 184, 202
Novelty-seeking, 45–46
Nurturance
gender differences, 111
genetic basis, 183
as problem, 166–167
work and, 11–13

Optimism, gender differences, 38
Organizations
competing in, 130–131
emotional intelligence and, 61–62
ethical basis of, 15–16
hierarchical competition and, 124–125
Originality, 91
Outrage, 170
Ownership, 91

Pain, response to emotional, 169–171

Parents, influence on children, 160–161
Parent's Journal, The (television program), 46
Parker, Anne Darby, 7, 25, 184
Pascal, Amy, 129
Passive excellence, 115–116
Paul, Heather, 64–65, 66, 184
Paula (Allende), 121
Peacemaker role, 51
Peak years, 74–75, 208
Permanent learning, 77
Perseverance, 3, 157–158
after failure, 178–179
Person, Ethel Spector, 10
Personal competition, 123–124
Personal development, 155–156
Personal experience, 97–98
Personality traits, effects on career, 164–166
Pessimism, gender differences, 38
Physical risk, gender differences, 35, 204
Physical space, personal development and, 80–81
Pleasing others, 119–121
Post-traumatic stress disorder (PTSD), 175
Powell, Colin, 160
Power
baiting and, 140–142
empowered mentoring and, 136–137
female resistance to, 131–134
gender differences and, 181–183
hierarchy and, 125–126, 135–136